致考研的自己:

_____

_____

_____

                              _____

考研英语词组
识记与应用大全

新东方考试研究中心 编著

新东方考研圈
考研资讯&指导，回复"赢"，赢小惊喜

群言出版社
QUNYAN PRESS
·北京·

时光荏苒，转眼恋练有词系列图书已经陪伴广大考研学子多年。在此期间，作为编者，我们因广大考生顺利通过考试后的灿烂笑容而备感欣慰，也为那些因为英语分差而与理想院校失之交臂的同学感到惋惜。为了更好地帮助考研学子备考考研英语，我们在充分研读历年真题的基础上，全新打造了这本考研英语词组书。

众所周知，词汇是英语学习的基础。无论考试的形式如何变化，打好坚实的词汇基础都是取得好成绩的关键，所谓"万变不离其宗"。通常，词汇的学习包含对单词及短语的学习：除了英语单词本身的词义，这些单词再与其他的词，如介词、名词、形容词等搭配使用，则可能衍生出全新的含义。以 come 一词为例，它的词义为"来；到达"，含义再简单不过，但当它和不同的介词、副词构成词组时，如 come about、come across、come after、come along、come at、come between、come down 等，却又各自呈现出与单独使用 come 时完全不同的语义。因此，如果考生只记住了 come 本身的含义，而不学习与之相关的词组，就会影响对语句的理解，导致理解偏差，甚至出现读不懂文章、答不对题的情况。

我们通过分析考研英语历年真题发现，每一年的真题都会至少涉及几十个词组。它们出现在真题的各个位置，是否能准确理解它们也会不同程度地影响到是否能顺利解题：词组出现在原文里，会加大考生理解整个篇章的难度；出现在题干和选项中，会影响考生做出正确的判断；而如果出现在翻译题里，甚至就直接决定了考生是得分还是失分。学习英语词组于考研的重要性，由此可见一斑。

本书结合考研英语大纲词表，在梳理近 20 年真题的基础上，精心筛选出了 1700 余个词组作为全书的主要内容，旨在帮助考生专项学习词组，夯实英语基础，熟悉真题考查内容，为考研英语考试做更充分的准备。本书具有以下特点：

1. 结合真题，精选词组

本书收录词组 1700 余个，分为真题词组（Day 01~Day 17）和加分词组（Day 18~Day 21）。其中，真题词组约 1300 个，加分词组约 400 个。真题词组为考研英语（一）和考研英语（二）历年真题中考查过的词组，需重点掌握。加分词组是与考研英语大纲词汇相关的词组，它们也属于考研英语考查的范畴，需要识记。只有将真题和大纲词汇结合起来学习，才能在考试时做到游刃有余。

2. 语境助记，讲解详细

本书所有词组都提供语境，助力理解和记忆，其中大多数为真题例句或切片，少量为题源例句。此外，本书对词组中的重难点单词给出了简要的讲解，并适当进行了拓展，包括近义词（组）、反义词（组）和形近词组，帮助考生建立知识点之间的联系，实现对知识点的灵活运用，从而提升整体英语水平。另外，为帮助不同英语水平的同学都能高效备考，特针对书中较为简单的词组做了语境的区分：简单的词组在书中仅提供例句切片，配套精讲视频中则给出切片对应的完整例句，方便大家按需选择。

3. 学练结合，便于自测

本书以天为单位，将所有内容划分到 21 天进行，便于考生更为科学地安排自己的学习进度。另配同步练习册 1 本，内含 21 个单元的同步练习，每单元均分为单项选择题和翻译填空题两部分，难度和题量适中，方便考生及时巩固自测，加强学习效果。

4. 视听结合，学习轻松

为了更好地帮助考生学习及记忆考研词组，我们邀请专业的词汇老师为本书精心录制了配套视频课程。考生只需扫描书内或封底二维码，即可聆听老师的生动讲解，学习起来更轻松！同步还提供全书词组、例句的纯正英音音频，以及适合日常背诵使用的带背视频，视听结合，让记忆效果加倍！

温馨提示

为帮助大家节约时间，高效备考，本书特参考初中英语课程标准及初中英语教材，利用图标 △ 和 ○，对书中词组进行了标记，其含义分别说明如下：

仅标 △：初中就应熟练掌握的词组，难度较小，建议快速复习。

标 △○：初中词组，但在高中或大学阶段有新增含义，建议查漏补缺。

标 ○○○：高中和大学阶段需掌握的词组，需要重点识记。

和单词一样，词组也需要不断地学习和积累。衷心祝愿各位考生能够坚持学习，顺利通过硕士研究生英语考试，梦圆理想学府！

新东方考试研究中心

目录 Contents

PART 01 真题词组   001

PART

02 加分词组   235

PART

03 附录：索引   291

PART 01
真题词组

本单元资源

collaborate with sb. (on sth.) 与某人合作（做某事）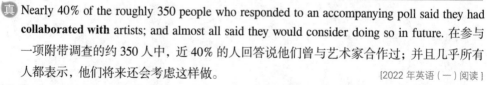

真 Nearly 40% of the roughly 350 people who responded to an accompanying poll said they had **collaborated with** artists; and almost all said they would consider doing so in future. 在参与一项附带调查的约 350 人中，近 40% 的人回答说他们曾与艺术家合作过；并且几乎所有人都表示，他们将来还会考虑这样做。 [2022 年英语（一）阅读]

拓 cooperate with 与……合作

hold down 保住（工作等）

真 If, like most writers these days, you're **holding down** a job to pay the bills, it's not easy to find the time to write. 如果像现在的大多数作家一样，你需要保住一份工作来支付账单，那么找时间进行写作并不容易。 [2022 年英语（二）完形填空]

a mass of 大量，众多；充满

真 However, the signaling in a plant is only superficially similar to the firing in a complex animal brain, which is more than "**a mass of** cells that communicate by electricity," Taiz said. 然而，植物发信号只是表面上类似于复杂的动物大脑中的放电，而动物大脑可并不只是"通过电流进行交流的一堆细胞"，塔伊兹说道。 [2022 年英语（一）完形填空]

拓 the mass of 大多数的

chalk up (to) 把……归因于

真 Some of the success of plant-based meat can be **chalked up to** shoppers wanting to signal their desire to protect the environment. 人造肉的成功在一定程度上可以归因于这类消费者：他们想要表达自己保护环境的愿望。 [2022 年英语（二）阅读]

拓 attribute to 把……归因于；认为是由……引起或产生 ‖ ascribe to 把……归因于 ‖ put down to 把……归因于

be immersed in 沉浸于，专心于

真 Artists and scientists alike **are immersed in** discovery and invention, and challenge and critique are core to both, too. 艺术家和科学家都沉浸在发现和发明中，挑战和批评也是这两者的核心。 [2022 年英语（一）阅读]

拓 immerse oneself in 使自己沉浸于；使自己深陷于或专心于

aim to do sth.　旨在做某事，以做某事为目标　○○○

真 According to the first two paragraphs, CCT programs **aim to** help poor families get better off. 根据前两段，有条件的现金援助项目（CCT）旨在帮助贫困家庭改善生活。

[2021 年英语（一）阅读]

align with　与……一致；与……结盟；将……排列在一条直线上　○○○

真 College students' ratings of strawberry jams and college courses **aligned** better **with** experts' opinions when the students weren't asked to analyze their rationale. 当学生们没有被要求分析他们（给出评价）的理由时，他们对草莓果酱和大学课程的评价与专家的意见更趋一致。

[2021 年英语（二）阅读]

拓 come into agreement with sb. 与某人意见一致

(be) preoccupied with (doing) sth.　专注于（做）某事　○○○

真 As a historian who's always searching for the text or the image that makes us re-evaluate the past, I've become **preoccupied with looking for** photographs that show our Victorian ancestors smiling (what better way to shatter the image of 19th-century prudery?). 作为一名总是在寻找能让我们重新评价过去的文稿或图像的历史学家，我变得专注于寻找那些能展示我们维多利亚时代祖先微笑的照片。（还有什么更好的方法能粉碎 19 世纪给人留下的拘谨的印象吗？）

[2021 年英语（一）阅读]

be under (...) investigation　接受……的调查；对……进行调查研究　○○○

真 It **is under** the FCC's **investigation**. 美国联邦通信委员会（FCC）正在调查它。

[2021 年英语（一）阅读]

wade into　介入；猛烈攻击　○○○

真 Although only a research project at this stage, the request has raised the prospect of regulators **wading into** early-stage tech markets that until now have been beyond their reach. 尽管这只是现阶段的一个研究项目，但这一要求增加了监管机构涉足早期科技市场的可能性，而这些市场迄今还不在监管机构的监管范围内。

[2021 年英语（二）阅读]

beyond one's reach　　够不到；非某人的能力、权力、影响等所能及　○○○

例 The glasses on the top shelf are **beyond her reach**. 顶层架子上的玻璃杯太高，她够不着。

拓 out of one's reach 够不到；非某人的能力、权力、影响等所能及

chew up　　破坏；损害　○○○

真 To Microsoft's critics, the fates of Wunderlist and Sunrise are examples of a remorseless drive by Big Tech to **chew up** any innovative companies that lie in their path. 在微软的批评者看来，奇妙清单和日出日历的命运表明，大型科技公司无情地想要摧毁任何挡在它们前进道路上的创新公司。

[2021 年英语（二）阅读]

cry out for　　迫切需要，急需；大声喊叫　○○○

真 The endless legal battles and back-and-forth at the FCC **cry out for** Congress to act. 没完没了的官司和美国联邦通信委员会（FCC）的反反复复都迫切需要国会采取行动。

[2021 年英语（一）阅读]

find out　　弄清，查明；发现，找出　○○○

真 But in addition to those trusted coworkers, you should expand your horizons and **find out** about all the people around you. 但是除了那些值得信任的同事之外，你应该放宽你的视野去了解你周围的所有人。

[2020 年英语（二）阅读]

a large sum of　　一大笔的；数额可观的　○○○

例 We'll have to spend **a large sum of** money to decorate the new house. 我们将不得不花一大笔钱来布置新房。

in line with　　与……一致；与……相符；与……成一条直线　○○○

例 His theory is found to be **in line with** the experimental results. 人们发现他的理论与这个实验结果一致。

拓 in tune with 与……一致

put aside　　把……暂放一边；把……留作后用　○○○

真 He quotes a giant of classical economics, Alfred Marshall, in describing this financial impatience as acting like "children who pick the plums out of their pudding to eat them at once" rather than **putting** them **aside** to be eaten last. 他引用了古典经济学家、巨匠艾尔弗雷德·马歇尔的话，将这种在金融上的不耐烦行为描述为像 "孩子从布丁里挖出梅子立刻吃掉"，而不是把梅子放在一边留到最后再吃的行为一样。

[2019 年英语（一）阅读]

---

read off　　读出；读取

🈲 What is in question is not the retrieval of an absolute, fixed or "true" meaning that can be **read off** and checked for accuracy, or some timeless relation of the text to the world. 问题不在于找到可以被读取出来和检验其准确性的绝对、固定或 "真正" 的含义，也不在于找到文本与世界之间某种永恒的关系。

[2015 年英语（一）阅读]

---

plenty of　　大量的，许多的

🈲 **plenty of** incentive 大量的动机

[2016 年英语（一）阅读]

---

eat out　　外出就餐

🈲 Wholesale demand from the food service sector is growing quickly as more Europeans **eat out** more often. 随着越来越多的欧洲人更加频繁地外出就餐，食品服务行业的批发需求正迅速增长。

[2010 年英语（一）阅读]

---

follow suit　　跟着做；学样

🈲 Other nations are likely to **follow suit**. 其他国家可能会效仿。

[2020 年英语（一）阅读]

---

as long as　　只要；如果；和……一样长

🈲 Under the plan, for example, the agency said it would not prosecute landowners or businesses that unintentionally kill, harm, or disturb the bird, **as long as** they had signed a range-wide management plan to restore prairie chicken habitat. 举例来说，在这个计划下，该机构声称不会起诉那些并非故意捕杀、伤害或是惊扰该鸟类的土地所有者或者企业，只要他们签署过重建草原榛鸡栖息地的一系列涉及面宽泛的管理计划。

[2016 年英语（二）阅读]

---

up in arms　　竭力反对；进行武装斗争

🈲 And in Europe, some are **up in arms** over a proposal to drop a specific funding category for social-science research and to integrate it within cross-cutting topics of sustainable development. 有人提议取消社会科学研究的特定资助类别，并将其纳入可持续发展的交叉课题，在欧洲，一些人对此竭力反对。

[2013 年英语（一）阅读]

far more than　远不止，远远超过　

真 In my own research, complaints from women about their husbands most often focused not on tangible inequities such as having given up the chance for a career to accompany a husband to his, or doing **far more than** their share of daily life-support work like cleaning, cooking and social arrangements. 我的研究发现，女性对丈夫抱怨最多的往往不是与一些切实存在的不平等有关，比如放弃自己的事业的机会以陪伴丈夫追求他的事业，或是承担了远超其分内的日常家务，比如打扫卫生、做饭和社交活动安排等。 [2010 年英语（二）阅读]

remind...of　使……记起，使……想起　

真 *Towards Avebury* **reminds** people **of** the English landscape painting tradition.《朝着埃夫伯里》让人们想起英国风景画的传统。 [2014 年英语（二）阅读]

拓 remind sb. about sth. 提醒某人某事

burst out　突然……起来；突然爆发出；突然发生

例 I told the whole story to my friend and then she **burst out** laughing. 我把整件事情告诉了我的朋友，她听后突然大笑起来。

take pride in　对……感到自豪，以……为骄傲

例 Each of us should **take pride in** our particular faith and heritage. 我们每个人都应对自己独特的信仰和传统感到自豪。

be contemptuous of　对……心怀蔑视，鄙视

例 As for me, the essay **was** totally **contemptuous of** science. 在我看来，那篇文章完全是对科学的蔑视。

at home　在家；在国内

真 A new study suggests that contrary to most surveys, people are actually more stressed **at home** than at work. 一项新研究表明，同大多数调查相悖的是：实际上人们在家中的压力比在工作中大。 [2015 年英语（二）阅读]

resort to　依靠，求助于；诉诸

例 They have to **resort to** taking these measures to settle the problem. 他们不得不依靠采取这些措施来解决这一问题。

a little bit　有点儿，有些

真 A small part of us hoped getting "the Rachel" might make us look just **a little bit** like Jennifer Aniston. 我们中的少数人希望理个瑞秋（《老友记》中漂亮的单身妈妈）式的发型可以使我们看起来有点儿像珍妮弗·安妮斯顿（瑞秋的扮演者）。

[2011 年英语（一）阅读]

take place　发生；举行

真 Many of the most celebrated national figures have participated in historical events that have **taken place** within the EEOB's granite walls. 国内许多极知名的人士参与了发生在艾森豪威尔行政办公楼的花岗岩墙内的历史事件。

[2018 年英语（一）阅读]

be of (...) importance　是（……）重要的

真 The quality of writing **is of** primary **importance**. 写作的质量是头等重要的。

[2015 年英语（一）阅读]

be competent to　足以胜任；有能力；合格

真 Many Americans regard the jury system as a concrete expression of crucial democratic values, including the principles that all citizens who meet minimal qualifications of age and literacy **are** equally **competent to** serve on juries. 许多美国人把陪审团制度看成基本民主价值观念的具体体现，包括以下几个原则：所有符合最低年龄限制和文化程度要求的公民都享有平等的担任陪审员的权利。

[2010 年英语（二）阅读]

clamp down　施加压力；强行压制；取缔；严加限制

真 As the cost to everyone else has become clearer, politicians have begun to **clamp down**. 随着带给其他人的损失渐趋明显，政治家们已开始施压。

[2012 年英语（一）阅读]

in one's view　在某人看来；依照某人的见解

例 You're taking a big risk **in my view**. 在我看来，你正在冒极大的风险。

turn to　转向；开始行动；求助于；变成；翻到（某页）

真 But the professional companies prospered in their permanent theaters, and university men with literary ambitions were quick to **turn to** these theaters as offering a means of livelihood. 但是，专业剧团因为有了固定的剧院而繁荣发展起来，而有文学抱负的大学生们迅速转向投身这些剧院，并以此谋生。

[2018 年英语（一）阅读]

break through　突破，（克服困难和障碍而）获得成功；冲破（障碍）　○○○

真 When women do **break through** to the summit of corporate power—as, for example, Sheryl Sandberg recently did at Facebook—they attract massive attention precisely because they remain the exception to the rule. 当女性突破重围，达到了公司权力的巅峰，就会引起很大的关注，比如最近脸书的谢丽尔·桑德伯格，只因为她们是这个社会规则的例外。

[2013 年英语（二）阅读]

draw a conclusion from　由……得出结论　○○○

例 We haven't got sufficient data **from** which to **draw a conclusion**. 我们还没有足够的数据来得出结论。

keep pace with　与……齐头并进；与……步调一致　○○○

真 Competition law cannot **keep pace with** the changing market. 竞争法跟不上不断变化的市场。

[2018 年英语（二）阅读]

拓 at one's own pace 按照某人自己的速度

the rest of　其余的，剩下的　○○○

真 These kids are going to be surrounded by computers—in their pockets, in their offices, in their homes—for **the rest of** their lives. 这些孩子将在到处是计算机的环境中——在他们的口袋里，在他们的办公室里，在他们的家里——度过余生。

[2016 年英语（二）阅读]

encourage sb. to do sth.　鼓励某人做某事　○○○

词 encourage [ɪnˈkʌrɪdʒ] v. 鼓励，激励；促使

真 And guilt, by prompting us to think more deeply about our goodness, can **encourage humans to** make up for errors and fix relationships. 通过促使我们更加深入地思考自己的善意，内疚可以激励人类对错误进行弥补，并对人际关系加以修复。

[2019 年英语（二）阅读]

拓 inspire sb. to do sth. 激发某人做某事

in other words　换句话说　○○○

真 **In other words**, they all share a view that the international tax system has failed to keep up with the current economy. 换句话说，他们都认为国际税收体系未能跟上当前经济的发展。

[2020 年英语（一）阅读]

拓 that is to say 换言之，也就是说

to put it another way　换句话说；换一个角度说

To put it another way: How can we make sure that the thinking of intelligent machines reflects humanity's highest values? 换句话说：我们如何才能保证智能机器的思维反映的是人类的最高价值？　[2019 年英语（一）阅读]

拓 namely 即；换言之

be obsessed with　对……着迷，痴迷于……

词 obsess [əb'ses] v. 使痴迷，使迷恋；困扰；心神不宁

真 Pretty in pink: adult women do not remember **being** so **obsessed with** the colour, yet it is pervasive in our young girls' lives. 粉红之美：成年女性不记得自己曾经如此迷恋粉红色，但在我们的少女时代，粉红色无处不在。　[2012 年英语（二）阅读]

force sb. to do sth.　迫使某人做某事

真 **force users to** be more conscious of their role 迫使用户更加留意自己的角色
　[2018 年英语（一）阅读]

拓 force sth. on sb. 勉强某人接受某事物 ‖ by force 强迫地；靠武力地；强行地

get the nod　获得认可；被选中；得到许可

真 As boards scrutinize succession plans in response to shareholder pressure, executives who don't **get the nod** also may wish to move on. 由于董事会迫于股东们的压力而严格审查公司的继任方案，那些未获得认可的经理人也可能想离职。　[2011 年英语（一）阅读]

拓 on the nod 点头表示同意，默许 ‖ nod off 打盹

ahead of　在……之前，在……前面；事先；胜过

真 These results suggest that imagining the outcome of following through on one's curiosity **ahead of** time can help determine whether it is worth the endeavor. 这些研究成果表明，事先设想自己的好奇心会带来何种后果会有助于人们决定其是否值得努力一试。

　[2018 年英语（二）完形填空]

拓 prior to 在（某个时间或事件）之前

afford to　支付得起；承担得起；（有条件）做

真 I can't **afford to** pay my monthly mortgage payments on my own, so I have to rent rooms out to people to make that happen. 我一个人负担不起房子的月供，所以必须把房间租给别人，这样才能够支付月供。

a ban on 对……的禁止，关于……的禁令

真 Thirty years ago, it would have been inconceivable to have imagined **a ban on** smoking in the workplace or in pubs, and yet that is what we have now. 三十年前，你会很难想象在工作场所或酒吧禁止吸烟，但这在如今已是事实。 [2011 年英语（二）阅读]

make up 构成；编造；补足（数量）；和好；配制（食物、药等）

真 Together, they **make up** the reading component of your overall literacy, or relationship to your surrounding textual environment. 它们（不同的阅读形式）共同构成了一个人的综合读写能力中的阅读部分，或者形成其与周围文本阅读环境的一种关联性。 [2015 年英语（一）阅读]

拓 consist of 构成 ‖ constitute ['kɒnstɪtjuːt] v. 构成

take the lead 带头；起带头作用

真 Lansley has alarmed health campaigners by suggesting he wants industry rather than government to **take the lead**. 兰斯利建议，应该由行业而非政府来带头处理此事，这提醒了健康生活倡导者。 [2011 年英语（二）阅读]

too...to... 太……而不能……

真 **too** complex **to** be understood 太复杂而难以理解 [2019 年英语（一）阅读]

result in 导致，结果是

真 Under the law, using a fashion model that does not meet a government-defined index of body mass could **result in** a $85,000 fine and six months in prison. 依照此项法规，聘用一名未达到政府规定的体重指标的时装模特可能会面临 85 000 美元的罚款和 6 个月的监禁。

[2016 年英语（一）阅读]

拓 result from 起因于……，由……造成

as it happens 碰巧，偶然发生

真 **As it happens**, America's armed forces are on the case already. 恰在此时，美国军方也已着手此项研究。 [2010 年英语（二）阅读]

拓 by coincidence 偶然

in trouble　惹上麻烦的；受训斥的；处于困难中的　

真 Public-sector unions seldom get **in trouble** for their actions. 公共部门的工会很少因为他们的举措而惹上麻烦。　[2012 年英语（一）阅读]

拓 make trouble 捣乱，制造麻烦 ‖ have trouble (in) doing sth. 在做某事上有困难 ‖ borrow trouble 自找麻烦，自寻苦恼

keep an eye out for　留意；当心；警惕　

真 If you've explored the area before, **keep an eye out for** familiar sights—you may be surprised how quickly identifying a distinctive rock or tree can restore your bearings. 如果你曾经来过这片区域，要特别留意熟悉的景象——你可能会惊喜地发现，认出一块特别的岩石或者一棵特别的树会多么迅速地帮你找回方向。　[2019 年英语（一）完形填空]

拓 keep one's eyes open 留意 ‖ keep an eye on 留意；密切注视

bring about　引起；导致　

真 Pillay believes that our brains' shift between being focused and unfocused can **bring about** greater efficiency. 皮莱认为我们的大脑在注意力集中和不集中这两种状态之间切换可以使效率更高。　[2018 年英语（二）阅读]

拓 give rise to 引起，使发生 ‖ lead to 导致

in question　争议中的；有关的；正考虑或讨论中的　

真 Colleges are partly responsible for the problem **in question**. 大学应该为这个有争议的问题负部分责任。　[2015 年英语（二）阅读]

拓 at issue 争议中的；讨论中的 ‖ out of the question 完全不可能的 ‖ out of question 毫无疑问的

be under way　在进行中；在航行中　

真 New research on transportation biofuels **is** already **under way**. 有关交通工具生物燃料的新研究已经在进行当中。　[2019 年英语（二）阅读]

拓 in motion 在运转中；在行进中

in the first place　起初；首先；从一开始　

真 And yet, John Hagel, author of *The Power of Pull* and other books, says Brynjolfsson and McAfee miss the reason why these jobs are so vulnerable to technology **in the first place**. 但

是《拉动的力量》等书的作者约翰·哈格尔说，布林约尔弗森和麦凯菲从一开始就没有领会到为什么这些工作在机器面前不堪一击。 [2014 年英语（二）阅读]

拓 at the beginning 首先；从一开始，从头开始 ‖ in the first instance 起初；首先

get on well with — 与……相处融洽

真 **get on well with** others 与他人相处融洽 [2014 年英语（二）阅读]

by accident — 偶然；意外地

例 I fell into this **by accident**, but have loved every minute of it because the work is so interesting. 我是偶然接触到这一行的，但打那时起我就爱上了这份工作，因为它太有趣了。

拓 by no accident 绝非偶然

in the face of — 面对

真 Hugging "is a marker of intimacy and helps generate the feeling that others are there to help **in the face of** difficulty." 拥抱"是亲密关系的一种象征，它可以帮助人们在面对困难时产生别人会伸出援助之手的感觉"。 [2017 年英语（一）完形填空]

拓 face to face 面对面 ‖ be faced with 面对；面临 ‖ on the face of 从……表面上判断

wear off — （感觉等）逐渐消失，消逝

例 The smell of the new paint will **wear off** in about a month. 新刷油漆的气味大约一个月会逐渐消失。

in short — 总之；简言之

真 **In short**, these are the types of jobs that machines can perform much better at than human beings. 简言之，这些类型的工作机器会比人类做得更好。 [2014 年英语（二）阅读]

拓 in brief 简言之

arise from — 由……产生；由……引起，起因于

真 It is speculated that gardens **arise from** a basic human need in the individuals who made them: the need for creative expression. 人们认为，花园源于其建造者的某种基本的人类需求，即创造性表达的需求。 [2013 年英语（一）阅读]

拓 arise out of 由……产生

be incapable of 无能力的；无法胜任的

真 This way you devalue your opinion and show that you **are incapable of** managing your own life. 这样，你就削弱了自己观点的价值，并且表明你无法掌控自己的生活。

[2015 年英语（二）阅读]

拓 incompetent [ɪnˈkɒmpɪtənt] *a.* 无能的；不称职的

in a word 总之；简言之

例 **In a word**, maintaining a common heart is not only necessary but also important. 总之，保持一颗平常心不仅必要，也很重要。

succeed in sth. 顺利完成；在……方面成功

真 **succeed in** higher education 顺利完成高等教育 [2015 年英语（二）阅读]

拓 succeed in doing sth. 成功做某事 ‖ be succeeded by 继……之后

respond to 回应；应对

真 Radesky's cites the "still face experiment" to show that parents need to **respond to** children's emotional needs. 瑞德斯基引用"静止脸实验"是为了表明父母需要对孩子的情感需求给予回应。

[2017 年英语（二）阅读]

serve on 担任（某职务）；成为……中的一员；履行义务

词 serve [sɜːv] *v.* 为……服务；供应；提供；满足；接待（顾客）

真 No citizen should be denied the right to **serve on** a jury on account of race, religion, sex, or national origin. 不得以种族、宗教、性别或民族血统等原因剥夺任何公民担任陪审员的权利。

[2010 年英语（二）阅读]

拓 serve up（给……）提供；上（菜、饮料）‖ serve out 分发（食物或饮料）；干完（任期）；服满（刑期）

divide into 将……分成

词 divide [dɪˈvaɪd] *v.* 分隔；分配；除以

真 Obesity, in turn, can be **divided into** moderately obese, severely obese, and very severely obese. 肥胖症依次又可以分为轻微肥胖、严重肥胖和超级肥胖。 [2014 年英语（二）完形填空]

拓 divide by 除以；用……除 ‖ divide up 分隔；均分

| of necessity | 必然地；不可避免地 | |

真 **Of necessity**, colonial America was a projection of Europe. 必然地，殖民地时期的美国成了欧洲的投影。 [2015 年英语（一）阅读]

拓 by necessity 必然地；不可避免地

| glare at | 怒视；瞪眼看 | |

真 In short, the image that best represents the current crisis is the stereotypical cartoon scene of a man sitting at the breakfast table with a newspaper held up in front of his face, while a woman **glares at** the back of it, wanting to talk. 简言之，一幅经典的卡通画最能描绘目前的婚姻危机：一个男人坐在早餐桌旁，面前举着一份报纸，而一位女士则怒视着报纸的背面，想要跟他说说话。 [2010 年英语（二）阅读]

| for example | 例如 | |

真 Jealousy and anger, **for example**, may have evolved to alert us to important inequalities. 比如说嫉妒和愤怒，可能会演变为提醒我们认识到重大的不平等。 [2019 年英语（二）阅读]

辨 for example, such as 和 for instance 都有举例说明的作用，但又存在一些区别：

for example 一般只举一个例子，可位于句首、句中或句末。

such as 一般列举多个例子，用在句子中间。

for instance 后面一般接一个句子或插入语，放在句子中间或末尾。

| look for | 寻找 | |

真 **look for** signs of human habitation 寻找人类居住的痕迹 [2019 年英语（一）完形填空]

拓 search for 寻找；搜索 ‖ seek for 寻找；追求；探索

| turn around | 转向反方向；反过来；（经济情况）好转 | |

真 Humans are unique in their capacity to not only make tools but then **turn around** and use them to create superfluous material goods—paintings, sculpture and architecture—and superfluous experiences—music, literature, religion and philosophy. 人类的独特之处在于他们不但能够制作工具，反过来还可以利用工具创造出大量的有形物质——绘画、雕塑和建筑，还有丰富的精神体验——音乐、文学、宗教和哲学。 [2012 年英语（一）阅读]

| invite...to | 请求，要求；邀请 | |

真 You infer information you feel the writer has **invited** you **to** grasp by presenting you with

specific evidence and clues. 你通过作者展示出的具体证据和线索来推断作者要求你掌握
的信息。 [2015 年英语（一）阅读]

instead of　　　　代替；而不是

真 **Instead of** wordy, worthy strategies, future governments need to do more to provide the conditions for sport to thrive. 与其制定冗长的、貌似有价值的方案，未来的政府倒不如多为体育运动的蓬勃发展努力创造条件。 [2017 年英语（二）阅读]

拓 rather than 而不是

in part　　　　部分地；在某种程度上

真 The advance is driven **in part** by vehicle manufacturers, who are placing big bets on battery-powered vehicles. 这样一种进步在某种程度上受到了汽车制造商的驱动，它们正就电动汽车进行一次"豪赌"。 [2018 年英语（二）阅读]

拓 to some degree 在某种程度上

be designed to　　　　旨在；设计目的在于

真 "Tech **is designed to** really suck you in," says Jenny Radesky in her study of digital play. 珍妮·瑞德斯基在其针对数码娱乐的研究中说道："技术设计的初衷就是真正地吸引住你。" [2017 年英语（二）阅读]

insure against　　　　以防；使预防

例 The organizers and promoters will take steps to **insure against** possible failure. 组织人员和推广人员将采取措施，以防可能出现的失败。

move on　　　　继续行进；进步，有进展；罢手去做别的事

真 Two years before graduating from secondary school, I took a sewing and design course thinking that I would **move on** to a fashion design course. 中学毕业前的两年里，我选修了一门有关缝纫和设计的课程，想着自己会去学习一门时尚设计课程。 [2017 年英语（二）翻译]

拓 move sb. on 命令某人走开

a group of　　　　一组；一群

真 But **a group of** researchers at Stanford University, led by Ilan Kroo, has suggested that airlines could take a more naturalistic approach to cutting jet-fuel use and it would not require them to buy new aircraft. 但是，由伊兰·克鲁领导的一个斯坦福大学研究小组指

出，航空公司可以通过更加自然的途径来降低飞机燃油的消耗，这样根本无需购买新的飞机。 [2010 年英语（二）阅读]

拓 a cluster of 一组；一群；一串 ‖ a flock of 一群（鸟或羊等）；一批（人或物）

consent to　同意，允许

词 consent [kən'sent] v. 同意，允许；赞同 n. 同意，准许；赞许；批文

例 Mr. Smith finally **consented to** answer our questions. 史密斯先生最终同意回答我们的问题。

拓 informed consent 知情同意 ‖ written consent 书面同意；同意书

辨 consent 为比较正式的用词，指同意别人的请求、建议或满足他人的愿望，其后常接介词 to 或动词不定式。

approve 侧重对认为正确或满意的事表示赞同或批准，常与 of 连用。

agree 为常见用词，指与其他人对某事有相同的意见或想法，后常接介词 to 或 with。

in the midst of　在……之中

真 One of these urges has to do with creating a state of peace **in the midst of** turbulence, a "still point of the turning world," to borrow a phrase from T. S. Eliot. 众多欲求中的一种就是关于如何在喧嚣中营造出一种平静的状态，借用 T. S. 艾略特的说法就是一个"旋转世界中的静止点"。 [2013 年英语（一）阅读]

辨 in the midst of 强调在某一过程中，指的是"正当……的时候"。
in the middle of 强调位置上的"中间"。

in fashion　流行的；时髦的

真 Keep Your Newspapers Forever **in Fashion** 让你的报纸永远流行 [2016 年英语（一）阅读]

rip off　欺骗（某人的钱财）；撕掉；偷窃

真 The common idea that high CEO pay is mainly about **ripping** people **off** doesn't explain history very well. 人们普遍认为，首席执行官的高薪主要是为了剥削员工，但这并不能很好地解释历史。 [2020 年英语（二）阅读]

for instance　例如，比如

词 instance ['ɪnstəns] n. 例子；实例；事例

真 **For instance**, failure can help you discover how strong a person you are. 例如，失败可以帮助你发现自己是多么的强大。 [2020 年英语（二）翻译]

DAY 02

本单元资源

account to　　对……负责；对……做出解释

词 account [ə'kaʊnt] v. 认为；视为 n. 账户；账号；解释，说明；赊购

真 While the conversation around our environment and our responsibility toward it remains centered on shopping bags and straws, we're ignoring the balance of power that implies that as "consumers" we must shop sustainably, rather than as "citizens" hold our governments and industries to **account to** push for real systemic change. 当围绕环境以及我们对环境的责任的讨论仍然集中在购物袋和吸管上时，我们正在忽视权利的平衡,这意味着作为"消费者",我们购物时必须注意可持续发展的问题,而不是作为 "公民" 要求政府和各行业承担起推动真正系统性变革的责任。　　　　　　　　　　　　　[2019 年英语（二）阅读]

embody in　　体现在……，使具体化

例 Our creativity should **embody in** the natural protection not the natural destruction. 我们的创造力应该体现在保护自然, 而不是破坏自然上。

拓 be embodied in 包含；收录

under stress　　在压力之下；在受力时

真 It is like the immune system of the body, which **under stress** or through lack of nutrition or exercise can be weakened, but which never leaves us. 它（心理健康）就好像身体的免疫系统, 在面临压力、处于营养不足或缺乏运动时可能会变得虚弱, 但它从不会离我们而去。

[2016 年英语（一）翻译]

拓 under pressure 在压力之下

come true　　成真，成为现实

真 You are the lucky inheritor of a dream **come true**. 你们是梦想成真的幸运后继者。

[2012 年英语（一）阅读]

thousands of　　数以千计的……，成千上万的……

真 **thousands of** volunteers 成千上万的志愿者　　　　　　　　[2017 年英语（二）阅读]

accord with　　同……相符合；与……一致

真 Since desire and will are damaged by the presence of thoughts that do not **accord with** desire,

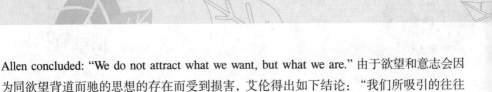

Allen concluded: "We do not attract what we want, but what we are." 由于欲望和意志会因为同欲望背道而驰的思想的存在而受到损害，艾伦得出如下结论："我们所吸引的往往不是自己渴望得到的东西，而是我们自身。"

[2011 年英语（一）阅读]

拓 with one accord 一致地 ‖ of one's own accord 自愿地；主动地

think of　　想到；想出

真 Carnegie would be right if arguments were fights, which is how we often **think of** them. 如果争论是一场对抗，正如我们往往认为的那样，那么卡耐基就是对的。[2019 年英语（一）阅读]

brand...as　　把……归为或列为（不好的事物）

真 We hail them as Americans in the making, or **brand** them **as** aliens to be kicked out. 我们要么把他们当作未来的美国人来欢迎，要么把他们列为终将被驱逐的异类。

[2013 年英语（二）阅读]

identify with　　理解；认同

例 You cannot only play the role that you **identify with** the character. 你不能只扮演你认同的角色。

be grateful for　　对……心存感激；感恩

真 Instead, **being grateful for** small things every day is a much better way to improve wellbeing. 与之相反，每天对细小的事物心存感恩是一种更好的提升幸福感的方式。

[2016 年英语（二）阅读]

think back　　回想，回忆

真 And afterwards, when we come to **think back** on it, we can't remember the journey well because we didn't pay much attention to it. 随后，当回想整个旅程时，由于我们没有对此太过留意，所以记忆会模糊。

[2015 年英语（二）翻译]

engage with　　与……接洽；与……建立友好关系；与（某人）交战

真 Toyota Motor, for example, alleviated some of the damage from its recall crisis earlier this year with a relatively quick and well-orchestrated social-media response campaign, which included efforts to **engage with** consumers directly on sites such as Twitter and the social-news site Digg. 例如，在今年早些时候的召回危机中，丰田汽车用一场相对迅速且精心策

划的社交媒体回应活动，挽回了部分损失，这些活动包括在推特和社会新闻网站 Digg 上直接与消费者交流。

[2011 年英语（一）阅读]

have nothing to do with 　与……无关

真 Although this is an interesting issue, it **has nothing to do with** the thesis, which explains how the setting influences Sammy's decision to quit his job. 尽管这是一个有趣的话题，但它与论题所讨论的"环境如何影响萨米决定放弃自己的工作"没有任何联系。

[2008 年英语（一）阅读]

拓 have little to do with 和……有些关系；和……关系不大

return the/a favor 　回报，报答

真 This could lead to the rats better remembering having freed it earlier, and wanting the robot to **return the favour** when they get trapped, says Quinn. 奎因说，这可能会让老鼠更好地记住早些时候把它（机器人老鼠）放出来的事，并希望当它们被困时，机器人老鼠能回报它们。

[2020 年英语（二）阅读]

拓 owe sb. a favor 欠某人一个人情

be applicable to 　适用于；能应用于

真 A lesson from the latter **is applicable to** the former. 后者带来的教训同样适用于前者。

[2005 年英语（一）阅读]

go through with 　将（决定的事）进行到底；完成

例 **go through with** the research 将研究进行下去

make fun of 　取笑，嘲笑

真 But this seems to be the irony of office speak: Everyone **makes fun of** it, but managers love it, companies depend on it, and regular people willingly absorb it. 但是这似乎是办公室语言的讽刺之处：每个人都嘲笑它，但是经理们却对此青睐有加，公司依赖它，普通人也乐于接受它。

[2015 年英语（二）阅读]

拓 laugh at 嘲笑；因……而发笑 ‖ mock [mɒk] v. 取笑，嘲弄；愚弄 ‖ ridicule ['rɪdɪkjuːl] v. 嘲笑，嘲弄

make efforts to/make an effort to 　做出努力

真 Several fast-fashion companies have **made efforts to** curb their impact on labor and the

environment. 几家快时尚公司已经在努力控制它们对劳动力和环境的影响。

[2013 年英语（一）阅读]

拓 it takes effort to（做某事）需要付出努力 ‖ with effort 吃力

in touch with　　同……有联系，和……有接触

真 "Healthy optimism means being **in touch with** reality," says Tal Ben-Shahar, a Harvard professor. 哈佛大学的教授塔尔·本 - 沙哈尔说："健康的乐观主义意味着不脱离现实。"

[2014 年英语（二）阅读]

拓 get in touch with 与……联系，与……接触 ‖ keep/stay in touch (with)（与……）保持联系，保持接触 ‖ be out of touch (with)（与……）失去联系 ‖ lose touch (with)（与……）失去联系

nothing more than　　无非，仅仅，只不过

真 "Dare to be different, please don't smoke!" pleads one billboard campaign aimed at reducing smoking among teenagers—teenagers, who desire **nothing more than** fitting in. "敢于与众不同，请不要吸烟！"一个旨在减少青少年吸烟的广告牌宣传活动提出了这样的忠告——这些青少年无非是想融入他人。

[2012 年英语（一）阅读]

拓 nothing but 仅仅，只不过 ‖ merely ['mɪəli] *ad.* 仅仅

rather than　　而不是

真 Second, it is surely a good thing that the money and attention come to science **rather than** go elsewhere. 其次，把资金和注意力投向科学而不是其他领域，这肯定是一件好事。

[2014 年英语（一）阅读]

without question　　毫无疑问

真 **Without question**, manufacturing has taken a significant hit during recent decades, and further trade deals raise questions about whether new shocks could hit manufacturing. 毫无疑问，近几十年来，制造业遭受了重大打击，而进一步的贸易协议引发了新的冲击是否会影响制造业的问题。

[2017 年英语（二）阅读]

拓 there is no doubt that... 毫无疑问…… ‖ without doubt 毫无疑问 ‖ beyond doubt 毫无疑问 ‖ out of question 毫无疑问的，没有问题的

stake out　　声称对……拥有所有权；用桩标出（地）界；监视

词 stake [steɪk] *v.* 用桩支撑；用……打赌或冒险；资助 *n.* 桩；赌注

真 That ruling produced an explosion in business-method patent filings, initially by emerging Internet companies trying to **stake out** exclusive rights to specific types of online transactions. 这一裁决导致了商业方法专利申请的激增，最初是新兴的互联网公司试图对特定类型的在线交易保有专有权。 [2010 年英语（一）阅读]

拓 at stake 在胜败关头；在紧要关头；冒风险

relate to   涉及，有关

真 This entails reducing our dependence on the North American market, whose programs **relate to** experiences and cultural traditions which are different from our own. 这让我们减少对北美市场的依赖成为必然，因为北美市场的节目涉及的经历和文化传统与我们的不同。

[2005 年英语（一）翻译]

拓 concerning [kən'sɜːnɪŋ] *prep.* 涉及，关于

place a burden on   增加……的负担

例 Road traffic accidents **place a** major **burden on** the healthcare system. 道路交通事故给医疗保健系统带来了沉重的负担。

拓 burden sb. with（使）某人担负 ‖ bear/carry/shoulder a heavy burden 承受 / 担负 / 肩负重担

tens of thousands of   成千上万，数以万计

真 Despite trade competition and outsourcing, American manufacturing still needs to replace **tens of thousands of** retiring boomers every year. 尽管存在贸易竞争和外包，美国的制造业每年仍然需要置换成千上万要退休的婴儿潮时期出生的工人。 [2017 年英语（二）阅读]

hundreds of millions of   数亿的

真 The companies that Dr. Curtis turned to—Procter & Gamble, Colgate-Palmolive and Unilever—had invested **hundreds of millions of** dollars finding the subtle cues in consumers' lives that corporations could use to introduce new routines. 柯蒂斯博士求助的公司包括宝洁、高露洁和联合利华，它们已经投入了数亿美元，寻找消费者生活中的微妙线索，以便企业能利用这些线索引入新的生活习惯。 [2010 年英语（二）阅读]

pray for   祈祷，祷告

例 Let's **pray for** world peace and make joint efforts to build a brighter future. 让我们为世界和平祈祷，为创造一个更加光明的未来而共同努力。

invest in 投资；买进

真 Transient investors, who demand high quarterly profits from companies, can hinder a firm's efforts to **invest in** long-term research or to build up customer loyalty. 那些要求从公司获得高额季度利润的短期投资者可能会阻碍公司在投资长期研究或建立客户忠诚度方面的努力。

[2019 年英语（一）阅读]

be eager to 渴望，盼望

真 According to Hans Sauer, companies **are eager to** win patents for establishing disease correlations. 根据汉斯·绍尔所说，各公司都渴望获得建立疾病相关性的专利。

[2012 年英语（二）阅读]

拓 be keen to 渴望，迫切希望 ‖ be keen on 热衷于 ‖ yearn for 渴望 ‖ long for 渴望

come into one's own 显出价值；得到承认；施展才能

例 This car really **comes into its own** on rough ground. 这辆汽车在崎岖的路上才真正显示出它的性能。

keep track of 了解……的动态；与……保持联系；记录……

真 Your pages will be easier to **keep track of** that way, and, if you have to clip a paragraph to place it elsewhere, you will not lose any writing on the other side. 那样的话，你所写的一页页的内容就更容易找到，而且，如果你不得不把某个段落剪下来放在其他地方，你也不会因此丢掉背面的任何文字。

[2008 年英语（一）阅读]

拓 lose track of 不了解……的动态；与……失去联系

clean up 清理，清除；整治

真 The FASB and IASB have been exactly that, **cleaning up** rules on stock options and pensions, for example, against hostility from special interests. 美国财务会计准则委员会和国际会计准则理事会正是这样做的，例如，整治股票期权和养老金方面的规则来对抗特殊利益集团的敌意。

[2010 年英语（一）阅读]

拓 clear up 清理，打扫；天气放晴

open up 开启，打开

真 "Each book **opens up** new avenues of knowledge," Gates says. 盖茨说："每一本书都开启了通向知识的新通道。"

[2018 年英语（二）翻译]

part of 部分

真 **Part of** the issue is that airports have only so much room for screening lanes. 造成这个问题的部分原因是机场拥有的安检通道空间有限。 [2017 年英语（一）阅读]

拓 in part 部分地；在某种程度上 ‖ partially ['pɑːʃəli] *ad.* 部分地；在一定程度上

common sense 常识

真 Mental health is the seed that contains self-esteem—confidence in ourselves and an ability to trust in our **common sense**. 心理健康是一颗种子，蕴含着自信——相信自己和信赖自身常识的能力。 [2016 年英语（一）翻译]

拓 make sense 有意义，讲得通；有道理

from the outset 从一开始

例 **From the outset** it was clear that he was guilty. 从一开始他有罪这件事就很明显。

拓 from the very beginning 从一开始

in favor of 支持，赞成；有利于

真 **in favor of** diffusionism 赞成文化传播论 [2009 年英语（一）阅读]

拓 be for 赞成，支持 ‖ oppose [əˈpəʊz] *v.* 反对 ‖ be against 反对

be seen to be 被看到成为；被视为

真 Professor Terence Stephenson, president of the Royal College of Paediatrics and Child Health, said that the consumption of unhealthy food should **be seen to be** just as damaging as smoking or excessive drinking. 英国皇家儿科及儿童健康学院院长特伦斯·斯蒂芬森教授说，吃不健康食品应该被视为与吸烟或酗酒一样危害巨大。 [2011 年英语（二）阅读]

拓 be seen as 被视为 ‖ be considered as/to be 被视为 ‖ be regarded as 被视为

or else 或者，要不然就是；否则，要不然；否则后果不妙

真 Sit down to read and the flywheel of work-related thoughts keeps spinning—**or else** you're so exhausted that a challenging book's the last thing you need. 坐下来阅读，而与工作相关的想法却像飞轮一样转个不停——或者，你太疲惫不堪了，读一本有挑战性的书是你最不想做的事。 [2016 年英语（二）阅读]

拓 or rather 更准确地说，倒不如说

talk of	谈到，说起	◠◠◠

真 Now even the project's greatest cheerleaders **talk of** a continent facing a "Bermuda triangle" of debt, population decline and lower growth. 现在，即使是该计划最坚定的一些支持者也在谈论一个面临债务、人口下降和低增长的"百慕大三角"大陆。 [2011 年英语（二）阅读]

拓 talk about 谈论，讨论 ‖ when it comes to 说起，谈及，提及

turn off	关闭，关掉（灯、电视、收银机或电源等）	◠◠◠

例 Let's **turn** the television **off** and go to the cinema. 咱们关了电视，去看电影吧。

拓 switch off 关掉，关闭（电源、电灯等）

look inside	往里看，向内看	◠◠◠

真 Each subject was then invited to **look inside**. 随后每一位调查对象都会受邀查看（容器的）内部。 [2018 年英语（一）完形填空]

in depth	深入地，全面地	◠◠◠

例 Graduate students pursue a specific aspect of a subject **in depth**. 研究生深入研究某一学科的某一方面。

拓 thoroughly ['θʌrəli] *ad.* 彻底地，完全地

work for	为……工作，效劳	◠◠◠

例 Smith have been **working for** the law firm for more than 20 years. 史密斯已经在这家法律事务所工作 20 多年了。

拓 work as 做，担任……职务 ‖ work on 致力于，从事

come to fruition	实现；完成；取得成果	◠◠◠

真 Indeed, predictions of such a society have been around for two decades but have not yet **come to fruition**. 事实上，关于这样一个社会的预言已经存在了 20 年，但尚未实现。

[2013 年英语（二）完形填空]

拓 come into being 形成，产生

in exchange (for)	（作为……的）交换	◠◠◠

词 exchange [ɪks'tʃeɪndʒ] *n./v.* 交换

真 In the world of capuchins, grapes are luxury goods (and much preferable to cucumbers). So when one monkey was handed a grape **in exchange for** her token, the second was reluctant to

PART 01

hand hers over for a mere piece of cucumber. 在卷尾猴的世界里，葡萄是奢侈品（比黄瓜受欢迎多了）。因此，当一只猴子用代币换回一颗葡萄时，另一只猴子不愿意用代币仅换回一片黄瓜。 [2005 年英语（一）阅读]

拓 exchange A for B 用 A 换 B

be interested in　　对……感兴趣

真 Millennials may not **be** that **interested in** taking their place. Other industries are recruiting them with similar or better pay. 千禧一代可能对于接替他们的职位并没有多大兴趣。其他行业也在以类似或更高的薪酬招聘他们。 [2017 年英语（二）阅读]

拓 be intrigued by 被……迷住，对……十分好奇

set limits on　　对……加以限制

真 "If we were really bold, we might even begin to think of high-calorie fast food in the same way as cigarettes—by **setting** strict **limits on** advertising, product placement and sponsorship of sports events," he said. 他说："如果我们真的大胆一点，我们甚至可以像对待香烟一样，通过严格限制广告、植入式广告和体育赛事的赞助来思考高热量快餐的问题。" [2011 年英语（二）阅读]

lean towards　　倾向于

真 "It surely seems plausible that happy people would be more forward-thinking and creative and **leans toward** R&D more than the average," said one researcher. 一位研究人员说，"快乐的人比普通人更有前瞻性、更有创造力，更倾向于研发，这的确似乎是合理的。" [2016 年英语（二）完形填空]

拓 lean against （背）靠着；斜靠

vary from...to...　　（根据情况）变化

词 vary ['veəri] v. 变化，改变；有不同，相异

真 During the late 1990s, national spending on social sciences and the humanities as a percentage of all research and development funds—including government, higher education, non-profit and corporate—**varied from** around 4% **to** 25%. 在 20 世纪 90 年代末，国家在社会科学和人文科学上的支出占所有研发基金的比例——包括政府、高等教育、非营利组织和企业——从 4% 到 25% 不等。 [2013 年英语（一）阅读]

| **shrug off** | 摆脱；对……不予理睬 | ◌◌◌ |

例 German and Brazilian papers have **shrugged off** the recession. 德国和巴西的报业已经摆脱了不景气。

| **not long ago** | 不久前 | ◌◌◌ |

真 **Not long ago**, with the country entering a recession and Japan at its pre-bubble peak, the U.S. workforce was derided as poorly educated and one of the primary causes of the poor U.S. economic performance. 不久前，随着美国进入经济衰退期以及日本处于泡沫前的顶峰，美国的劳动力被嘲笑受教育程度低，并且是美国经济表现不佳的主要原因之一。

[2009 年英语（一）阅读]

拓 before long 不久以后，很快

| **rest on** | 依靠，依赖；（目光等）停留在……上 | ◌◌◌ |

真 Good governance **rests on** an understanding of the inherent worth of each individual. 良好的治理建立在对每个个体固有价值的理解之上。

[2017 年英语（一）阅读]

拓 lie in 在于

| **keep...away from** | 使……远离；回避 | ◌◌◌ |

真 Ants **keep** predatory insects **away from** where their aphids feed; Gmail keeps the spammers out of our inboxes. 蚂蚁让食肉昆虫远离蚜虫觅食的地方；谷歌邮箱使垃圾邮件发送者远离我们的收件箱。

[2018 年英语（二）阅读]

| **with confidence** | 满怀信心地，有把握地，放心地 | ◌◌◌ |

真 Mr. Schmidt described it as a "voluntary ecosystem" in which "individuals and organizations can complete online transactions **with confidence** trusting the identities of each other and the identities of the infrastructure on which the transaction runs." 施密特先生将其描述为一个"自愿的生态系统"，在这个系统中，"个人和组织可以放心地完成在线交易，信任彼此的身份以及交易所运行的基础设施的身份。"

[2011 年英语（二）完形填空]

拓 boost/increase sb.'s confidence 增强某人的自信心 ‖ shake/damage sb.'s confidence 动摇 / 损害某人的自信心

| **appear to** | 似乎，看起来 | ◌◌◌ |

真 Not surprisingly, newly published discovery claims and credible discoveries that **appear to** be important and convincing will always be open to challenge and potential modification or refutation by future researchers. 不足为奇的是，看起来重要又令人信服的、新发表的发现声明和可信的发现将永远乐于接受质疑和潜在的修订，或来自未来研究人员的反驳。

[2012 年英语（一）阅读]

拓 seem to 似乎

provide sth. for sb.　为某人提供某物

真 **provide** a comfortable life **for** their children 为他们的孩子提供舒适的生活

[2016 年英语（二）阅读]

拓 supply/provide sb. with sth. 为某人提供某物 ‖ furnish sb./sth. with sth. 为某人 / 某物提供某事物

be expected to　有望，被期待

真 If software promises to save lives on the scale that drugs now can, big data may **be expected to** behave as a big pharma has done. 如果软件能够像现在的药物能做到的那样拯救生命，那么大数据就有望像大型制药公司那样发挥作用。 [2018 年英语（一）阅读]

pledge to　承诺，保证

词 pledge [pledʒ] v. 承诺，保证

真 It also **pledged** not **to** deploy AI whose use would violate international laws or human rights. 它还承诺不会部署用途会违反国际法或侵犯人权的人工智能。 [2017 年英语（二）阅读]

拓 promise to do sth. 承诺做某事

substitute for　代替，取代

词 substitute ['sʌbstɪtjuːt] v. 代替 n. 代替者；代替物

真 And vice versa: High sympathy can **substitute for** low guilt. 反之亦然，高同情可以代替低内疚。 [2019 年英语（二）阅读]

拓 replace A with B 用 B 代替 A

wait for　等待

真 **wait for** confidence to return 等待信心的回归 [2010 年英语（二）阅读]

拓 expect for 期待，期盼

draw (sb.'s) attention to　吸引（某人的）注意，令（某人）注意　○○○

真 These benefactors have succeeded in their chosen fields, they say, and they want to use their wealth to **draw attention to** those who have succeeded in science. 他们表示，这些捐助者在他们选择的领域取得了成功，他们想用自己的财富来吸引人们对那些在科学上取得成功的人的关注。　　　　　　　　　　　　　　　　　　　　　　　　[2014 年英语（一）阅读]

拓 catch sb.'s attention/eye 吸引某人的注意

none of...　……之中没有任何一个　○○○

真 **None of** these will be easy but you can start even if others refuse to. 这些方式没有一个是容易的，但是即便其他人拒绝，你也可以尝试开始。　　　　　　　　　　[2019 年英语（一）阅读]

decide to　决定　○○○

真 The crash was a major reason the U.S. Fish and Wildlife Service (USFWS) **decided to** formally list the bird as threatened. 这一数量骤减是美国鱼类和野生动植物管理局决定正式将这种鸟列为受威胁物种的主要原因。　　　　　　　　　　[2016 年英语（二）阅读]

拓 determine to 决定 ‖ make up one's mind 决定

in the long term　从长期来看；从长远来看　○○○

例 **In the long term,** the deal will have positive results for both sides. 从长远来看，这次交易对双方都将产生积极的影响。

拓 in the long run 从长远来看

break up　使分裂；解散；分手　◇

真 It's like the teacher who **breaks up** the troublemakers in the back row by pairing them with better-behaved classmates. 这就像老师把后排的捣乱分子与表现较好的同学组成一对，用这种方式把这些捣乱分子分开一样。　　　　　　　　　　[2012 年英语（一）阅读]

拓 break up with 与……分手 ‖ break away from 脱离

do without　没有……也行　○○○

真 Certainly, no homework should be assigned that students cannot complete on their own or that they cannot **do without** expensive equipment. 当然，不应该布置一些学生靠自己不能完成的作业，或者他们不借助昂贵设备难以完成的作业。　　　　　　　　[2012 英语（二）阅读]

| **come about** | 产生；发生 | |

例 If you don't like your life, instead of wallowing in self-pity, see yourself changing it and then what you envision will **come about**. 如果不喜欢自己的生活，不要沉溺于自怜之中，而要靠自己去改变，然后你预想的就会发生。

| **comment on** | 评论 | |

真 Even after the advent of widespread social media, a pyramid of production remains, with a small number of people uploading material, a slightly larger group **commenting on** or modifying that content, and a huge percentage remaining content to just consume. 甚至在社交媒体广泛出现之后，仍然存在金字塔式的生产结构，即只有一小部分人上传信息，稍多的人对此信息进行评论或修改，而绝大部分人仅仅满足于消费这些信息。

[2012 英语（一）阅读]

| **a number of** | 若干；许多 | |

真 While all of these countries face their own challenges, there are **a number of** consistent themes. 尽管这些国家自身都面临一些问题，还是有若干始终一致的主题。

[2017 英语（一）阅读]

| **by nature** | 天生，就其本性而言 | |

真 This movement, driven by powerful and diverse motivations, built a nation out of a wilderness and, **by** its **nature**, shaped the character and destiny of an uncharted continent. 这场移民运动由各种强大的动机所推动，在一片荒野之中创立了一个国家，而且就其本质而言，该运动也塑造了一个未知大陆的性格并决定了它的命运。

[2015 年英语（一）翻译]

| **bring out** | 使出现，使显明；公布，出版 | |

真 In fact, circumstances seem to be designed to **bring out** the best in us. 事实上，环境似乎旨在激发我们的最大潜能。

[2011 年英语（一）翻译]

| **make no difference** | 没有影响，没有作用 | |

真 It **makes no difference** how you write, just so you do. 如何写并不重要，重要的是你要付诸笔端。

[2008 年英语（一）阅读]

本单元资源

be hostile to/towards 对……怀有敌意，对……极不友好

例 Many of those disgruntled people **are** actively **hostile to** Obamacare. But they might **be** even more **hostile to** any effort to kill the law. 牢骚满腹的民众可能对奥巴马医疗改革充满敌意，但是他们可能对任何要废除该法案的举动更为不满。

be linked to 与……有关

真 That's because happiness **is linked to** the kind of longer-term thinking necessary for making investments for the future. 那是因为快乐与一种更长远的思维方式有关，而这种长远思维是对未来进行投资所必需的。

[2016 年英语（二）完形填空]

拓 link...with... 将……与……连接、联系起来

be packed with 充满，填满，塞满

真 This slim volume **is packed with** tips to help wage slaves as well as lottery winners get the most "happiness bang for your buck." 这本薄薄的小书涵盖了许多建议，这些建议既可以帮助工薪阶层也可以帮助乐透幸运儿们最大程度地享受"金钱带来的快乐"。

[2014 年英语（二）阅读]

be apt to 易于；倾向于

真 The digital services tax **is apt to** arouse criticism at home and abroad. 数字服务税容易引起国内外的批评。

[2020 年英语（二）阅读]

assign sb. to (do) sth. 指定或委派某人做某事

真 The student union of your university has **assigned** you **to** inform the international students about an upcoming singing contest. 你们学校的学生会让你通知留学生关于即将举行的歌唱比赛的事情。

[2020 年英语（二）阅读]

拓 assign sth. to sb. 将某事物分配给某人

stick with 坚持；紧跟

真 Human nature being what it is, most people **stick with** default settings. 人性就是这样，大多数人都坚持使用默认设置。

[2013 年英语（一）阅读]

拓 stick to 坚持 ‖ persevere with 坚持 ‖ persist in 坚持，固执于

tease out　梳理，提炼

词 tease [tiːz] *v.* 梳理；取笑；招惹

真 It is really important to understand and try and **tease out** what is the human connection with fire today. 理解并尝试梳理出当今人类与火的关系是非常重要的。　　[2017 年英语（二）阅读]

rise above　克服；不受……的影响

真 We still have the imaginative capacity to **rise above** temptation and reverse the high-speed trend. 我们仍然有摆脱诱惑、扭转高速发展趋势的想象力。　　[2013 年英语（二）阅读]

拓 overcome [ˌəʊvəˈkʌm] *v.* 克服

wipe out　摧毁；使灭绝

例 Many historical buildings were **wiped out** in the endless chaos of war. 在无穷尽的战乱中，许多历史建筑遭到了摧毁。

拓 demolish [dɪˈmɒlɪʃ] *v.* 摧毁

strip sb. of sth.　剥夺某人的某事物

词 strip [strɪp] *v.* 剥夺；除去；剥去；拆卸

真 Downloading and consuming culture requires great skills, but failing to move beyond downloading is to **strip** oneself **of** a defining constituent of humanity. 下载和消费文化需要高超的技巧，但如果不能超越下载，就等于剥夺了人类的一种决定性成分。

　　[2012 年英语（一）阅读]

come to terms with　接受，适应；达成妥协

真 Professor Balch points out that fire is something man should **come to terms with**. 鲍尔奇教授指出，人类应该接受火这一事实。　　[2012 年英语（一）阅读]

拓 compromise [ˈkɒmprəmaɪz] *n./v.* 妥协，让步 ‖ make a compromise 做出让步

place/put emphasis on　强调，重视

真 And **placing** too much **emphasis on** their opinions can ruin a fantastic home purchase. 过分强调他们的观点会毁掉一场美妙的购房之旅。　　[2019 年英语（二）阅读]

拓 emphasize [ˈemfəsaɪz] *v.* 强调；重视 ‖ highlight [ˈhaɪlaɪt] *v.* 突出；强调 ‖ stress [stres] *v.* 强调；着重；重读

DAY 03

side with 支持；站在……的一边

例 It chooses to **side with** information behemoths rather than promote competition. 它选择支持信息业巨头，而不是促进竞争。

拓 be for 支持 ‖ back sb./sth. up 支持某人 / 某事物

look after 照顾；照管

真 **look after** their wellbeing 照管好他们的幸福 [2016 年英语（二）阅读]

rush to 匆忙，急于

真 In fact, **rushing to** get your own ideas out there can cause colleagues to feel you don't value their opinions. 事实上，急于把自己的想法说出来会让同事觉得你不重视他们的意见。

[2020 年英语（二）阅读]

set off 出发，动身；引起，使发生

真 **set off** to run 5km around their local park 开始绕着他们当地的公园跑 5000 米

[2017 年英语（二）阅读]

拓 set out 出发 ‖ start off 出发，开始

flee to 逃往

真 Yet two years before Dickens's birth, his mother's father was caught stealing and **fled to** Europe, never to return. 然而，就在狄更斯出生前两年，他的外祖父因盗窃被抓现行，逃往欧洲，再也没有回来。

[2017 年英语（一）阅读]

拓 escape from 从……逃离；免于……

out of line 出格；越轨；不成直线

例 The hostess stepped **out of line** when she laughed at the guest in the program. 当女主持人在节目中嘲笑嘉宾的时候，她的行为出格了。

with the exception of 除了……之外

真 Unfortunately, L.A. Unified has produced an inflexible policy which mandates that **with the exception of** some advanced courses, homework may no longer count for more than 10% of a student's academic grade. 不幸的是，洛杉矶联合大学制定了一项不灵活的政策，规定除了一些高级课程外，家庭作业在学生学业成绩中的占比不得超过 10%。 [2012 年英语（二）阅读]

lay off
解雇；停止工作 ○○○

真 Millennials remember their father and mother both were **laid off**. 千禧一代记得他们的父亲和母亲曾双双失业。
[2017 年英语（二）阅读]

set back
阻碍，使受挫；推迟，延误 ○○○

真 Yet its report may well **set back** reform by obscuring the depth and breadth of the challenge that Congress asked it to illuminate. 然而，其报告很可能因为模糊了国会要求它阐明的挑战的深度和广度而阻碍改革。
[2014 年英语（一）阅读]

拓 obstruct [əb'strʌkt] v. 阻挡；妨碍 ‖ hinder ['hɪndə(r)] v. 阻碍，妨碍

be born with
与生俱来，天生 ○○○

真 The most famous of these efforts was initiated by Noam Chomsky, who suggested that humans **are born with** an innate language-acquisition capacity that dictates a universal grammar. 这些成果中最著名的是由诺姆·乔姆斯基提出的，他认为人类天生就具有支配通用语法的语言习得能力。
[2012 年英语（一）翻译]

拓 innate [ɪ'neɪt] a. 固有的；与生俱来的 ‖ inborn [ˌɪn'bɔːn] a. 天生的

no less than
不少于，多达 ○○○

真 This alone demonstrates that the television business is not an easy world to survive in, a fact underlined by statistics that show that out of eighty European television networks, **no less than** 50% took a loss in 1989. 仅这一点就表明，在电视行业生存并不容易。统计数据显示，在 1989 年 80 家欧洲电视网中，亏损的不下 50%。
[2005 年英语（一）翻译]

in such a case
在这种情况下 ○○○

真 **In such a case**, the company's response may not be sufficiently quick or thoughtful, and the learning curve has been steep. 在这种情况下，企业的回应也许不够快或深思熟虑，而且学习曲线一直都很陡峭（即时间紧，任务重）。
[2011 年英语（一）阅读]

拓 in this case 在这种情况下

all the more so
更是如此 ○○○

真 But they certainly will reshape it, and **all the more so** the longer they extend. 但它们肯定会重塑美国，而且时间越长，影响就越大。
[2012 年英语（二）阅读]

DAY
03

be accessible to 容易接近的，容易进入的

真 They **are** easily **accessible to** the general public. 对普通大众来说它们很容易获得。

[2011 年英语（一）阅读]

in essence 本质上；大体上

真 The administration was **in essence** asserting that because it didn't want to carry out Congress's immigration wishes, no state should be allowed to do so either. 政府本质上是在宣称，因为它不想执行国会在移民方面的意愿，所以任何州都不应该被允许这样做。[2013 年英语（一）阅读]

拓 in nature 本质上 ‖ essentially [ɪ'senʃəli] *ad.* 本质上 ‖ substantially [səb'stænʃəli] *ad.* 基本上；大体上

cling to 紧握；依附；坚持

真 Everyone around us seems to agree by the way they **cling to** their phones, even without a signal on a subway. 我们周围的每个人似乎都认同，即使地铁里没有信号，他们也会紧握手机。

[2015 年英语（二）完形填空]

拓 persevere with 坚持

do harm to 对……不利；伤害

例 **do harm to** the environment 对环境造成破坏

拓 do good to 对……有利

make it 做成某事；获得成功

真 Will the European Union **make it**? 欧盟会成功吗？ [2011 年英语（二）阅读]

for the better 好转，向好的方向发展

真 On first hearing, this was the socially concerned chancellor, trying to change lives **for the better**, complete with "reforms" to an obviously indulgent system that demands too little effort from the newly unemployed to find work, and subsidises laziness. 乍一听来，这是一位关注社会的财政大臣，他试图让生活变得更好，完成了对一个明显放纵的体制的"改革"，这个体制对新失业者找工作的要求太低，而且助长了懒惰。 [2014 年英语（一）阅读]

拓 for the worse 变糟糕，向坏的方向发展

for fear of/that 为了避免，唯恐

真 Dead markets partly reflect the paralysis of banks which will not sell assets **for fear of** booking losses, yet are reluctant to buy all those supposed bargains. 市场失灵部分反映了银行的瘫痪，它们不愿出售资产，因为担心出现亏损，但又不愿购买所有这些所谓的便宜货。

[2010 年英语（一）阅读]

拓 lest [lest] *conj.* 以免，免得 ‖ in case of 以防万一

take control of 控制

真 Once a discovery claim becomes public, the discoverer receives intellectual credit. But, unlike with mining claims, the community **takes control of** what happens next. 一旦一项研究发现被公开，发现者就会获得学术声望。但是，与矿藏发现不同的是，科学界会控制接下来发生的事情。

[2012 年英语（一）阅读]

拓 in control of 控制 ‖ under the control of 处于……的控制之下

bear on/upon 对……有影响；与……有关

例 Countries differ in a large number of respects that **bear on** economic performance. 国家之间在诸多方面都有所差异，这些差异都会对国家的经济表现产生影响。

拓 in/with relation to 与……有关；涉及

flag up 使……注意；指出

真 Manuscript will be **flagged up** for additional scrutiny by the journal's internal editors, or by its existing Board of Reviewing Editors or by outside peer reviewers. 原稿将由期刊的内部编辑，或现有的审查编辑委员会或外部同行审稿人进行额外的审查。 [2015 年英语（一）阅读]

in need of 需要；缺少 ○○○

真 The French tax is not just a unilateral move by one country **in need of** revenue. 法国的这一征税并不是一个需要税收的国家单方面采取的行动。 [2020 年英语（一）阅读]

拓 a friend in need 患难之交

turn on 取决于；打开（电视、收音机等）；以……为主要议题 ○○○

真 For the low-sympathy kids, how much they shared appeared to **turn on** how inclined they were to feel guilty. 对于缺乏同情心的孩子来说，他们分享的多少取决于他们有多容易感到内疚。

[2019 年英语（二）阅读]

拓 depend on 取决于 ‖ lie on 取决于

in the meantime　与此同时，在此期间

真 **In the meantime**, thriving Spanish colonies had been established in Mexico, the West Indies, and South America. 与此同时，西班牙在墨西哥、西印度群岛和南美洲建立了繁荣的殖民地。 [2015 年英语（一）翻译]

拓 simultaneously [ˌsɪml'teɪnɪəsli] *ad.* 同时

participate in　参加，参与

词 participate [pɑːˈtɪsɪpeɪt] *v.* 参加，参与

真 If you have no friends or relatives, try to **participate in** several online communities, full of people who are always willing to share advice and encouragement. 如果你没有朋友或亲戚，可以试着参加一些线上社区，那里到处都是愿意分享建议和鼓励的人。[2015 年英语（二）阅读]

apply to　应用于；适用于

真 We become defensive when criticised, and **apply** negative stereotypes **to** others to boost our own esteem. 当受到批评时，我们会变得具有防御性，并把负面的刻板印象施加于他人，以此来提升自己的自尊。 [2014 年英语（二）阅读]

out of necessity　出于必要，由于需要

词 necessity [nəˈsesəti] *n.* 必要；需要；必然

真 At the same time, people continue to treat fire as an event that needs to be wholly controlled and unleashed only **out of necessity**. 与此同时，人们一如既往地认为火是一个需要被彻底控制住的事物，并且只有在必要的时候才能释放。 [2017 年英语（二）阅读]

manage to　设法（做成）

真 **manage to** select 设法选择 [2015 年英语（一）阅读]

leave behind　留下；落后；永远离开

真 There is often much housework **left behind**. 经常有很多家务活被落下。

[2015 年英语（二）阅读]

on the one hand　一方面

真 **On the one hand**, it's a necessary condition for many worthwhile things: child care,

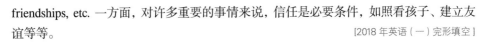

friendships, etc. 一方面，对许多重要的事情来说，信任是必要条件，如照看孩子、建立友谊等等。

[2018 年英语（一）完形填空]

on the other hand　　另一方面

真 **On the other hand**, putting your faith in the wrong place often carries a high price. 另一方面，在错误的地方施以信任往往会付出高昂的代价。

[2018 年英语（一）阅读]

concern for　　对（人、组织等）重要的事情；……负责的事；担心，忧虑

真 And anything that raises GPAs will likely make students—who, at the end of the day, are paying the bill—feel they've gotten a better value for their tuition dollars, which is another big **concern for** colleges. 任何一个提高平均成绩的做法都可能会让学生——说到底，是他们在支付学费——觉得他们交的学费是值得的，这是各个大学要考虑到的另一个重大问题。

[2019 年英语（一）阅读]

at a time　　每次；依次；逐一

真 Buy all your clothes at once with a stylist instead of shopping alone, one article of clothing **at a time**. 和造型师一起一次买完所有的衣服，而不是自己独自购物，每次只买一件。

[2016 年英语（一）阅读]

differentiate...from...　　构成……间的差别；使……有差别

词 differentiate [ˌdɪfəˈrenʃieɪt] v. 使有差别；区分

真 Our ability to mute our hard-wired reactions by pausing is what **differentiates** us **from** animals: dogs can think about the future only intermittently or for a few minutes. 我们有通过暂停来减少本能回应的能力，这是我们和动物的区别：狗会考虑未来，但这种思考不连续，或者只有几分钟。

[2013 年英语（二）阅读]

correspond to　　相一致，符合；相当于，类似于

词 correspond [ˌkɒrəˈspɒnd] v. 相一致；相对应

真 In the end, credibility "happens" to a discovery claim—a process that **corresponds to** what philosopher Annette Baier has described as the commons of the mind. 最终，一项科学发现声明被人们所相信——这个过程恰与哲学家安妮特·拜尔所描述的"思想的共性"是一致的。

[2012 年英语（一）阅读]

split up　　（使）分开；（使）分手；（使）朝不同方向去　　

词 split [splɪt] v. （使）裂开；（使）分开

例 They cooked breakfast, drank coffee, and then **split up** to go to school. 他们做了早餐，喝了咖啡，然后分头上学去了。

keep to　　不偏离，不离开；遵循；忠于，信守（诺言等）

例 The key to mastering the art of deep work is to **keep to** your focus time. 掌握深度工作艺术的关键是保持你的专注时间。

at night　　在晚上

真 to sleep **at night** 晚上睡觉　　　　　　　　　　　　　　[2006 年英语（一）完形填空]

拓 in the morning 在早上；上午 ‖ at noon 中午

fend off　　抵御，抵挡；回避，避开　　

真 Healthy trees are also better able to **fend off** insects. 健康的树木也能够更好地抵御昆虫。

[2019 年英语（二）阅读]

拓 fend for oneself 照顾自己；自谋生计；独立生活

be another matter　　是另外一个问题；另当别论　　

真 Whether the separation distances involved would satisfy air-traffic-control regulations **is another matter**. （飞行）间距是否符合空中交通管制条例则是另外一个问题。

[2010 年英语（二）阅读]

prove to be　　后来被发现是；最终显现为　　

真 *Happy Money* may **prove to be** a worthwhile purchase.《幸福金钱》可能会被证明是值得购买的。　　　　　　　　　　　　　　　　　　　　　　　　　[2014 年英语（二）阅读]

the hard way　　艰难地　　

真 Everything he achieved in life was earned **the hard way** and his success in the literary field was no exception. 他一生所获得的成就，每一样都来之不易，他在文学领域获得的成功也不例外。　　　　　　　　　　　　　　　　　　　　　　　　　[2019 年英语（二）翻译]

a kind of　　一种；某种，几分，隐约

真 **a kind of** insidious prejudice 一种隐性的偏见　　　　　　[2018 年英语（二）阅读]

拓 kind of 稍微，有几分，有点儿

| **in total** | 总计，共计 | |

真 Roughly one out of every three manufacturing jobs—about 6 million **in total**—disappeared. 大约三分之一的制造业岗位消失了，也就是总数约 600 万个岗位。 [2013 年英语（二）阅读]

| **compensate for** | 弥补；补偿；赔偿 | |

真 Health-savings plans will **compensate for** the reduced pensions. 医疗储蓄计划将弥补减少的养老金。 [2007 年英语（一）阅读]

| **need to** | 需要 | |

真 That tells me whether I **need to** confirm my training program. 那会告诉我是否需要调整自己的训练计划。 [2019 年英语（二）完形填空]

| **be biased against/towards** | 对……有偏见 | |

词 biased ['baɪəst] *a.* 有偏见的；倾向性的；片面的

真 Professors **are biased against** classical liberal ideas. 教授们对古典自由主义思想有偏见。 [2014 年英语（一）阅读]

| **pop into** | 突然出现；冷不防冒出 | |

词 pop [pɒp] *v.* 发出砰的响声；突然出现 *n.* 流行乐

真 I also remember that the musical play *Hair* opened on Broadway on the same day—they both just **pop into** my mind in the same way. 我也还记得音乐剧《发》也在那一天在百老汇首演——这两件事就那么以同样的方式突然浮现在我的脑海中。 [2013 年英语（二）翻译]

拓 pop up 突然出现或浮现

| **for sale** | 待售，供出售（尤指从主人手里） | |

例 The owner of the painting was putting it up **for sale** in good faith, but he or she is likely to lose it without compensation when it is returned to France. 此画的所有者基于善意将作品拿出来出售，但是当作品送还法国时，他或她很可能失去该画，并且得不到任何赔偿。

拓 on sale 出售，上市；减价出售

| **work against** | 努力反对，对抗 | |

例 These antibodies **work against** such kind of virus. 这些抗体能够对抗这种病毒。

拓 work for 努力促成

wake up　　醒来

（真）**wake up** in the middle of the night 在半夜醒来　　[2010 年英语（二）翻译]

at the same time　　同时

（真）**At the same time**, the European Union, Spain, Britain and several other countries have all seriously contemplated digital services taxes. 与此同时，欧盟、西班牙、英国和其他几个国家都在认真考虑征收数字服务税。　　[2020 年英语（一）阅读]

（拓）meanwhile ['miːnwaɪl] *ad.* 其间，同时

cannot but / cannot help (but)　　禁不住

（例）I **cannot but** feel excited whenever I visit the city. 无论何时来到这个城市，我都会情不自禁感到激动。

be better off (doing)　　更好的；更幸福的；是较为明智的

（真）It seems most people would **be better off** if they could shorten their commutes to work, spend more time with friends and family and less of it watching television. 看起来，如果人们能缩短通勤时间，用更多时间陪伴家人和朋友，减少看电视的时间，就能更快乐。

[2014 年英语（二）阅读]

classify...into...　　把……分成……

（词）classify ['klæsɪfaɪ] *v.* 将……分类；划分

（真）Department stores were advised to **classify** consumers **into** smaller groups. 百货商店被建议把消费者细分成更小的群体。　　[2012 年英语（二）阅读]

cast/shed/throw light on sth.　　使某事物清楚些，阐明某事物

（真）A recent annual study of countries and their ability to convert growth into well-being **sheds** some **light on** that question. 最近一份关于各国及其将经济增长转化为福祉的能力的年度研究阐明了这一问题。　　[2017 年英语（一）阅读]

above average　　在平均水平之上

（真）The best jobs will require workers to have more and better education to make themselves **above average**. 最好的工作会要求员工有更多、更好的教育，以使自己远在平均水平之上。

[2013 年英语（二）阅读]

be cautious about　对……持谨慎态度

词 cautious ['kɔːʃəs] *a.* 谨慎的；小心的；细心的

真 Professors **are cautious about** intellectual investigation. 教授们对智力调查持谨慎态度。

[2014 年英语（一）阅读]

give away　赠送，免费送出；分发；丧失（优势）；暴露

真 Americans, she finds, buy roughly 20 billion garments a year—about 64 items per person—and no matter how much they **give away**, this excess leads to waste. 她发现，美国人一年大约要购置 200 亿件服装——平均每人约 64 件——无论他们会捐赠多少，这种过量还是会导致浪费。

[2013 年英语（一）阅读]

to say nothing of　更不用说

真 Both the Romanow commission and the Kirby committee on health care—**to say nothing of** reports from other experts—recommended the creation of a national drug agency. 罗曼诺委员会和科比健康委员会——且不说其他专家的报告——都建议成立一个全国性的药物机构。

[2005 年英语（一）阅读]

obstacle to　成为……的障碍

真 But, when one considers the **obstacles to** achieving the meritocratic ideal, it does look as if a fairer world must be temporarily ordered. 但是，当考虑到实现一个英才制度的理想所面临的障碍，确实看上去一个更加公平的世界需要暂时被管理。

[2013 年英语（二）阅读]

apart from　除去

真 Even today, in our industrial life, **apart from** certain values of industriousness and thrift, the intellectual and emotional reaction of the forms of human association under which the world's work is carried on receives little attention as compared with physical output. 甚至在今天，在我们的工业社会中，除了某些勤奋和节俭的价值观念之外，整个世界得以运转的各种形式的人类联合所产生的对于人类理智和情感的影响，和物质产出比较起来，所受到的关注微乎其微。

[2009 年英语（一）翻译]

more often than not　通常，多半

真 Soon you'll feel comfortable asking if they've any knuckles of ham for soups and stews, or beef bones, chicken carcasses and fish heads for stock which, **more often than not**, they'll let you have for free. 很快你就会发现，当你问店主们是否有做汤和炖菜用的猪腿骨或者煲原汤用的牛骨、鸡骨架和鱼头时，自己就不会觉得尴尬了，而且这些东西他们经常会免费送给你。

[2013 年英语（二）阅读]

in particular　　特别地，尤其；详细地

真 Another approach to getting more done in less time is to rethink how you prioritize your day—**in particular** how we craft our to-do lists. 想要在更少的时间里做更多的事还有一个方法，那就是重新考虑一天之中的事情孰轻孰重，特别是该如何精巧地安排我们的待办事项清单。

[2018 年英语（二）阅读]

nothing but　　只有，仅仅

真 Alvarez cared about **nothing but** making money. 阿尔瓦雷斯只关心赚钱。

[2008 年英语（一）阅读]

appeal to　　对……有吸引力；向……上诉；要求，请求，呼吁

真 Lower-income jobs like gardening or day care don't **appeal to** robots. 低收入的工作，比如园艺或者日托，对机器人没有什么吸引力。

[2018 年英语（一）阅读]

on paper　　以书面的形式；理论上；表面上；在筹划中

真 Once you have a first draft **on paper**, you can delete material that is unrelated to your thesis and add material necessary to illustrate your points and make your paper convincing. 一旦初稿完成，你就可以删除与主题无关的内容，并增加必要的内容以阐述你的观点，并使文章更具有说服力。

[2008 年英语（一）阅读]

in/with relation to　　关于，涉及；与……有关

真 In Europe, as elsewhere, multi-media groups have been increasingly successful: groups which bring together television, radio, newspapers, magazines and publishing houses that work **in relation to** one another 在欧洲，同其他地方一样，传媒集团越来越成功：这些集团将协同运作的电视、广播、报纸、杂志和出版社融合在一起。

[2005 年英语（一）阅读]

in spite of　　尽管，虽然；不管，不顾

真 **In spite of** "endless talk of difference," American society is an amazing machine for homogenizing people. 尽管"人们不停地谈论着差异"，美国社会却是一台惊人的同化人的机器。

[2006 年英语（一）阅读]

拓 even so 尽管如此，虽然这样

account for （数量等）占；解释，说明（原因等）

真 The move to renewables is picking up momentum around the world: They now **account for** more than half of new power sources going on line. 使用可再生能源在全球范围内呈现增长势头：现在使用的新能源中，半数以上都是可再生能源。 [2018 年英语（二）阅读]

拓 make clear 解释清楚

from the bottom up 从下到上

真 Only over the past 20 years have scholars examined history **from the bottom up**. 学者们仅在过去的二十年间才开始从头彻底地研究历史。 [2008 年英语（一）阅读]

拓 from bottom to top 自下而上 ‖ from the bottom of one's heart 由衷地

本单元资源

for the benefit of　　为了……的利益

真 Both the wildlife park and zoo claimed to be operating **for the benefit of** the animals and for conservation purposes. 野生动物园和动物园都声称其运营是为了动物的利益和出于保护动物的目的。 [2022 年英语（一）阅读]

拓 for sb's benefit 以对某人进行帮助、指引、指导等

be beneficial to　　对……有利

真 It can be inferred that the "high-income threshold" in Australia **is beneficial to** business owners. 可以推断，澳大利亚的"高收入门槛"对企业主是有利的。 [2022 年英语（一）阅读]

拓 be detrimental to 对……有害，不利于……

back off/down　　放弃；放手；屈服

真 If you're breathing too hard to talk in complete sentences, **back off**.（运动时）如果你呼吸困难而无法说出完整的句子，那就先别做了。 [2022 年英语（二）阅读]

拓 give up 放弃

accountable to　　对……负责

真 Dark patterns also can be addressed on a self-regulatory basis, but only if organizations hold themselves **accountable**, not just **to** legal requirements, but also **to** industry best practices and standards. "暗黑设计"也可以在自我监管的基础上得到解决，但前提是各机构不仅要对法律规定负责，还要对行业最佳范例和标准负责。 [2022 年英语（二）阅读]

Dark Pattern：指一种精心布局以诱导用户完成某件事的界面设计。

拓 be responsible for (doing) sth. 对（做）某事负责

by design　　故意地，有意地

真 This all seems random, but it's **by design**, part of what the $6.1 billion U.S. egg industry bets will be its next big thing: climate-friendly eggs. 这一切似乎都是随机的，但却是有意为之，美国鸡蛋行业投资 61 亿美元的下一件大事就是气候友好型鸡蛋。 [2022 年英语（二）阅读]

拓 on purpose 故意地

decline to do sth.　　婉言拒绝做某事

真 Microsoft **declined to** comment. 微软谢绝发表评论。 [2021 年英语（二）阅读]

from the ground up 完全，彻底地

真 Microsoft's own Office dominates the market for "productivity" software, but the start-ups represented a new wave of technology designed **from the ground up** for the smartphone world. 微软自己的 Office 软件主导着"生产力"软件市场，但这些初创企业代表了完全为智能手机世界设计的新一波技术。 [2021 年英语（二）阅读]

hear about 听到关于……的消息

例 When it comes to AI in business, we often **hear about** it in relation to automation and the impending loss of jobs, but in what ways is AI changing companies and the larger economy that don't involve doom-and-gloom mass unemployment predictions? 说到商业中的人工智能，我们经常会听闻它与自动化和即将到来的失业有关，但是人工智能是以什么方式改变那些预计不会面临惨淡的大规模裁员的公司和更大的经济体的呢？ [2021 年英语（一）阅读]

hold off 推迟；拖延

真 You may decide it's best to **hold off** on voicing your opinion. 你可能会决定最好还是暂时不要说出自己的意见。 [2021 年英语（二）阅读]

in private 私下地；无他人在场

真 Discussing the issue **in private** will make the powerful person feel less threatened. 私下讨论这个问题会让有权的人感觉不那么受威胁。 [2021 年英语（二）阅读]

拓 privately ['praɪvətli] *ad.* 私下地

in short order 立即，迅速地

真 The threat of nationalisation may have been seen off for now, but it will return with a vengeance if the justified anger of passengers is not addressed **in short order**. 目前国有化的威胁可能已经被消除，但如果乘客合理的愤怒不能立即得到处理，国有化的威胁将会大肆卷土重来。 [2021 年英语（一）阅读]

with a vengeance （比正常或预期）程度更深或更甚；猛烈地

例 Last year's Greek bailout didn't solve the problem and now it's back **with a vengeance**. 去年的希腊救助方案并未解决问题，如今它又气势汹汹地卷土重来了。

拓 to a greater degree 程度更深或更甚

level out/off（升或跌之后）呈平稳状态；水平飞行 ⟅⟅⟅

It peaks in young adulthood, **levels out** for a period of time, and then generally starts to slowly decline as we age. 它（流体智力）在成年早期达到最高水平，在一段时间内保持稳定，然后通常会随着我们年龄的增长而开始慢慢下降。 [2021 年英语（一）完形]

shy away from (doing) sth.避免或逃避（做）某事 ⟅⟅⟅

The researchers also argued that when we **shy away from** casual interactions with strangers, it is often due to a misplaced anxiety that they might not want to talk to us. 研究人员还声称，我们羞于与陌生人进行随意的互动往往是出于一种不应该有的焦虑，担心他们可能不想和我们说话。 [2021 年英语（二）翻译]

strike up (with)（与……）开始（交往、认识、交谈等） ⟅⟅⟅

In one series of studies, researchers instructed Chicago-area commuters using public transportation to **strike up** a conversation with someone near them. 在一系列研究中，研究人员让芝加哥地区乘坐公共交通工具的通勤者主动与其周围的人攀谈。[2021 年英语（二）翻译]

draw in（指白天的时间）渐短；使参与 ⟅⟅⟅

It won't be easy for you to **draw** him **in**. 你要让他参与进来可不容易。

proceed to前往；继续前进；继续进行 ⟅⟅⟅

Dr. Kroo and his team modeled what would happen if three passenger jets departing from Los Angeles, San Francisco and Las Vegas were to assemble over Utah, assume an inverted V-formation, occasionally change places so all could have a turn in the most favourable positions, and **proceed to** London. 克鲁教授和他的团队模拟了如下情形的后果：三架客机分别从洛杉矶、旧金山和拉斯维加斯起飞，在犹他州集合，采用反 V 字形并偶尔换一下位置，以便所有飞机轮流利用最有利位置，最后飞到伦敦。 [2010 年英语（二）阅读]

or so大约，左右 ⟅⟅⟅

In the last decade **or so**, advances in technology have allowed mass-market labels such as Zara, H&M, and Uniqlo to react to trends more quickly and anticipate demand more precisely. 在过去约十年的时间里，科技的进步使得诸如 Zara、H&M 和 Uniqlo 等大众品牌能对时尚趋势做出迅速反应，并且能更加准确地预估市场需求。 [2013 年英语（一）阅读]

depart from 起飞；离开；偏离，违背 〇〇〇

例 Flight F307 will **depart from** Dubai at 9:00 am. 航班 F307 将于上午 9 点从迪拜起飞。

拓 depart for 去往

amount to 总计，共达 〇〇〇

真 Given the current divorce rate of nearly 50 percent, that **amounts to** millions of cases in the United States every year—a virtual epidemic of failed conversation. 考虑到当前离婚率将近 50%，每年美国离婚案例总计可达上百万，不得不说这是由交流不畅引发的一场流行病。

[2010 年英语（二）阅读]

insist on 坚持，坚决主张；一定要；坚持说 〇〇〇

真 In the real world, as in school, we **insist on** choosing our own friends. 在现实生活中，就像在学校一样，我们都坚持自己选择朋友。 [2012 年英语（一）阅读]

peculiar to 特有；独特 〇〇〇

真 But the force of geographic conditions **peculiar to** America, the interplay of the varied national groups upon one another, and the sheer difficulty of maintaining old-world ways in a raw, new continent caused significant changes. 但是美国特有的地理条件的作用，不同民族之间的相互影响，以及在这个原始的新大陆上维持欧洲移民原有的生活方式所面临的极大困难引起了显著的变化。 [2015 年英语（一）阅读]

do/try one's utmost 竭力，竭尽所能 〇〇〇

真 Colleges continue to **do their utmost** to keep students in school (and paying tuition) and improve their graduation rates. 大学继续竭力让学生留在学校（并支付学费），提高他们的毕业率。 [2019 年英语（一）阅读]

be independent of 独立于……之外；不依赖 〇〇〇

真 Chomsky's grammar should show patterns of language change that **are independent of** the family tree or the pathway tracked through it. 乔姆斯基的语法应该体现语言变化的模式，不论这种模式是独立于该系谱，还是独立于贯穿该系谱所经由的路径。

[2012 年英语（一）翻译]

provide...with sth. 给……提供某事物 〇〇〇

真 The same dramatic technological changes that have **provided** marketers **with** more (and more diverse) communications choices have also increased the risk that passionate consumers will voice their opinions in quicker, more visible, and much more damaging ways. 同样剧烈的技术变革为营销人员提供了更多的（以及更加多样的）交流方式，但同时也增加了这样的风险——情绪激动的消费者会以更快、更明显和更具破坏性的方式去表达他们的意见。

[2011 年英语（一）阅读]

body of　　大量；大批；大堆

真 Yet only one of his books is now in print, and his vast **body of** writings on music is unknown save to specialists. 然而，他那么多书现在只有一本在出版，除了专家之外，其关于音乐的大量著作无人知晓。

[2010 年英语（一）阅读]

come along　　一起来；不期而至，突然出现；在进展

例 Miracles don't **come along** very often. 奇迹不会常常出现。

be concerned with　　关注

真 He was not interested in daily politics, but **concerned with** questions of moral behavior and the larger questions of right and wrong affecting the entire society. 他对日常发生的政治事件并不感兴趣，但他很关注道德行为问题以及可对整个社会造成影响的是非观念这些更为重要的问题。

[2014 年英语（一）翻译]

struggle against　　与……斗争

真 The recession has made people **struggle against** each other. 经济衰退使人们互相争斗。

[2012 年英语（二）阅读]

struggle to　　极力挣扎；努力

真 Schneider, a 27-year-old auto technician from the Chicago suburbs, says he **struggled to** find a job after graduating from college. 施耐德 27 岁，是一个来自芝加哥郊区的汽车技师，他说他在大学毕业后费了很大的力气才找到工作。

[2016 年英语（二）阅读]

take turns　　轮流

真 **take turns** governing themselves 轮流管理他们自己

[2010 年英语（二）阅读]

roll out　　推出（新产品或服务）

真 Madrid was hailed as a public health guiding light last November when it **rolled out** ambitious

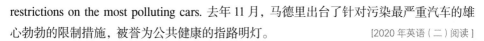

restrictions on the most polluting cars. 去年 11 月，马德里出台了针对污染最严重汽车的雄心勃勃的限制措施，被誉为公共健康的指路明灯。 [2020 年英语（二）阅读]

| **be full of** | 充满 | ◇ |

真 **be full of** potential 充满了潜力 [2012 年英语（一）阅读]

| **prefer to** | 选择；更喜欢 | ◇ |

真 **prefer to** smile and value their life 选择笑对并珍视生活 [2015 年英语（二）阅读]

| **make the most of** | 最大限度地利用 | ◯◯◯ |

真 In order to **make the most of** our focus and energy, we also need to embrace downtime, or as Newport suggests, "be lazy." 为了最大限度地利用我们的注意力和精力，我们还需要欣然接受停工休息，或者像纽波特所说的：犯懒。 [2018 年英语（二）阅读]

拓 make full use of 充分利用

| **in principle** | 原则上；大体上；在理论上 | ◯◯◯ |

词 principle ['prɪnsəpl] *n*. 原则；原理

例 Even if it supported sanctions **in principle**, it was not disposed to support measures that would harm its national economic self-interest. 即使它在原则上支持制裁，它也不愿意支持有损其自身经济利益的措施。

拓 on principle 依据原则

| **outside of** | 在……的外面；除……以外 | ◯◯◯ |

真 A few decades ago, many people didn't drink water **outside of** a meal. 几十年前，许多人不会在用餐以外的时间喝水。 [2010 年英语（二）阅读]

| **receptive to** | 善于接受，敏于接受 | ◯◯◯ |

词 receptive [rɪ'septɪv] *a*. 易于接受的，接受得快的

真 Just as important as being honest about yourself is being **receptive to** others. 和坦诚对待自己一样重要的是要善于接纳他人。 [2020 年英语（二）阅读]

| **(be) second only to** | 仅次于 | ◯◯◯ |

词 second ['sekənd] *a*. 第二的；（重要性、规模、质量等）居第二位的；另外的

例 It has a 27% share of the market, **second only to** Baidu's. 它占据了整个市场份额的 27%，

仅次于百度。

拓 second to last 倒数第二 ‖ second to none 不亚于任何人

middle ground 中间立场，中间观点

真 Looking beyond the culture war logic of right or wrong means opening up the **middle ground**. 要超越这种非对即错的文化战争逻辑就意味着我们要开辟一个折中的地带。

[2013 年英语（二）阅读]

take a/one's stand (on sth.) 宣布（对某事物的）立场、意见等；表明态度

词 stand [stænd] n. 态度；立场；观点

真 In so doing they give composure to a segment of the inarticulate environment in which they **take their stand**. 通过这样做，他们为自身所在的不善表达的局部环境带来了沉静。

[2013 年英语（一）翻译]

hail from 来自

真 This argument has attracted a lot of attention, via the success of the book *Race Against the Machine*, by Erik Brynjolfsson and Andrew McAfee, who both **hail from** MIT's Center for Digital Business. 通过艾立克·布林约尔弗森和安德鲁·麦凯菲共同的著作《同机器赛跑》一书的成功，这一观点受到人们的极大关注，两位作者都来自麻省理工学院的数字化经济中心。

[2014 年英语（二）阅读]

at work 在工作的地方；在起作用，在运转

例 As for Lina, she said, "I feel like I can be more myself than I have ever been and enjoying every minute of that at home or **at work**." 至于莉娜，她说，"我感觉我比以前更能活出自我，我享受这样的每一分钟，不论是在家里还是在工作的地方。"

lead to 导致，造成

真 This could **lead to** the rats better remembering having freed it earlier, and wanting the robot to return the favour when they get trapped, says Quinn. 奎因说，这可能会让老鼠更好地记住早些时候把它放出来的事，并希望当它们被困时，机器老鼠能回报它们。

[2020 年英语（二）阅读]

keep...from doing sth. 防止或阻止……做某事

真 **keep us from sleeping** 使我们无法入睡

[2005 年英语（一）]

all of a sudden 突然；出乎意料地

真 When you start a conversation from there and then move outwards, you will find **all of a sudden** that the conversation becomes a lot easier. 当你从这里发起对话并向外拓展话题时，突然，你就会发现对话变得容易多了。 [2018 年英语（二）阅读]

evolve from 由……演变而来；由……进化而来

词 evolve [ɪˈvɒlv] v. （使）逐渐形成；进化

真 Human indignation **evolved from** an uncertain source. 人类的义愤来源不明。 [2005 年英语（一）阅读]

a few 少数；几个

真 Most of the women she interviewed—but only **a few** of the men—gave lack of communication as the reason for their divorces. 她采访的大多数女性把缺乏交流看作是离婚的原因，而只有少数男性有这样的看法。 [2010 年英语（二）阅读]

拓 a good few (= not a few) 相当多，不少

work with 与……共事；对……起作用

真 **Work with** a professional photographer instead of your spouse or friend. 让专业摄影师而不是你的配偶或朋友来为你拍照。 [2016 年英语（一）阅读]

press on/ahead (with) 坚决地继续（进行）；坚持（做）

真 Unable to tell whether someone really objects to behavioral ads or whether they are sticking with Microsoft's default, some may ignore a DNT signal and **press on** anyway. 由于尚不清楚一些用户到底是反感行为广告还是保留了微软的默认设置，有些公司可能将漠视 DNT 信号，继续我行我素。 [2013 年英语（一）阅读]

have an impact on/upon 对……产生影响

真 While seemingly innocent, this loss of mental focus can potentially **have a(n)** damaging **impact on** our professional, social, and personal wellbeing. 虽然表面上看起来没有什么危害，但精神集中能力的丧失会对我们的职业、社交以及个人的健康都产生有害影响。 [2014 年英语（一）完形填空]

be possible to ……有可能；做得到

真 Unhealthy curiosity **is possible to** resist, however. 然而，有害身心的好奇心是有可能抵制的。 [2018 年英语（二）完形填空]

rein in　　　严格控制；（用缰绳）勒住（马）（使之放慢或止住脚步）

词 rein [reɪn] *n.* 缰绳；控制手段 *v.* 严格控制

真 Some kids who are low in sympathy may make up for that shortfall by experiencing more guilt, which can **rein in** their nastier impulses. 一些缺乏同情心的孩子可能会通过体验到更多内疚来弥补这种不足，这些内疚可以抑制他们更恶劣的冲动。　　[2019 年英语（二）阅读]

seize on/upon　　　突然对……大为关注；抓住

真 No disciplines have **seized on** professionalism with as much enthusiasm as the humanities. 没有哪门学科像人文学科这样突然热衷于学科的专业化。　　[2011 年英语（一）]

persuade sb. into (doing) sth.　　　说服或劝说某人做某事

真 Toyota Motor's experience is cited as an example of **persuading** customers **into** boycotting products. 丰田汽车的事例被引用来作了一个说服消费者抵制产品的例证。

[2011 年英语（一）阅读]

not to mention　　　且不说，更不用说

词 mention ['menʃn] *v.* 提到，说到，写到

真 Wasted time is a drag on Americans' economic and private lives, **not to mention** infuriating. 且不说它令人恼火，浪费掉的时间本身就是对美国人经济和私人生活的一种拖累。

[2017 年英语（一）阅读]

be necessary to　　　对……来说是必要的

真 They argue that government action **is necessary to** curb Britain's addiction to unhealthy food. 他们认为为了遏制英国人食用垃圾食品成瘾，政府采取行动是很有必要的。

[2011 年英语（二）阅读]

a bit　　　有一点儿

真 Today, the virtue of work may be **a bit** overblown. 如今，工作的优点可能有些被夸大了。

[2017 年英语（一）完形填空]

seek...from　　　从……寻找，寻求

真 Those suffering from persistent nightmares should **seek** help **from** a therapist. 那些长期受到噩梦困扰的人应该寻求心理专家的帮助。　　[2005 年英语（一）阅读]

be vulnerable to 易受……的影响或侵害

词 vulnerable ['vʌlnərəbl] *a.* 易受攻击的；易受伤害的；脆弱的

真 They **are** more **vulnerable to** changes in family economics. 他们更容易受到家庭经济变化的影响。 [2017 年英语（一）阅读]

out of control 失去控制

真 Global climate change may get **out of control**. 全球气候变化可能会失控。[2019 年英语（二）阅读]

in front of 在……前面

例 opportunities that are **in front of** you 你面前的那些机会

look down on 看不起，鄙视

真 Even very young children tend to **look down on** the overweight, and teasing about body build has long been a problem in schools. 就连小孩子都会看不起肥胖的伙伴，嘲弄身材也是学校里长期存在的一个问题。 [2014 年英语（二）完形填空]

拓 despise [dɪ'spaɪz] *v.* 轻视，藐视，看不起

disagree about/on sth. 存在分歧，对某事物持有不同观点

真 It is stuck because the euro zone's dominant powers, France and Germany, agree on the need for greater harmonization within the euro zone, but **disagree about** what to harmonize. 陷入僵局的原因在于，欧元区的两大主导力量——法国和德国，一致同意有必要在欧元区内进一步协调统一，但在对哪些方面协调统一的问题上存在分歧。 [2011 年英语（二）阅读]

拓 disagree with sb. 与某人的观点不同；使某人不舒服

be unfamiliar with 对……不熟悉

词 unfamiliar [ˌʌnfə'mɪliə(r)] *a.* 不熟悉的，陌生的；没经验的；无……知识的

真 If you **are unfamiliar with** words or idioms, you guess at their meaning, using clues presented in the context. 如果你不熟悉单词或习语，你可以通过上下文提供的线索来猜测它们的意思。 [2015 年英语（一）阅读]

拓 be familiar with 对……熟悉

arrive at/in 到达，抵达

真 **arrive at** the jobcentre with a CV 拿着简历到就业中心 [2014 年英语（一）阅读]

DAY
04

take over 控制，管理；接收，接管，接手

真 I don't believe that "technology" can **take over** our lives — unless we choose to let it. 我不相信"技术"能控制我们的生活——除非我们自己主动让它控制。

take effort 需要付出努力

例 It **takes** a lot of time and **effort** to pass the examination. 通过这项考试需要投入很多时间并需要付出大量努力。

be about to 即将；正要

真 Even he, however, might tremble at the thought of what he **is about to** do. 然而，一想到接下来将要做的事情，甚至连他自己也会感到不寒而栗。 [2008 年英语（一）完形填空]

lure sb. into (doing) sth. 引诱或说服某人做某事（尤指坏事或危险的事）

词 lure [ljʊə(r)] v. 诱惑；吸引

真 The supermarket is designed to **lure** customers **into** spending as much time as possible within its doors. 超市旨在引诱消费者尽可能在店里多逗留一段时间。 [2016 年英语（二）翻译]

tell apart 区分，辨别

例 It's easy to **tell** our pens **apart** because they're all different colors. 我们的笔很容易区分，因为它们的颜色不一样。

辨 tell...apart 指在同一类人或事物中分辨，常用 tell sb./sth. apart（将某人 / 某事物区分开）。

tell...from 指两个或两类之间的区别，常用 tell A from B（将 A 和 B 区分开来）。

sum up 总结，概括；形成对……的看法

真 To **sum up**: a system of conservation based solely on economic self-interest is hopelessly lopsided. 总之，一个仅仅基于经济利益的保护体系存在着无可救药的片面性。

[2010 年英语（一）翻译]

be/feel disappointed at 对……感到失望

真 People **feel disappointed at** the realities of modern society. 人们对现代社会的现实情况感到失望。 [2006 年英语（一）阅读]

in the form of　以……的形式

真 gained weight **in the form of** muscle mass 以增肌的形式增加了体重

[2019 年英语（二）完形填空]

decide on/upon　决定；选定

例 can't **decide on** something 在某些问题上无法做出决定

拓 determine on/upon sth. 决定做某事；对某事下定决心 ‖ be determined to do sth. 决心做某事

in the end　最后，最终

例 **In the end**, however, Bella agreed with her boyfriend. 然而，最后贝拉还是同意了她男朋友的说法。

in dispute　有争议的，处于争议中

真 His reputation as a music critic has long been **in dispute**. 作为音乐评论家，他的名声一直饱受争议。

[2010 年英语（一）阅读]

be essential to　对……是必要的，对……是必不可少的

真 It **is essential to** consider factors beyond GDP. 考虑除 GDP 以外的因素也很有必要。

[2017 年英语（一）阅读]

let rip　（使）全速行使或运转；尽情地做；激烈或激昂地说话

真 Development should be planned, not **let rip**. 发展应讲求计划性，而不是任意妄为。

[2016 年英语（一）阅读]

after all　毕竟

真 **After all**, if everyone you know is going to college in the fall, it seems silly to stay back a year, doesn't it? 毕竟，如果每个你认识的人都在秋天上大学，你却延迟一年才去，这样看上去会很傻，是吧？

[2017 年英语（二）阅读]

comply with　遵从；服从

真 After all, it has an ad business too, which it says will **comply with** DNT requests, though it is still working out how. 毕竟，它本身也有广告业务，尽管微软承诺在广告业务中会遵守"禁止追踪"（DNT）要求，但如何遵守尚待研究。

[2013 年英语（一）阅读]

拓 subject to 受……支配；服从于

be suspicious of/about　　对……感到怀疑，不信任

词 suspicious [sə'spɪʃəs] *a.* 有疑心的；表示怀疑的；可疑的

真 A few premiers **are suspicious of** any federal-provincial deal-making. 一些省份的省长对于联邦政府和各省之间的任何合作都抱着怀疑的态度。　　[2005 年英语（一）阅读]

ascribe...to　　认为……具有；把……归因于

真 Rather, we **ascribe** meanings **to** texts on the basis of interaction between what we might call textual and contextual material. 相反，读者对文本含义的推测是基于他们与所谓的文本资料和语境资料之间的互动。　　[2015 年英语（一）阅读]

aim for　　（向某方向）努力；力争

真 In face of the present situation, the *Times* (*The New York Times*) should **aim for** efficient management. 面对目前的形势，《纽约时报》应努力高效管理。

[2016 年英语（一）阅读]

be aimed at　　目的是，旨在；针对

真 **be aimed at** preventing the income gap from widening 以防止收入差距扩大为目标

[2018 年英语（一）阅读]

拓 aim at 力求做到；瞄准

as a whole　　整体上；作为一个整体；总的来说

真 At least, that is how it looks **as a whole**. 至少从整体上来看是这样。　　[2010 年英语（一）阅读]

filter out　　过滤掉；筛除；淘汰

真 To **filter out** what is unique from what is shared might enable us to understand how complex cultural behaviour arose. 从共性中筛选出特性，或许能让我们明白复杂的文化行为是如何产生的。

[2012 年英语（一）翻译]

as opposed to　　而非，相对于

真 A sacred place of peace, however crude it may be, is a distinctly human need, **as opposed to** shelter, which is a distinctly animal need. 那是一片宁静的圣土，不管多么简陋，都是人类特有的需求，它不同于遮风避雨的地方，那明显是动物的需求。　　[2013 年英语（一）翻译]

have confidence in　对……有信心

真 Readers must **have confidence in** the conclusions published in our journal. 读者必须对发表在我们杂志上的研究结论有信心。 [2015 年英语（一）阅读]

tax on　对……征税

真 These unilateral developments differ in their specifics, but they are all designed to **tax** multinationals **on** income and revenue that countries believe they should have a right to tax, even if international tax rules do not grant them that right. （这些国家）各自的进展在细节上有所不同，但它们的目的都是对跨国公司的收入征税，以及对这些国家认为它们有权征税的收益上征税，即使国际税收规则不授予它们这种权利。 [2020 年英语（一）阅读]

(be) relative to　与……相比，与……有关

真 It's not popular to say, but one reason their pay has gone up so much is that CEOs really have upped their game **relative to** many other workers in the U.S. economy. 虽然这种说法并不普遍，但首席执行官们的薪酬增长如此之快的一个原因是：与美国经济中的许多其他员工相比，他们的技能确实提高了。 [2020 年英语（二）阅读]

such as　比如，例如

真 It is designed to apply primarily to companies **such as** Google, Apple, Facebook and Amazon —in other words, multinational tech companies based in the United States. 它主要适用于谷歌、苹果、脸书和亚马逊等公司，换句话说，也就是总部设在美国的跨国科技公司。 [2020 年英语（一）阅读]

react to　对……做出反应，回应

真 Personality can affect how a person **reacts to** eye contact. 性格会影响一个人对眼神交流的反应。 [2020 年英语（一）阅读]

本单元资源

drop back to　回到；降低到　○○○

例 It is difficult for me to **drop back to** business after a 7-day foreign holiday. 我去国外度了7天的假后，很难回归到工作状态中。

go against　对……不利；违背（意愿等）　○○○

例 The jury's verdict **went against** her. 陪审团的裁定对她不利。

make the best of　充分利用；尽力而为　○○○

例 He **made the best of** the opportunity and finally succeeded. 他充分利用了这次机会，最终取得了成功。

be bound to do sth.　一定做某事；有法律责任或义务做某事　○○○

真 Someone **is bound to** point out that it amounts to the bare, bare minimum necessary to keep the Postal Service afloat, not comprehensive reform. 一定会有人指出这充其量也就是保持邮政业务运转的基本条件，而不是全面改革。　　　　　[2018 年英语（一）阅读]

拓 have an obligation to do sth. 有义务做某事

keep away (from)　避免接近，远离　○○○

真 McCreevy objects to the IASB's attempt to **keep away from** political influences. 迈克里维反对国际会计委员会（IASB）远离政治影响的意图。　　　　　[2010 年英语（一）阅读]

along with　与……同样；与……一起　◐○

真 **Along with** Singapore, other governments and mega-corporations are beginning to establish their own guidelines. 和新加坡一样，其他国家的政府和大型企业也开始制定它们自己的指导方针。　　　　　[2019 年英语（一）阅读]

拓 get along with 与……和睦相处

at large　整个，全部；普遍地；一般地；自由的　○○○

例 The chances of getting reforms accepted by the community **at large** remain remote. 让社会普遍都接受改革的希望仍然渺茫。

in detail 详细地，详尽地

真 It was taken for granted that the critics of major papers would write **in detail** and at length about the events they covered. 各大报纸的评论员们对所报道的事件进行详尽的评述是理所当然的事情。 [2010 年英语（一）阅读]

lose faith in 对……失去信心；不再信任

真 It has more or less **lost faith in** markets. 它已经或多或少地对市场失去了信心。 [2011 年英语（二）阅读]

拓 lose confidence in 失去对……的信心

under fire 受到攻击或批判；在战火下

真 Ms. Simmons was **under fire** for having sat on Goldman's compensation committee. 西蒙斯女士因就职于高盛的薪酬委员会而受到猛烈抨击。 [2011 年英语（二）阅读]

work out 找到（解决方法）；进展顺利；锻炼

真 Yet the new system has not **worked out** any cheaper for the universities. 然而，新系统并没有实现为大学提供更便宜的服务。 [2020 年英语（一）阅读]

adapt to 适应

真 The original purpose of grade forgiveness is to help freshmen **adapt to** college learning. "分数宽恕"的初衷是为了帮助大学新生适应大学的学习。 [2019 年英语（一）阅读]

look at 看；检查；研究；看待

真 **look at** someone else in a pleasant way 以一种令人愉快的方式看着别人 [2020 年英语（一）阅读]

be representative of 代表；可作为典型

真 The Supreme Court extended the requirement that juries **be representative of** all parts of the community to the state level. 最高法院要求陪审团要代表社会的各个阶层。 [2010 年英语（二）阅读]

on that count 就这个问题，在这方面

真 The firm has compared some of its other products favorably with Google's **on that count** before. 在这方面，该公司曾经将其一些其他产品与谷歌的产品进行过比较。 [2013 年英语（一）阅读]

function as	起……作用，具有……功能	

真 The second half of the 20th century saw a collection of geniuses, warriors, entrepreneurs and visionaries labour to create a fabulous machine that could **function as** a typewriter and printing press, studio and theatre, paintbrush and gallery, piano and radio, the mail as well as the mail carrier. 20 世纪下半叶出现了一批天才、勇士、企业家和畅想家，他们合力创造了一台不可思议的神奇机器，它集打字机和印刷机、摄影室和剧院、画笔和美术馆、钢琴和收音机、邮件以及邮递员等诸多功能于一身。 [2012 年英语（一）阅读]

(be) eligible for sth.	有资格获得某事物	

真 It was not until the 1940s that a majority of states made women **eligible for** jury duty. 直到 20 世纪 40 年代，大多数州才让女性有资格加入陪审团。 [2010 年英语（二）阅读]

拓 be eligible to do sth. 有资格做某事

be qualified to	有资格……	

例 The renowned author **is** eminently **qualified to** explore the topic. 那位著名的作家非常有资格探讨这一主题。

free from	解放；使摆脱；免于	

真 Likewise, automation should eventually boost productivity, stimulate demand by driving down prices, and **free** workers **from** hard, boring work. 同理，自动化最终也会推动生产力的发展，通过降低物价来刺激需求，将工人们从繁重、枯燥的工作中解放出来。[2018 年英语（一）阅读]

sign on	办理失业登记	

真 Those first few days should be spent looking for work, not looking to **sign on**.（失业）最初的那几天应该用来找工作，而不是指望被登记在册。 [2014 年英语（一）阅读]

at times	有时，偶尔	

例 Several tests may fail **at times**, which proves designers need to put more effort. 几个测试有时候可能会失败，这证明设计师需要付出更多的努力。

拓 once in a while 偶尔，有时

come out	说出；出现；发表；公开表明	

真 You wanted to say something—the first word—but it just won't **come out**. 你想要说点什么——第一个字——但是就是说不出口。 [2018 年英语（二）阅读]

be parallel with/to 与……类似；与……相同；与……平行 ○○○

真 On the other, it links these concepts to everyday realities in a manner which **is parallel to** the links journalists forge on a daily basis as they cover and comment on the news. 另一方面，这一学科将这些概念同日常生活结合起来，这种做法与新闻记者日常报道和评论新闻时的做法是相似的。 [2007 年英语（一）翻译]

try to do sth. 努力做某事 ○○○

真 **Try to** slot it in as a to-do list item and you'll manage only goal-focused reading. 试着把它放到待办事项列表里，这样你就可以只处理目标明确的阅读了。 [2016 年英语（二）阅读]

kick out 用脚踢；撵走；开除 ○○○

例 In 1985, he was effectively **kicked out** of Apple for being unproductive and uncontrollable. 事实上，1985 年，他因为效率低下和不好控制而被从苹果公司赶了出去。

talk about 谈论，讨论 ◇

真 **talk about** passion 谈论热情 [2015 年英语（二）阅读]

be reluctant to do sth. 不愿意做某事 ○○○

真 Despite these factors, many social scientists seem **reluctant to** tackle such problems. 尽管存在这些因素，但许多社会科学家却似乎不情愿解决这些问题。 [2013 年英语（一）阅读]

拓 be unwilling to do sth. 不愿意做某事

emigrate to 移民到…… ○○○

真 The architect **emigrated to** the United States before World War II and took up posts at American architecture schools. 那位建筑师在二战前移民到美国，并在美国的一些建筑大学从事工作。 [2011 年英语（二）阅读]

sort out 解决；整理；将……拣出 ○○○

真 The justices had to specify novel rules for the new personal domain of the passenger car then; they must **sort out** how the Fourth Amendment applies to digital information now. 那时法官们不得不为轿车作为新的私人领域细化新的准则；现在他们则必须解决如何让第四条修正案适用于数字信息这一问题。 [2015 年英语（一）阅读]

| knock off | 迅速完成；效仿，模仿 | 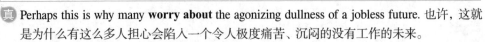 |

真 It took Beaumont decades to perfect her craft; her example can't be **knocked off**. 博蒙特花了几十年时间来完善自己的技艺；她的例子是无法效仿的。 [2013 年英语（一）阅读]

| worry about | 担心，担忧 | |

真 Perhaps this is why many **worry about** the agonizing dullness of a jobless future. 也许，这就是为什么有这么多人担心会陷入一个令人极度痛苦、沉闷的没有工作的未来。

[2017 年英语（二）完形填空]

| up to | 达到；由……决定；是……的职责 | |

真 The European Union is now considering legislation to compel corporate boards to maintain a certain proportion of women—**up to** 60 percent. 欧盟正考虑立法，强制公司董事会吸收一定比例的女性，这个比例可高达 60%。 [2013 年英语（二）阅读]

拓 be down to 由……负责

| by default | 默认情况下；由于对手缺席（而胜出） | |

真 There is no guarantee that DNT **by default** will become the norm. 没有人能保证默认设置"禁止追踪"（DNT）会成为一种规范。 [2013 年英语（一）阅读]

| for use | 供使用 | |

真 Chewing gum, once bought primarily by adolescent boys, is now featured in commercials as a breath freshener and teeth cleanser **for use** after a meal. 口香糖曾经主要由青春期男孩购买，现在在商业广告中作为饭后的口气清新剂和牙齿清洁剂大肆宣传。 [2010 年英语（二）阅读]

| bring forth | 产生；发表 | |

例 Their efforts they made during the two years will surely **bring forth** good fruit. 他们在那两年中付出的努力必将产生好的结果。

| attribute to | 把……归因于 | |

真 Some **attributed** virtually every important cultural achievement **to** the inventions of a few, especially gifted peoples. 有些人（人类学家）把每一项重要的文化成就都归功于少数几个民族，尤其是有天赋的民族的发明创造。 [2009 年英语（一）阅读]

see/perceive...as　把……看作；认为

真 More artists began **seeing** happiness **as** meaningless, phony or, worst of all, boring. 许多艺术家开始把快乐看作无意义的、虚伪的，甚至是令人厌烦的东西。　[2006 年英语（一）阅读]

compete with　与……竞争

真 However, during that course I realised that I was not good enough in this area to **compete with** other creative personalities in the future, so I decided that it was not the right path for me. 然而，在学习那门课程期间我发现，在时尚设计领域，我并没有优秀到将来可以和其他那些极具创意的精英人物竞争，所以我断定那条路不适合我。　[2017 年英语（二）翻译]

jump at　欣然或急切地接受（建议等）

例 Surely any smart entrepreneur would **jump at** a chance to make profits on those deals. 显然，任何一个聪明的企业家都不会错过从这些买卖中赚钱的机会。

拓 accept [ək'sept] *v.* 接受 ‖ embrace [ɪm'breɪs] *v.* 欣然接受或采取（意见等）

pay attention to　关注；留意

真 **pay** particular **attention to** the introductory and concluding paragraphs 要特别注意引言和结束部分　[2008 年英语（一）阅读]

拓 value ['væl]uː] *v.* 重视

listen to　听；听从

真 He doesn't **listen to** me. 他不听我说话。　[2010 年英语（二）阅读]

be licensed to　得到授权或许可去……

真 Drivers must **be licensed to** drive on public roads. 驾驶员必须拿到驾照才可以在公共道路上开车。　[2011 年英语（二）完形填空]

be obliged to　被迫；感谢

真 Advertisers **are obliged to** offer behavioral ads. 广告商被迫提供行为广告。　[2013 年英语（一）阅读]

guard against　提防，防止，防范

例 To **guard against** accidents, the government is trying to take strict measures. 为防范意外的发生，政府正努力采取严格的措施。

to come　　即将来临

真 Some art dealers were awaiting better chances **to come**. 一些艺术品交易商正等待好机会的来临。　　　　　　　　　　　　　　　　　　　　　　　　　[2010 年英语（二）阅读]

turn out　　结果是，证明是；制造，生产；关掉（灯），出现

真 "We humans seem to be fascinated by robots, and it **turns out** other animals are too," says Wiles. "我们人类似乎对机器人很着迷，结果表明，其他动物也一样。" 怀尔斯说道。　　　　　　　　　　　　　　　　　　　　　　　　　　　　　　[2020 年英语（二）阅读]

let alone　　更不用说，更别提

真 While few craftsmen or farmers, **let alone** dependents and servants, left literary compositions to be analyzed, it is obvious that their views were less fully intellectualized. 虽然极少数工匠或农民（更不用说随从或仆人）留下了一些文学作品以待分析，但是很明显，他们的见解不够理智。　　　　　　　　　　　　　　　　　　　　　　　　　　[2009 年英语（一）阅读]

half of　　一半的；半程的；二分之一

真 **Half of** them found a toy; the other half discovered the container was empty—and realized the tester had fooled them. 他们当中一半的人会发现一个玩具；另一半的人会发现容器是空的，并意识到测试员愚弄了他们。　　　　　　　　　　　　　　　　　　[2018 年英语（一）完形填空]

拓 half off 打五折

come to mind　　出现在脑海中

真 One Italian example would be the Berlusconi group, while abroad Maxwell and Murdoch **come to mind**. 意大利的贝卢斯科尼集团就是一个例子，此外我们能想到的外国集团还有麦斯威尔和默多克。　　　　　　　　　　　　　　　　　　　　　　　　[2005 年英语（一）翻译]

拓 spring to one's mind 出现在某人的脑海中

promise to　　承诺，保证；可能；答应

例 By it's very nature many of these responsibilities are things we have **promised to** do for other people—whether that's someone at work, a friend or family member. 就本质而言，这些责任中很多是我们对其他人承诺要去做的事——不管是与工作相关的人、朋友还是家人。

拓 keep one's promise 信守承诺

out of style	过时	

真 These are disciplines that are going **out of style**. 这些学科正日趋没落。 [2011 年英语（一）阅读]

renege on	违背（诺言、契约等）	

真 It announced it was **reneging on** a longstanding commitment to abide by the state's strict nuclear regulations. 它宣布不再履行其长期信守的遵守该州严格的核能法规的承诺。

[2012 年英语（一）阅读]

for my part	就我来说	

真 **For my part**, I have no idea whether Gilbert is a great conductor or even a good one. 对于我而言，我不知道吉尔伯特是否是一位伟大的指挥家，甚至连他是否是一位好指挥我都不知道。

[2011 年英语（一）阅读]

for the best	（所有因素考虑在内）能产生的最好结果	

真 Realistic optimists are these who make the best of things that happen, but not those who believe everything happens **for the best**. 现实的乐观主义者在现有的情况下尽力而为，而不会指望每件事都会有最好的结果。 [2014 年英语（二）翻译]

拓 at one's/its best 处于最佳状态 ‖ all the best（尤用于告别时）一切顺利

evolve into	逐渐发展成，逐渐演变成	

真 It was only after "toddler" became a common shoppers' term that it **evolved into** a broadly accepted developmental stage. 直到"幼童"这个词常常为顾客所用，它才逐渐演变为人们广泛接受的一个成长阶段。 [2012 年英语（二）阅读]

suck in	吸引；把……卷入（某事）	

真 Tech is designed to really **suck** you **in** and digital products are there to promote maximal engagement. 技术设计的初衷就是真正地吸引住你，而数码产品的存在实现了人们最大程度的参与度。 [2017 年英语（二）阅读]

exclusive to	专为……所有；局限于	

真 But snap decisions in reaction to rapid stimuli aren't **exclusive to** the interpersonal realm. 但是，应对突然刺激的快速决定并不只限于人际交往领域。 [2013 年英语（二）阅读]

| **take up** | 开始从事；占用（时间、精力等）；接受（建议等） | ○○○ |

真 A lot of students **take up** law as their profession due to the attraction of financial rewards. 许多学生从事法律职业是被该行业的薪资报酬所吸引。

[2014 年英语（一）阅读]

| **look back** | 回顾，回忆 | ○○○ |

真 The notion is that people have failed to detect the massive changes which have happened in the ocean because they have been **looking back** only a relatively short time into the past. 这种观点认为，人们尚未发觉海洋中已经发生的巨大变化，因为他们只回顾了过去相对较短的一段时期内的情况。

[2006 年英语（一）阅读]

| **lack of** | 缺乏，不足 | ○○○ |

真 Stereotypes associated with obesity include laziness, **lack of** will power, and lower prospects for success. 与肥胖有关的成见包括懒惰、意志薄弱和成功的可能性较低。

[2014 年英语（二）完形填空]

| **approve of** | 赞成，同意 | ○○○ |

例 My mother doesn't **approve of** my going abroad for further education. 我母亲不同意我出国进修。

拓 disapprove of 不赞成，不同意

| **weigh in** | 提出重要的或令人信服的意见；自信地提出看法 | ○○○ |

真 Leading doctors today **weigh in** on the debate over the government's role in promoting public health. 关于政府在促进公共卫生方面的角色，当今一流的医生在讨论中发表了重要的意见。

[2011 年英语（二）阅读]

| **call out** | 大声喊出；召集 | ○○○ |

真 As the auctioneer **called out** bids, in New York one of the oldest banks on Wall Street, Lehman Brothers, filed for bankruptcy. 当拍卖商喊出报价时，纽约华尔街历史最悠久的银行之一雷曼兄弟申请破产。

[2010 年英语（二）阅读]

| **no exception** | 不例外 | ○○○ |

例 People love to get their hands on the latest and greatest technology, and scientists had long believed that early humans were **no exception**. 人们总喜欢设法得到最新的和最伟大的技术，长期以来，科学家们都相信早期的人类也不例外。

拓 make an exception (of sb./sth.) 将某人／某事物作为例外

set out	阐述，提出；启程，出发

真 Some were advised to **set out** monthly goals and study activities. 一些人被建议阐述月度目标和学习活动计划。 [2018 年英语（二）阅读]

speed up	加速，加快

例 help you **speed up** your success 有助于加速你的成功

fit in	适应；适合；相处融洽；发挥作用

真 There are two extra choices, which do not **fit in** any of the blanks. 有两个多余的选项，不适合填入任何空格中。 [2015 年英语（一）阅读]

in a dilemma	进退两难，左右为难

词 dilemma [dɪ'lemə] *n.* （进退两难的）窘境，困境

真 The Supreme Court decision on Thursday will put most online business **in a dilemma**. 最高法院周四的裁定将使大多数在线业务处于进退两难的境地。 [2019 年英语（一）阅读]

in charge	负责，主管

真 And if Peretti were **in charge** at the *Times* (*The New York Times*), "I wouldn't pick a year to end print," he said. 如果佩雷蒂掌管《纽约时报》，他说："我不会选择要在哪一年结束印刷版。" [2016 年英语（一）阅读]

day by day	一天天；逐日

真 Others were told to plan activities and goals in much time detail **day by day**. 其余的人被告知要尽可能详细地制订每一天的活动和目标计划。 [2018 年英语（二）阅读]

in the name of	以……的名义；代表

真 Write them an email **in the name of** the Students' Union. 以学生会的名义给他们写一封电子邮件。 [2012 年英语（一）写作]

拓 under/by the name of 以……的名义

infuse sb./sth. with sth.	使某人/某物具有（某特性）；将（某特性）灌输或注入某人/某物

词 infuse [ɪn'fjuːz] *v.* 灌输；注入

真 These terms are also intended to **infuse** work **with** meaning—and, as Rakesh Khurana, another professor, points out, increase allegiance to the firm. 这些词语也试图给工作赋予意

义，正如另一位教授拉凯什·库兰纳指出的，这可以增强人们对公司的忠诚度。

[2015 年英语（二）阅读]

拓 **infuse sth. into sb./sth.** 使某人 / 某物具有（某特性）；将（某特性）灌输给或注入某人 / 某物

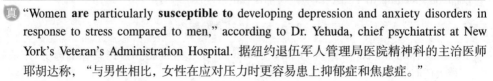

be susceptible to 易患……的；对……敏感的；容易受……影响的

真 "Women **are** particularly **susceptible to** developing depression and anxiety disorders in response to stress compared to men," according to Dr. Yehuda, chief psychiatrist at New York's Veteran's Administration Hospital. 据纽约退伍军人管理局医院精神科的主治医师耶胡达称，"与男性相比，女性在应对压力时更容易患上抑郁症和焦虑症。"

[2008 年英语（一）阅读]

be/become sympathetic to 对……表示同情；赞同

词 sympathetic [ˌsɪmpəˈθetɪk] *a.* 同情的；表示同情的；赞同的

真 The guilt-prone ones shared more, even though they hadn't magically **become** more **sympathetic to** the other child's deprivation. 那些更容易产生负罪感的孩子分享得更多，尽管不可思议的是他们并没有对另一个孩子没有这些东西感到更加同情。[2019 年英语（二）翻译]

give priority to 优先考虑

词 priority [praɪˈɒrəti] *n.* 优先；优先权；优先考虑的事

真 Generation Zs **give** top **priority to** professional training. "Z 一代"把专业培训放在首位。

[2020 年英语（一）阅读]

拓 prioritize [praɪˈɒrətaɪz] *v.* 按优先顺序列出；优先处理，优先考虑

detect...from... 从……中发现……

真 To find out if this extends to non-living beings, Laleh Quinn at the University of California, San Diego, and her colleagues tested whether rats can **detect** social signals **from** robotic rats. 为了查明这一情况是否适用于非生物，加州大学圣地亚哥分校的拉蕾·奎恩及其同事测试了老鼠是否能够觉察到机器鼠发出的社交信号。

[2020 年英语（二）阅读]

do damage to... 对……造成破坏

真 This may not only **do damage to** your relationship with your child but also affect your child's self-esteem. 这不仅可能会破坏你和孩子之间的关系，而且还可能会影响孩子的自尊。

[2020 年英语（二）完形填空]

get together
聚集；组织；开会；聚会

真 to **get together** 15 people 把 15 个人聚在一起
[2020 年英语（二）阅读]

revolve around
围绕……转动；以……为中心

真 Copernicus theorized in 1543 that all of the planets that we knew of **revolved** not **around** the Earth, but the Sun, a system that was later upheld by Galileo at his own expense. 哥白尼在 1543 年提出了一个理论：我们所知道的所有行星都不是围绕着地球转的，而是围绕着太阳转的，后来伽利略以牺牲自己的方式维护了这一理论体系。
[2020 年英语（一）翻译]

catch one's attention
吸引某人的注意

真 It can **catch someone's attention** in a crowded room. 在拥挤的房间里，它能引起别人的注意。
[2020 年英语（一）阅读]

gaze into
凝视

真 We know that a typical infant will instinctively **gaze into** its mother's eyes, and she will look back. 我们知道，一个典型的婴儿会本能地注视妈妈的眼睛，然后妈妈也会回看。
[2020 年英语（一）阅读]

lose one's job
失业

真 many of their parents **lost their jobs** 他们的父母中有很多人失去了工作
[2020 年英语（二）阅读]

all too often
时常，经常

真 But **all too often** such policies are an insincere form of virtue-signaling that benefits only the most privileged and does little to help average people. 但是，这些政策经常是一种虚伪的道德信号，只惠及最有特权的人，而对普通人帮助甚微。
[2020 年英语（一）阅读]

be hailed as...
被誉为……

真 Madrid **was hailed as** a public health guiding light last November when it rolled out ambitious restrictions on the most polluting cars. 去年 11 月，马德里出台了针对污染最严重的汽车的雄心勃勃的限制措施，被誉为公共健康的指明灯。
[2020 年英语（二）阅读]

push sb. too far
特别让某人生气；过分逼迫某人

真 You're only human, and sometimes your kids can **push** you just a little **too far**. 你只是个凡人，有时候，你的孩子可能会让你有点忍无可忍。
[2020 年英语（二）完形填空]

DAY
05

from time to time　有时，不时；偶尔

例 How much the overall sales would increase depends on the ratio between the rabid adherents of this artist and the people who simply like some jazz **from time to time**. 整体销售额的增长量取决于这位艺术家的狂热追随者与只是偶尔喜欢听爵士的人们的比例。

拓 once in a while 偶尔地；间或 ‖ between times 有时候

put pen to paper　落笔，下笔，开始写

真 While even the modestly educated sought an elevated tone when they **put pen to paper** before the 1960s, even the most well regarded writing since then has sought to capture spoken English on the page. 在 20 世纪 60 年代以前，仅受过一点教育的人在落笔时都会追求一种更高雅的格调；而在那之后，即使是最受关注的文章也都力求使用英语口语。

[2005 年英语（一）阅读]

under...conditions　在……条件下

真 Studies of both animals and humans have shown that sex hormones somehow affect the stress response, causing females under stress to produce more of the trigger chemicals than do males **under** the same **conditions**. 对动物和人的研究都已表明，性激素会以某种方式影响对压力的反应，使雌性在承受压力时比处于同等条件下的雄性分泌更多引发不安反应的化学物质。

[2008 年英语（一）阅读]

拓 in the condition of 在……情况下；在……条件下

get into　进入，卷入，陷入

真 At least they have demonstrated that when companies **get into** trouble with the law, evidence of good character can win them a less costly punishment. 至少他们已经证实，当公司遇到法律麻烦的时候，能证明其优良品德的证据可以使其少受惩罚。　[2016 年英语（一）阅读]

拓 be involved in 被卷入……中；涉及……

DAY 06

本单元资源

---

at the moment   此刻，现在，目前

(真) the biggest problem **at the moment** 目前最大的问题   [2010 年英语（二）阅读]

(拓) for now 目前，暂时 ‖ temporary ['temprəri] *a.* 暂时的；临时的

---

at the speed of   以……的速度

(真) In addition, new digital technologies have allowed more rapid trading of equities, quicker use of information **at the speed of** Twitter, and thus shorter attention spans in financial markets. 此外，新的数字技术使股票交易更加迅速，信息的使用速度可以达到推特的速度，因而金融市场也越来越急功近利。   [2019 年英语（一）阅读]

---

similar to   与……相似

(真) Yet humans remain fascinated by the idea of robots that would look, move, and respond like humans, **similar to** those recently depicted on popular sci-fi TV series such as "Westworld" and "Humans". 然而，人类依旧对机器人这一概念着迷，这些机器人会像人类一样观察、做动作和反应，就像最近大受欢迎的科幻电视连续剧《西部世界》和《人类》中所展现的那些机器人那样。   [2019 年英语（一）阅读]

---

differentiate between A and B   区分 A 和 B

(词) differentiate [ˌdɪfəˈrenʃieɪt] *v.* 区别，辨别

(真) A Canadian study found that children as young as 14 months can **differentiate between** a credible person **and** a dishonest one. 加拿大的一项研究发现，年仅 14 个月的孩子就可以区分可信的人和不诚实的人。   [2018 年英语（一）完形填空]

(拓) A differs from B   A 与 B 不同

---

rely on   依靠，依赖

(真) **rely on** researchers passing on copies they have themselves legally accessed 依靠研究人员传递他们合法获取的副本   [2020 年英语（一）阅读]

---

by the end of   到……结束时；在……之前

(真) **by the end of** this decade 到这个十年结束之时   [2006 年英语（一）完形填空]

register for　　注册；报名参加

真 Only if the jobless arrive at the job centre with a CV, **register for** online job search, and start looking for work will they be eligible for benefit. 只有失业者拿着简历到就业中心，注册网上求职并开始找工作，他们才有资格获得救济金。 [2014 年英语（一）阅读]

拓 enter for 报名参加（比赛）

be dominant over　　对……有主导权；主导

词 dominant ['dɒmɪnənt] *a.* 最突出的；占支配地位的

真 The Administration **is dominant over** immigration issues. 行政管理部门在移民问题上有主导权。 [2013 年英语（一）阅读]

doze off　　打瞌睡；困倦

词 doze [dəʊz] *v./n.* 小睡；（打）瞌睡

例 That boy closed his eyes for a minute and must have **dozed off**. 那个男孩闭了会儿眼，后来一定是睡着了。

pin down　　确定；发现，查明

真 This suggests that the alleged "Hawthorne effect" is hard to **pin down**. 这表明所谓的"霍桑效应"很难确定。 [2010 年英语（一）完形填空]

at that point　　在那时；在那个阶段

真 To Egypt, France, and a dozen more countries, G.I. Joe was any American soldier, **at that point** the most important person in their lives. 对于埃及、法国和其他诸多国家来讲，大兵乔可以是任何一位美国士兵，在那个时候，他是他们生命中最重要的人。

[2012 年英语（二）完形填空]

拓 at that time 在那时

empower sb. to do sth.　　授权或允许某人做某事

词 empower [ɪm'paʊə(r)] *v.* 授权

真 Yet rather than **empowering** teachers **to** find what works best for their students, the policy imposes a flat, across-the-board rule. 但是，这项规定并没有赋予教师权力去探寻什么（家庭作业）最适合学生，而是强加了一个全盘性的原则。 [2012 年英语（二）阅读]

拓 grant [grɑːnt] *v.* 同意给予或允许（所求）

be prone to　　易于……；有……的倾向

真 Scientists have found that although we **are prone to** snap overreactions, if we take a moment and think about how we are likely to react, we can reduce or even eliminate the negative effects of our quick, hard-wired responses. 科学家发现，尽管我们很容易突然做出过度反应，但是如果我们花点时间思考一下自己可能会作何反应，我们就能减少甚至消除快速反应的负面影响。

[2013 年英语（二）阅读]

devote to　　致力于；献身于

真 If your work is your "passion," you'll be more likely to **devote** yourself **to** it, even if that means going home for dinner and then working long after the kids are in bed. 如果你的工作就是你的热情所在，你将更有可能全身心地投入其中，即使那意味着你要回家吃晚饭，然后等孩子们睡着后还要工作很久。

[2015 年英语（二）阅读]

in advance　　预先，提前

真 Consider the person that you're dealing with **in advance** and what will get you to your desired outcome. 提前想想你要打交道的那个人，以及什么会让你达到你预期的结果。

[2020 年英语（二）阅读]

拓 ahead of time 提前，提早

far beyond　　远远超出，大大超越

真 But the market generates interest **far beyond** its size because it brings together great wealth, enormous egos, greed, passion and controversy in a way matched by few other industries. 但是（艺术品）市场产生的利益远远超出它本身的规模，因为它集中了巨大的财富、膨胀的自我意识、贪婪、激情和争议，从这个意义来说，很少有其他行业能与之相比。

[2010 年英语（二）阅读]

point out　　指出，指明，点出

真 Optimists **point out** that technological upheaval has benefited workers in the past. 乐观主义者指出，技术进步过去曾让工人们受益。

[2018 年英语（一）阅读]

拓 indicate ['ɪndɪkeɪt] v. 表明；指出；明示

be enthusiastic about　　热衷于；对……充满热情

真 Consumers may create "earned" media when they **are enthusiastic about** recommending their favourite products. 当消费者们热衷于推荐他们最喜爱的产品时，他们也许会创建一种"免费"媒体。

[2011 年英语（一）阅读]

拓 be indifferent to 不在乎……；对……漠不关心

sit for the bar　　参加律师资格考试；获得律师资格

真 Another is to let students **sit for the bar** after only two years of law school. 另一个办法是允许学生在法学院学习两年以后就参加律师资格考试。

[2014 年英语（一）阅读]

put on　　上演；穿戴；涂抹；增加

真 So keep it simple: "Hi", "Hey" or "Hello"—do the best you can to gather all of the enthusiasm and energy you can, **put on** a big smile and say "Hi". 所以简单说一声："嗨""嘿"或者"你好"——尽可能地让自己展现全部的热情和精力，面带灿烂的笑容，道一声"嗨"。

[2018 年英语（二）阅读]

be put on hold　　暂停，暂缓

真 The homework rules should **be put on hold** while the school board, which is responsible for setting educational policy, looks into the matter and conducts public hearings. 在负责制定教育政策的学校董事调查这件事并举行公众听证会期间，关于家庭作业的规定应当暂缓。

[2012 年英语（二）阅读]

拓 put off 推迟；延期

come with　　与……一起；伴随……发生

真 The danger will **come with** Charles, who has both an expensive taste of lifestyle and a pretty hierarchical view of the world. 危险将随查尔斯王子而至，他不仅有着品位奢华的生活方式，而且用颇具等级观念的眼光看待世人。

[2015 年英语（一）阅读]

拓 accompany [əˈkʌmpəni] v. 伴随；陪伴；伴奏

value in　　在……方面的价值

真 If you're not convinced of the inherent **value in** taking a year off to explore interests, then consider its financial impact on future academic choices. 如果你还质疑休整一年去发掘兴趣爱好的内在价值，那么考虑一下它对你未来学业选择的经济影响吧。

[2017 年英语（二）阅读]

| **lose control of** | 失去对……的控制 | |

🔒 They fear **losing control of** Mauna Kea. 他们害怕失去对莫纳克亚山的控制。

[2017 年英语（一）阅读]

拓 out of control 失控

| **in prison** | 在狱中，坐牢；监禁 | |

例 She was illiterate almost all her life; she only learned to read and write **in prison**. 她几乎一辈子都不识字；她只是在监狱里才学会了读写。

拓 put in jail 囚禁，关押

| **make up for** | 弥补；补偿 | |

例 To **make up for** this we have decided to send Teresa to a local middle school, giving her an opportunity to mix with other children. 为了弥补这一点，我们决定送泰丽莎去当地的一所中学，给她融入其他孩子的机会。

| **be willing to** | 乐意，愿意 | |

🔒 managers have **been** more than **willing to** adjust team uniforms 经理们很乐意调整队服

[2008 年英语（一）阅读]

| **most often** | 通常来说；很多时候 | |

🔒 Good writing **most often** occurs when you are in hot pursuit of an idea rather than in a nervous search for errors. 只有当你集中全部精力地阐述某个观点，而非紧张兮兮地寻找错误的时候，好文章才通常会被创作出来。

[2008 年英语（一）阅读]

| **be confronted with** | 面临，面对；对照 | |

词 confront [kən'frʌnt] 使正视，使面对

🔒 In its early days the U.S. **was confronted with** delicate situations. 美国在早些年面临着微妙的处境。

[2008 年英语（一）阅读]

| **be afraid to** | 害怕（去做） | |

🔒 So don't **be afraid to** ask more personal questions. 所以，不要害怕问更私人的问题。

[2018 年英语（二）阅读]

拓 be afraid of 畏惧，害怕；担忧 ‖ be fearful of 害怕，担忧 ‖ dare to 敢于

make conversation　交谈；闲聊

🈚 Five amazing ways that you can **make conversation** with almost anyone. 五种让你几乎可以和任何人对话的好办法。

[2018 年英语（二）阅读]

🈹 have a chat with sb. 与某人交谈，与某人聊天

show sympathy for　对……表示同情

🈹 Indeed, friends are those who willingly help us when we are in trouble, and **show sympathy for** us when we are in misery. 事实上，朋友是那些在我们困难时愿意帮助我们的人，以及在我们悲伤时对我们表示同情的人。

🈹 be sympathetic to/towards/with 对……表示同情

take...for granted　认为……是理所当然的

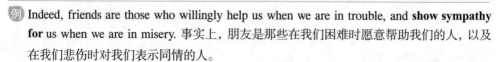

🈚 During most of his waking life he will **take** his code **for granted**, as the businessman takes his ethics. 在其生命中的大部分时间里，他会把自己的行为准则视为理所当然，就像商人对待自己的道德准则一样。

[2006 年英语（一）翻译]

most of　大部分，大多数的

🈚 There are a lot of tasks to be done; there are inadequate rewards for **most of** them. 有太多任务需要完成，而大多数得不到足够的回报。

[2015 年英语（二）阅读]

at all　（用于否定句中）根本，究竟

🈚 Children were not colour-coded **at all** until the early 20th century: in the era before domestic washing machines all babies wore white as a practical matter, since the only way of getting clothes clean was to boil them. 在 20 世纪初之前，孩子们（对衣服）根本没有色彩偏好：在家用洗衣机出现之前，所有的婴儿实际上都穿白色衣服，因为把衣服洗干净的唯一方法就是把它们煮开。

[2012 年英语（二）阅读]

🈺 at all 一般用于否定句中，用于加强语气，强调否定的意味。如：I do not know him at all! 我根本就不认识他！

on earth 意为"究竟，到底"，一般用于疑问句中，表示强调。如：Well, who on earth was doing it? 那么，究竟当时是什么人在做呢？

weigh down　使感到沉重；使颓丧；压低

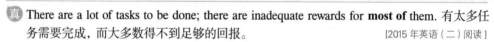

🈐 weigh [weɪ] v. 权衡；重量为；称（重）

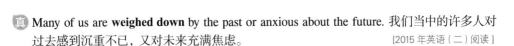

真 Many of us are **weighed down** by the past or anxious about the future. 我们当中的许多人对过去感到沉重不已，又对未来充满焦虑。 [2015 年英语（二）阅读]

follow the example of　　效仿；学习……的榜样　　○○○

真 Otherwise outside directors will **follow the example of** Ms. Simmons, once again very popular on campus. 否则，外部董事们就会像西蒙斯女士那样，摇身一变，再次成为校园里大受欢迎的人。 [2011 年英语（二）阅读]

DAY 06

go away　　消失；走开；离去　　○○○

例 Yet, almost at that moment, the problem began to **go away**. 然而，几乎就是从那时起，问题开始消失。

拓 disappear [dɪsəˈpɪə(r)] v. 消失，失踪

as a means of　　作为一种……的手段　　○○○

真 By using the first draft **as a means of** thinking about what you want to say, you will very likely discover more than your notes originally suggested. 通过用初稿来梳理自己想要表达的内容，你很可能会发现比你原本想表达的更多的内容。

[2008 年英语（一）阅读]

around the clock　　夜以继日地，昼夜不停地　　○○○

真 But a boost in the storage capacity of batteries is making their ability to keep power flowing **around the clock** more likely. 但是电池电容的增加使得它们（风力发电机）更有可能做到昼夜不停转动。 [2018 年英语（二）阅读]

拓 off the reel 不停地；滔滔不绝地

be serious about　　对……是认真的；严肃对待　　○○○

真 If we **are serious about** ensuring that our science is both meaningful and reproducible, we must ensure that our institutions encourage that kind of science. 如果我们真想确保科学既有意义还可再现，我们就必须确保现有机制要鼓励这样的科学研究。 [2019 年英语（一）翻译]

拓 take...seriously 重视；认真对待

search for　　寻找，搜索　　◇

例 **search for** an artist 搜索艺术家
拓 seek [siːk] v. 寻找，寻求

| **lean on** | 依靠；倚靠 | |

真 No shock there, considering how much work it is to raise a kid without a partner to **lean on**. 没有什么可惊讶的，仔细想想，没有伴侣可以依靠，独自抚养孩子是需要付出很多的。

[2011 年英语（一）阅读]

| **in reality** | 实际上，事实上 | |

真 While we may be able to sustain the illusion of control through the conscious mind alone, **in reality** we are continually faced with a question: "Why cannot I make myself do this or achieve that?" 虽然我们或许仅仅靠有意识的思维活动就可以维持这种能控制自己思想的错觉，但事实上我们却不断面临一个问题："为什么我不能让自己去做这件事情或者实现那个目标呢？"

[2011 年英语（一）翻译]

拓 as a matter of fact 事实上 ‖ actually ['æktʃuəli] ad. 实际上，事实上

| **quick fix** | 权宜之计 | |

真 Markets have lost faith that the euro zone's economies, weaker or stronger, will one day converge thanks to the discipline of sharing a single currency, which denies uncompetitive members the **quick fix** of devaluation. 市场已经失去了对欧元区经济的信心，不管它是更弱还是更强，总有一天会因为共同使用单一货币的原则而趋同，而单一货币的原则让缺乏竞争力的成员国无法迅速采取货币贬值的权宜之计。

[2011 年英语（二）阅读]

| **in conjunction with** | 连同，共同；与……协力 | |

词 conjunction [kən'dʒʌŋkʃn] n. 结合；混合；同时发生

真 The scores were then used **in conjunction with** an applicant's score on the Graduate Management Admission Test, or GMAT, a standardised exam which is marked out of 800 points, to make a decision on whether to accept him or her. 然后，这些分数将与申请者的 GMAT（经企管理研究生入学考试，一项满分为 800 分的标准化考试）成绩共同决定是否录取他或她。

[2013 年英语（一）完形填空]

| **look up to** | 尊敬，敬仰；仰望 | |

真 How do the people you respect and **look up to** present themselves? 你尊重和敬仰的人是如何展现他们自己的？

[2016 年英语（一）阅读]

拓 respect [rɪ'spekt] v./n. 尊敬 ‖ show respect to 尊敬 ‖ have little respect to 不尊重

PART 01

a big deal　重要的事；至关重要；大买卖

真 Let's not forget sports—in male-dominated corporate America, it's still **a big deal**. 让我们不要忘了运动——在男性为主导的美国公司中，运动依然是一件大事。[2015 年英语（二）阅读]

拓 a good/great deal of 很多，大量

switch to　转到；切换到；转变成

真 At Boston College, for example, you would have to complete an extra year were you to **switch to** the nursing school from another department. 举例来说，在波士顿学院，如果你想从其他院系转到护理学院，那你就必须额外多读一年。[2017 年英语（二）阅读]

volunteer to　自愿，志愿

真 They **volunteer to** set up an equally big habitat. 他们自愿建立一个同样大的栖息地。[2016 年英语（二）阅读]

拓 of one's own accord 自愿地，主动地 ‖ voluntarily ['vɒləntrəli] ad. 自愿地，主动地

for good　永久地；一劳永逸地

真 Certain jobs have gone away **for good**, outmoded by machines. 一些工作岗位已经被机器淘汰，一去不复返了。[2014 年英语（二）阅读]

拓 once and for all 一劳永逸地；彻底地

cater to　迎合；为……服务

真 Demand comes mainly from two sources: independent mom-and-pop grocery stores which, unlike large retail chains, are too small to buy straight from producers, and food service operators that **cater to** consumers when they don't eat at home. （市场）需求主要源于两个方面：一是独立经营的夫妻杂货店，一是饮食服务运营商。前者不同于大型零售连锁店，其规模太小，因此无力从厂商直接进货；后者则主要是迎合那些外出就餐的消费者。[2010 年英语（一）阅读]

a piece of cake　小菜一碟；轻松的事

真 Yet to hear Sandra and Britney tell it, raising a kid on their "own" (read: with round-the-clock help) is **a piece of cake**. 然而，桑德拉和布兰妮却说，"独自"抚养孩子（注意：身边有全天候的助手帮忙）简直是小菜一碟。[2011 年英语（一）阅读]

get rid of　除去，除掉；摆脱

真 Even though there is plenty of evidence that the quality of the teachers is the most important variable, teachers' unions have fought against **getting rid of** bad ones and promoting good ones. 尽管许多证据都表明，教师素质是影响教育水平最重要的变量，但教师工会还是反对开除差老师、提拔好老师。

[2012 年英语（一）阅读]

on average　按平均数计算

真 It is true that CEO pay has gone up—top ones may make 300 times the pay of typical workers **on average**, and since the mid-1970s, CEO pay for large publicly traded American corporations has, by varying estimates, gone up by about 500%. 没错，首席执行官的薪酬上涨了——最高的首席执行官薪酬可能是普通员工平均薪酬的 300 倍，而且，据多方估计，自 20 世纪 70 年代中期以来，美国大型上市公司首席执行官的薪酬约上涨了 500%。

[2020 年英语（二）阅读]

拓 above/below average 高于 / 低于平均水平

escape from　逃离，逃脱

真 In fact, circumstances seem to be designed to bring out the best in us, and if we feel that we have been "wronged" then we are unlikely to begin a conscious effort to **escape from** our situation. 事实上，环境似乎旨在激发我们的最大潜能，如果我们总感觉"上天不公"，那么就不太可能有意识地去努力摆脱现状。

[2011 年英语（一）翻译]

拓 get away from 摆脱；逃离 ‖ flee [fliː] v. 逃离；逃跑

bring back　拿回来；返回；使……恢复

例 You can **bring back** your recyclable cans and bottles, but please rinse them out first. 你可以把可回收的瓶瓶罐罐带回来，但是请先把它们清理干净。

fall short　不符合标准；不足；功亏一篑

例 They **fell** far **short** of the required qualifications. 她们远达不到要求的资格。

thirst for　对于……的渴望，热望

例 The **thirst for** better education is strong for those people. 那些人强烈渴望获得更好的教育。

拓 yearn for 渴望，向往

to the effect that　大意是

真 Scientists jumped to the rescue with some distinctly shaky evidence **to the effect that** insects would eat us up if birds failed to control them. 科学家们急忙介入，但是提出的证据显然站不住脚，其大意是：如果鸟类不能控制害虫的数量，害虫就会吞噬我们人类。

[2010 年英语（一）翻译]

拓 general idea 大意

take measures　采取措施

真 They could still invalidate Fourth Amendment protections when facing severe, urgent circumstances, and they could **take** reasonable **measures** to ensure that phone data are not erased or altered while waiting for a warrant. 在面临严重和紧急的情况时，他们还可以不受第四条修正案保护条款的约束，在等搜查令下来的过程中采取合理的措施确保手机中的数据不被删除或修改。

[2015 年英语（一）阅读]

offer to　提供；提议；出价

真 DNA testing is also the latest rage among passionate genealogists—and supports businesses that **offer to** search for a family's geographic roots. 基因检测不仅受到热心的谱系学家的热烈追捧，而且也成为提供家族地域溯源服务的公司的技术支持。

[2009 年英语（一）阅读]

in the wake of　随着……而来；作为……的结果

真 The Federal Circuit's action comes **in the wake of** a series of recent decisions by the Supreme Court that has narrowed the scope of protections for patent holders. 联邦巡回法院的行动是继最高法院最近出台的一系列决议之后展开的，这些决议缩小了专利持有人的保护范围。

[2010 年英语（一）阅读]

cast doubt on　质疑，对……产生怀疑

真 History has never **cast doubt on** them. 历史从未质疑过它们（诺贝尔奖）。

[2014 年英语（一）阅读]

leave sb. in the dark　使某人（对某事）一无所知

真 While more families buck an older-generation proclivity to **leave** kids **in the dark** about real estate decisions, realty agents and psychologists have mixed views about the financial, personal and long-term effects kids' opinions may have. 越来越多的家庭反对老一辈人让孩

子们对房产决策一无所知的倾向，与此同时，房地产中介和心理学家对孩子的意见可能带来的财务、个人和长期影响看法不一。

[2019 年英语（二）阅读]

hand out　　　分发；施舍；把……拿出来

真 G.I. is just a military abbreviation implying Government Issue, and it was on all of the articles **handed out** to soldiers. "G.I." 只不过是"政府事务"的军事缩写，在分发给士兵们的所有物品中都有这个名称。

[2012 年英语（二）完形填空]

not...until　　　直到……才

真 Because our conscious mind is occupied with daily life we do**n't** always think about the emotional significance of the day's events—**until**, it appears, we begin to dream. 因为清醒时我们的意识被日常琐事占据着，所以并不总去思考白天发生的事情对我们情绪的影响，似乎直到我们开始做梦，这种影响才会显现。

[2005 年英语（一）阅读]

die of　　　死于，因（病）而死亡

真 Many of the ships were lost in storms, many passengers **died of** disease, and infants rarely survived the journey. 许多船只在暴风雨中迷失，许多乘客被疾病夺去了生命，很少有婴儿能在这次旅程中存活下来。

[2015 年英语（一）翻译]

辨 die of 更多的是指死于内因，如疾病、衰老等自身的原因。如：die of cancer 死于癌症。die from 主要指死于外因，如交通事故、地震等。如：die from a car accident 死于一场车祸。

press forward　　　奋力向前；向前逼近

真 When our time of mourning is over, we **press forward**, stronger with a greater understanding and respect for life. 哀伤过后，我们要努力向前，我们会因为对生活的更多理解和敬重而变得愈加坚强。

[2015 年英语（二）阅读]

live with　　　适应；忍受；承认；与……同居

真 During the Depression and the war, Americans had learned to **live with** less, and that restraint, in combination with the postwar confidence in the future, made small, efficient housing positively stylish. 在大萧条和二战期间，美国人已经学会了适应物资匮乏。于是，这种对物欲的克制，连同战后人们特有的对未来的信心，使得窄小但利用率高的房子绝对风靡。

[2011 年英语（二）阅读]

over the years 多年以来

真 Priestly explains how the deep blue color of the assistant's sweater descended **over the years** from fashion shows to department stores and to the bargain bin in which the poor girl doubtless found her garment. 普里斯特利解释了助理身上所穿的深蓝色毛衣在这些年中是如何从时装表演的舞台降格到了百货商店，再被丢到打折品货架上，而这个可怜的姑娘无疑就是从那里买到她的这件衣服的。 [2013 年英语（一）阅读]

拓 through the years 这些年来

DAY 06

if only 要是，只要，但愿

真 Later, more established companies raced to add such patents to their files, **if only** as a defensive move against rivals that might beat them to the punch. 此后，越来越多的知名企业也竞相将此类专利归入自家卷宗，以求将其作为防止竞争对手占得先机的防御性措施。

[2010 年英语（一）阅读]

agree with 同意；与……一致，相符合

真 Not everyone will **agree with** the authors' policy ideas, which range from mandating more holiday time to reducing tax incentives for American homebuyers. 并不是所有人都赞同作者提出的政策，例如提供更多的假期时间以及减少美国购房者的税收。

[2014 年英语（二）阅读]

拓 in accord with 与……一致

boast of/about 吹嘘，吹牛，自夸

例 Not every village can **boast of** having a picture gallery. And it is worth to say that ordinary villagers are usually far from high art. 不是每个村子都敢夸口说有美术展览馆，并且值得一提的是，普通村民通常离高级艺术较远。

拓 talk big 吹牛

enthusiasm for 对……的热情

真 The American Academy of Arts and Sciences (AAAS) displays great **enthusiasm for** liberal education. 美国人文与科学院对于文科教育显示出了极大的热情。 [2014 年英语（一）阅读]

view...as... 认为……是……

真 First, scientific work tends to focus on some aspect of prevailing knowledge that is **viewed as** incomplete or incorrect. 首先，科学研究倾向于重点关注被视为不完整或不正确的主流知识的某些方面。

[2012 年英语（一）阅读]

拓 regard...as... 把……认作…… ‖ take for 认为，以为

at random　　　　随机地，随便地；任意地

真 This law abolished special educational requirements for federal jurors and required them to be selected **at random** from a cross section of the entire community. 该法案废除了对联邦陪审员特殊学历的要求，并要求从社会各阶层民众中随机挑选陪审员。 [2010 年英语（二）阅读]

拓 at a venture 随便地

owing to 由于，因为 ○○○

（真）Monarchs are kept as heads of state in Europe mostly **owing to** their undoubted and respectable status. 在欧洲，君主之所以被保留为国家元首，主要是因为他们的地位不容置疑且令人尊敬。 [2015 年英语（一）阅读]

be meant to 旨在；有意要；注定 ○○○

（真）This rule **is meant to** address the difficulty that students from impoverished or chaotic homes might have in completing their homework. 这项规定旨在解决来自贫困或混乱家庭的学生在完成家庭作业时可能遇到的困难。 [2012 年英语（二）阅读]

in so far as 至于；在……的限度内 ○○○

（真）Thinking of time as a resource to be maximized means you approach it instrumentally, judging any given moment as well spent only **in so far as** it advances progress toward some goal. 将时间视为有待最大化利用的资源意味着你把时间当作工具来对待，只有当每个既定时刻对某个目标起推进作用时，你才会把这一时刻视为用得恰到好处。

[2016 年英语（二）阅读]

be generous to 对……慷慨的，对……大方的 ○○○

（例）She **is** always extremely **generous to** friends. 她对待朋友总是极其大方。

be popular with 受……欢迎的，为……所喜欢的 ○○○

（真）Homework has never **been** terribly **popular with** students and even many parents, but in recent years it has been particularly scorned. 家庭作业从来不受学生甚至许多家长的欢迎，但近年来它尤其受到了蔑视。 [2012 年英语（二）阅读]

emerge from （从隐蔽处或暗处）出现，浮现，露出 ○○○

（真）Pairs of opponents hit the ball back and forth until one winner **emerges from** all who entered. 成对的对手来来回回地击球，直到有一个胜者从所有的选手中脱颖而出。

[2019 年英语（一）阅读]

look into 调查；观察；窥视，往里看 ◇

（真）But Congress should **look into** doing so directly, by helping to finance PreCheck enrollment or to cut costs in other ways. 但是国会应该考虑直接这么做，通过为 PreCheck 登记提供资金支持或者通过其他方式削减成本。

[2017 年英语（一）阅读]

| **pay for** | 为……付费，为……付酬；为……付出代价；赔偿 | |

真 **pay for** new vehicles 支付新车费用　　　　　　　　　[2018 年英语（一）阅读]

| **keep an eye on** | 密切注视；照看；留意 | |

真 The teachers' unions **keep an eye on** schools, the CCPOA on prisons and a variety of labor groups on health care. 教师工会盯着学校；加州监狱和平促进委员会（CCPOA）盯着监狱；而各种各样的劳工团体则监视着医疗保健部门。　　　　　　　　　[2012 年英语（一）阅读]

拓 pay/give close attention to 对……密切关注

| **to say the least** | 至少可以说，最起码，退一步说 | |

真 For the most part, the response has been favorable, **to say the least**. 至少可以说，大部分人的回答都是赞同的。　　　　　　　　　[2011 年英语（一）阅读]

| **come across** | 给人留下……印象；偶然遇到，偶然发现 | |

真 However, its campaign risks **coming across** as being pushy and overprotective. 然而，这种做法可能会给人留下咄咄逼人、保护过度的印象。　　　　　　　　　[2020 年英语（一）完形填空]

拓 run into/across 偶然遇到，无意中碰到

| **at the start of** | 在……开始的时候，在……初期 | |

真 **At the start of** this century, about one-third of crop workers were over the age of 35. 在本世纪初，种植农作物的工人大约有三分之一在 35 岁以上。　　　　　　　　　[2019 年英语（二）阅读]

| **want to** | 愿意，想要，想要做 | |

真 This advice is more relevant now than ever before, even as more parents **want to** embrace the ideas of their children, despite the current housing crunch. 这条建议现在比以往任何时候都更有意义，尽管目前的住房紧张，但越来越多的父母愿意接受孩子的想法。

[2019 年英语（二）阅读]

拓 long for 渴望，向往

| **(be) known as** | 被称为……；被认为是……；以……而著称 | |

真 a phenomenon **known as** upwash 被称为上升流的现象　　　　　　　　　[2010 年英语（二）阅读]

in some cases　　在某些情况下，有时候

真 But **in some cases**, one marketer's owned media become another marketer's paid media—for instance, when an e-commerce retailer sells ad space on its Web site. 但在某些情况下，某一营销者的"赢得媒体"成了另一营销者的付费媒体——例如，电子商务零售商出售其网站上的广告位。　　[2011 年英语（一）阅读]

pile into　　涌入，挤进，挤入

真 The best lawyers made skyscrapers-full of money, tempting ever more students to **pile into** law schools. 顶级律师的收入极其丰厚，这吸引了更多学生涌入法学院。　　[2014 年英语（一）阅读]

拓 stream into 涌入

stand out　　突出，杰出；显眼；站出来

真 Therefore, everyone needs to find their extra—their unique value contribution that makes them **stand out** in whatever is their field of employment. 因此，每个人都必须找到自身独特的价值——使其在任何职业领域都突出的特有的价值贡献。　　[2013 年英语（二）阅读]

at the beginning of　　在……的开始，在……伊始

真 **at the beginning of** the century 在本世纪初　　[2010 年英语（一）阅读]

send out　　发送，发出（信号、声音、光、热等）；分发，散发；派遣

例 The processor monitors the properties of the nerve when they take in stimuli and **send out** signals to the brain. 当接收到刺激并向大脑发送信号时，传感器便可以监测神经的特性。

reflect on　　认真思考，沉思；回想，回顾

真 Senior executives' quitting may be spurred by their need to **reflect on** their private life. 高级管理人员辞职可能是因为他们需要认真思考自己的个人生活。　　[2011 年英语（一）阅读]

a lot of　　许多的，大量的；非常

真 **a lot of** ethical questions 很多伦理问题　　[2019 年英语（一）阅读]

拓 numerous ['njuːmərəs] *a.* 众多的，许多的

boot up　　启动，打开

真 All I have to do is to go to my CD shelf, or **boot up** my computer and download still more recorded music from iTunes. 我要做的仅仅是到走到我的唱片架，或者打开电脑从 iTunes 下载更多的录制音乐作品。

[2011 年英语（一）阅读]

in the manner of   以……方式，按照……的方式   ◯◯◯

真 The challenge the computer mounts to television thus bears little similarity to one format being replaced by another **in the manner of** record players being replaced by CD players. 因此，计算机施加给电视的挑战与一种格式被另一种格式所取代（就像唱片机被 CD 播放器所取代一样）没有什么相似之处。

[2012 年英语（一）阅读]

pose sth. to   给……造成（问题、危险、困难等）   ◯◯◯

真 Ryan Hooper remarks that significant moves may **pose challenges to** children. 瑞恩·胡珀说重大的变迁可能会给孩子带来挑战。

[2019 年英语（二）阅读]

enter into   进入；达成（协议）；参与（讨论）；结成（关系）   ◌◯

例 **enter into** something like the fullness of her life experience 进入她生活经历的所有细节

a list of   ……的清单；一系列   ◯◯◯

真 A fifth grader gets a homework assignment to select his future career path from **a list of** occupations. 一个五年级孩子获得一份这样的家庭作业：从一份职业清单上挑选自己将来的职业道路。

[2018 年英语（二）翻译]

at the brink of   处于……的边缘   ◯◯◯

真 There are many reasons this formerly stable federal institution finds itself **at the brink of** bankruptcies. 这个曾经稳定的联邦机构发现自己处于破产边缘的原因有很多。

[2018 年英语（一）阅读]

拓 at the edge of 在……边缘

apply for   申请；请求   ◯◯◯

真 Nowadays anyone **applying for** a research post has to have published twice the number of papers that would have been required for the same post only 10 years ago. 如今，任何申请研究职位的人必须发表的论文数量是仅在 10 年前同一职位所需论文数量的两倍。

[2019 年英语（一）翻译]

on the charge of   以……罪名；因，以   ◯◯◯

例 The woman, whose nine-year-old son died of leukemia last year, stood trial **on the charge of** attempted murder for withholding from him at least six months of chemotherapy medications. 这位女士 9 岁的儿子去年死于白血病，她因禁止自己的孩子接受至少 6 个月的化疗而被指控谋杀未遂，受到审判。

be inferior to　　劣于，次于，差于，低于　

🈚 They **are** often **inferior to** live concerts in quality. 它们（录音）的音效通常不如现场音乐会的效果好。　[2011 年英语（一）阅读]

🈯 be worse than 差于

make one's way　　行走；前进　◇

🈚 **make his way** up the promotion ladder 在晋升的阶梯上奋力向上攀爬　[2022 年英语（一）翻译]

all in all　　总而言之，总的来说　◇

🈚 **All in all**, this clearly seems to be a market in which big retailers could profitably apply their gigantic scale, existing infrastructure, and proven skills in the management of product ranges, logistics, and marketing intelligence. 总之，这显然是一个大型零售商可以获利的市场。大型零售商可以利用自己的庞大规模、现有的基础设施，以及在产品种类、物流和营销情报等方面的技术优势来获得利润。　[2010 年英语（一）阅读]

🈯 in sum 总而言之，总的来说

in the absence of　　在缺少……的情况下　

🈚 But the epidemic is "moderate" in severity, according to Margaret Chan, the organization's director general, with the overwhelming majority of patients experiencing only mild symptoms and a full recovery, often **in the absence of** any medical treatment. 但世界卫生组织总干事陈冯富珍表示，疫情的严重程度是"中等"，绝大多数患者只出现轻微症状，而且往往无须治疗就可以完全康复。　[2010 年英语（二）完形填空]

take hold　　显现；抓住；生根　

🈚 As the first signs of recovery begin to **take hold**, deputy chiefs may be more willing to make the jump without a net. 当经济复苏的种种迹象开始显现时，二把手们也许会更愿意在没有找到新的工作时就辞职。　[2011 年英语（一）阅读]

eat up　　吞噬，耗尽；吃光　

🈚 **eat up** human jobs 吞噬人们的工作　[2014 年英语（二）阅读]

ban...from 禁止；取缔

真 My own hospital system has **banned** sugary drinks **from** its facilities. 我所在的医院系统禁止提供含糖饮料。 [2014 年英语（二）完形填空]

拓 to impose/lift a ban 颁布 / 解除禁令

by all accounts 根据大家所说，据大家所知

真 **By all accounts** he was a freethinking person, and a courageous one, and I find courage an essential quality for the understanding, let alone the performance, of his works. 人们普遍认为他是个思想自由的人，是个勇敢无畏的人，我发现勇敢这一特征是理解他作品的关键，更不必说是演奏其作品的关键了。 [2014 年英语（一）翻译]

learn from 向……学习，从……中学习

真 **learn from** private industry 向私营企业学习 [2010 年英语（二）阅读]

solution to ……的解决方法，……的解决途径

真 The **solution to** the ethical issues brought by autonomous vehicles is still beyond our capacity. 解决无人驾驶车辆所带来的伦理问题仍在我们的能力范围之外。

[2019 年英语（一）阅读]

in need 需要帮助的；在危难中的，在穷困中的

例 My brother and I had our clashes, but we always had each other when we were **in need**. 我和哥哥之间也有矛盾，但当有需要时，我们总是就在彼此身边。

dedicate to 投入（时间、精力等）于，致力于，献身于

真 There are a number of approaches to mastering the art of deep work—be it lengthy retreats, **dedicated to** a specific task; developing a daily ritual; or taking a "journalistic" approach to seizing moments of deep work when you can throughout the day. 掌握深度工作技能有多种方法——为了投入一项特定的任务而长时间闭关；养成每天的习惯；或者是采用"新闻工作者"的办法，抓住一天中能够深度工作的时刻。 [2018 年英语（二）阅读]

on campus 在校的；在校内

真 Write an email to all international experts **on campus**, inviting them to attend the graduation ceremony. 给所有在校的国际专家写一封电子邮件，邀请他们参加毕业典礼。

[2018 年英语（一）写作]

mess up	弄糟；把……弄乱，弄脏	

例 One of the primary reasons people **mess up** their lives is that they have no devout friends to give them advice. 使人们生活一片混乱的一个主要原因是他们没有忠诚的朋友为其提供建议。

tempt sb. into (doing) sth.	诱惑或怂恿某人做某事	

真 Writers are likely to be **tempted into** journalism. 作家们很可能会因为受到诱惑而从事新闻工作。   [2010 年英语（一）阅读]

would rather	宁愿，宁可	

例 Many people have great ideals, but achieving them takes lots of time and effort, so they **would rather** work at their own projects than join yours. 很多人有远大的理想，但是实现它们需要付出大量时间和努力，所以他们宁愿做自己的工作也不愿加入你的团队。

make progress	取得进步，取得进展	

真 I also found that weighing myself daily did not provide an accurate distribution of the hard work and **progress** I was **making** in the gym. 我还发现，每天称体重并不能准确地反映我在健身房所做的努力以及我所取得的进步。   [2019 年英语（二）完形填空]

拓 improvement [ɪm'pruːvmənt] n. 改善，改进

differ from	与……不同，区别于……	

真 Ways of reading on a train or in bed are likely to **differ** considerably **from** reading in a seminar room. 在火车上阅读或在床上躺着阅读，可能与在会议室里阅读大为不同。

[2015 年英语（一）阅读]

put up with	容忍，忍受	

例 It becomes much more economical to automate some respects of the work, employing machines to do those tedious and dull toil that men and women are no longer willing to **put up with**. 把一部分工作变得自动化，使用机器去做那些男人和女人都不愿再忍受的单调乏味的劳累工作将会变得更加经济。

拓 bear [beə(r)] v. 忍受 ‖ endure [ɪn'djʊə(r)] v. 忍耐，容忍；持续

| **hundreds of** | 成百上千的；数以百计的；许许多多的 | ◇ |

真 **hundreds of** simpler apartment complexes 成百上千个较为简朴的平民住宅群

[2014 年英语（一）阅读]

拓 hundreds of thousands of 成千上万；几十万

| **look to** | 关注，注意；指望；照看 | ◯◯◯ |

真 And perhaps faintly, they hint that people should **look to** intangible qualities like character and intellect rather than dieting their way to size zero or wasp-waist physiques. 而且它们还可能隐晦地暗示人们应该关注性格和智慧等无形的品质，而不是一直节食以达到零码身材或蜂腰体型。

[2016 年英语（一）阅读]

| **in the future** | 在将来，在未来 | ◇ |

真 to compete with other creative personalities **in the future** 将来和其他极具创意的精英人物一较高低

[2017 年英语（二）翻译]

| **on account of** | 因为，由于，出于……的缘故 | ◯◯ |

例 The game was postponed **on account of** the bad weather. 比赛由于天气恶劣而被推迟了。

| **do with** | 利用；处理；忍受 | ◇ |

真 What would you **do with** $590m? 你会如何利用 5.9 亿美元？　　[2014 年英语（二）阅读]

| **in the way of** | 在……方面，关于；按照；妨碍 | ◯◯◯ |

真 First, they can shut things down without suffering much **in the way of** consequences. 其一，他们可以罢工停业，却无需承担太多后果。

[2012 年英语（一）阅读]

| **be going to** | 将要，打算，计划 | ◯◯◯ |

真 Suppose you **are going to** study abroad and share an apartment with John, a local student. 假设你要出国留学，和当地的学生约翰合住一间公寓。

[2014 年英语（二）写作]

| **be busy doing sth.** | 忙于做某事 | ◯◯◯ |

真 The dominant powers **are busy handling** their own crises. 主要大国忙于处理自己的危机。

[2011 年英语（二）阅读]

拓 occupy oneself (in doing sth./with sth.) 忙着（做某事物），忙于（某事务）

| **an array of** | 一系列，一大批，一大群 | ◯◯◯ |

词 array [əˈreɪ] *n.* 一系列；陈列；展示；服装

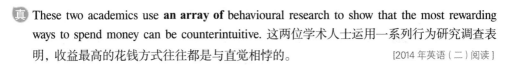 These two academics use **an array of** behavioural research to show that the most rewarding ways to spend money can be counterintuitive. 这两位学术人士运用一系列行为研究调查表明，收益最高的花钱方式往往都是与直觉相悖的。 [2014 年英语（二）阅读]

in place of	取代，代替	

 In place of Thomas Carlyle, Britain nurtured Christopher Hill, EP Thompson and Eric Hobsbawm. 英国培养出了克里斯托弗·希尔、汤普森、埃里克·霍布斯鲍姆，他们取代了之前的托马斯·克莱尔。 [2012 年英语（二）阅读]

go along with	与……意见一致，赞同	

I'm afraid I can't **go along with** you on this question. 在这个问题上，我恐怕无法赞同你的观点。

refrain from	避免；克制，忍住	

refrain [rɪ'freɪn] v. 克制，抑制

California has asked the justices to **refrain from** a sweeping ruling. 加利福尼亚州已经请求法官们在引用最高法院的指导性别例时要有所克制。 [2015 年英语（一）阅读]

look out of	看向……的外面，向外看	

Think of those fleeting moments when you **look out of** an aeroplane window and realise that you are flying, higher than a bird. 想想当你坐在飞机上，眼望窗外时，突然意识到自己正在飞翔，飞得比鸟儿还要高。 [2012 年英语（一）阅读]

in one way	从某种意义上来讲	

None of these tricks will help you understand them, their positions or the issues that divide you, but they can help you win—**in one way**. 这些技巧都不会帮助你理解他们，也不会帮助你理解他们的立场以及让你们产生分歧的问题，但是这些技巧能帮助你获胜——从某种意义上来讲。 [2019 年英语（一）阅读]

in a certain sense 从某种意义上来说

research into	关于……的调查	

Social psychologists have amassed oceans of **research into** what they call the "above average effect" or "illusory superiority". 社会心理学家已经开展了很多针对所谓的"超过平均效应"或"幻想优越性"的调查。 [2014 年英语（一）阅读]

to the letter　严格地，不折不扣地；严格按照字句　○○○

例 We should certainly carry out these plans **to the letter**. 我们一定要严格执行这些计划。

take a page from　借鉴，从……吸取经验　○○○

真 Rosenberg argues convincingly that public-health advocates ought to **take a page from** advertisers, so skilled at applying peer pressure. 罗森伯格有力地论证道，公共卫生倡导者应从广告人那里吸取经验，因为他们能熟练地运用同辈压力。　[2012 年英语（一）阅读]

for the long term　长期，从长远来看　○○○

真 Britain's new rule is a reminder to bankers that society has an interest in their performance, not just for the short term but **for the long term**. 英国的新规定让银行家意识到，社会不仅仅在短期内关注其表现，长期也是。　[2019 年英语（一）阅读]

拓 for the long run 从长远来看 ‖ for the short term/run 在短期内

ask for　寻求；请求；求见　◇

真 **ask for** honest feedback 寻求坦诚的反馈　[2016 年英语（一）阅读]

adjust to　根据……进行调整，改变……以适应　○○

真 We need to **adjust to** this changing climate. 我们需要依据气候变化做出调整。　[2014 年英语（二）阅读]

be able to　能够　◇

真 not **be able to** visit professor Smith 无法去拜访史密斯教授　[2018 年英语（二）写作]

at the very least　至少　○○○

真 **At the very least**, it has awoken us from our national fever dream of easy riches and bigger houses. 至少，这种状况让整个国家从轻易致富、买到豪宅的美梦中醒来。　[2012 年英语（二）阅读]

as soon as　一……就……　◇

真 **As soon as** you awaken, identify what is upsetting about the dream. 当你一醒过来，立刻找出梦中有什么在困扰你。　[2005 年英语（一）阅读]

bound for　驶向　○○○

真 The first shiploads of immigrants **bound for** the territory which is now the United States

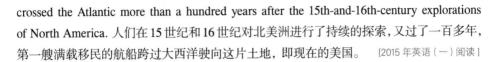

crossed the Atlantic more than a hundred years after the 15th-and-16th-century explorations of North America. 人们在 15 世纪和 16 世纪对北美洲进行了持续的探索，又过了一百多年，第一艘满载移民的航船跨过大西洋驶向这片土地，即现在的美国。 [2015 年英语（一）阅读]

in the case of　　至于；在……的情况下

(真) **In the case of** Hamish Fulton, you can't help feeling that the Scottish artist has simply found a way of making his love of walking pay. 至于哈米什·富尔顿，你一定会觉得这位苏格兰艺术家已经找到了从行走这一爱好中挣钱的方法。 [2014 年英语（二）阅读]

give up　　放弃；戒除；认输；辞去（工作）；把……让给；自首

(真) The web's full of articles offering tips on making time to read: "**Give up** TV" or "Carry a book with you at all times." 网络上充斥着各种关于找时间阅读的建议文章："戒掉看电视的习惯"或是"随时随身携带一本书"。 [2016 年英语（二）阅读]

go off　　变质；对……不再喜欢；爆炸；停止运转；进展；（警报器）突然响起

(真) If you have surplus vegetables you'll do a vegetable soup, and all fruits threatening to "**go off**" will be cooked or juiced. 如果你有多余的蔬菜，你就会做个蔬菜汤，而所有即将变质的水果都会用来做菜或者榨汁。 [2013 年英语（二）阅读]

write off　　取消；注销；忽视；报废（车辆）；（向公司等）去函

(真) It is too soon to **write off** the EU. 取消欧盟还为时尚早。 [2011 年英语（二）阅读]

embed...in　　将……深而牢固地固定于（周围的物体中）

(词) embed [ɪm'bed] v. 使根深蒂固；将……嵌入（或插入）

(真) Not only did they develop such a device but by the turn of the millennium they had also managed to **embed** it **in** a worldwide system accessed by billions of people every day. 这些人不但发明了这个设备，而且在世纪之交时还将这台机器纳入了一个世界性的体系内，从而使几十亿人每天都可以使用它。 [2012 年英语（一）阅读]

faint praise　　轻描淡写的赞扬，敷衍或无心的赞美

(词) faint [feɪnt] a. 不热情的，不积极的；微小的

(真) As a description of the next music director of an orchestra that has hitherto been led by musicians like Gustav Mahler and Pierre Boulez, that seems likely to have struck at least some *Times* (*The New York Times*) readers as **faint praise**. 但对于一个迄今一直由像古斯塔

夫·马勒和皮埃尔·布列兹那样的音乐家带领的乐团来说，这样描述其下一任指挥者，至少对《纽约时报》的某些读者而言，可能像是轻描淡写的赞扬。 [2011 年英语（一）阅读]

in addition　此外，另外

真 **In addition**, "AI looks at résumés in greater numbers than humans would be able to, and selects the more promising candidates." 此外，"比起人类，人工智能软件远能查看更多数量的简历，还能选择更有前途的应聘者。" [2021 年英语（一）阅读]

stand for　代表；是……的缩写；支持，主张；容忍（常用否定）

真 to **stand for** rail travelers 代表铁路旅客 [2021 年英语（一）阅读]

be correlated with　和……相互关联；和……相互影响

真 That's because economic growth can **be correlated with** environmental degradation, while protecting the environment **is** sometimes **correlated with** greater poverty. 这是因为经济增长可能与环境退化有关，而环境保护有时与更为严重的贫困有关。 [2021 年英语（一）阅读]

in silence　安静地，无声地

真 On average, participants who followed this instruction felt better than those who had been told to stand or sit **in silence**. 一般来说，遵循这一指令的参与者比那些被告知去安静地站着或坐着的人感觉更好。 [2021 年英语（二）翻译]

connect to　（使）连接；结合

真 You're more likely to be heard if you can **connect** your disagreement **to** a higher purpose. 如果你能把你的异议与更高的目标联系起来，你的意见更有可能被听到。[2021 年英语（二）阅读]

focus on　集中（注意力、精力等）于

真 And people made car-buying decisions that were both objectively better and more personally satisfying when asked to **focus on** their feelings rather than on details, but only if the decision was complex—when they had a lot of information to process. 当人们被要求将注意力集中在他们的感觉而不是细节上时，他们做出的购车决定在客观上更好，也更能令自己心满意足，但仅限于这个决定很复杂，即当他们需要处理大量信息的时候。 [2021 年英语（二）阅读]

put an end to　　结束；终止　　

真 "They bought the seedlings and closed them down," complained Paul Arnold, a partner at San Francisco-based Switch Ventures, **putting an end to** businesses that might one day turn into competitors. 总部位于旧金山的 Switch Ventures 的合伙人保罗·阿诺德抱怨道："他们买下这些刚刚崭露头角的小公司，又将它们关闭。"此举终结了那些可能有朝一日会变成其竞争对手的企业。 [2021 年英语（二）阅读]

regardless of　　不管，尽管，不顾　　

真 And **regardless of** transferability, the study shows that what's good for people may also be good for the environment. 抛开可转移性不谈，该研究表明，对人有益的事物可能也对环境有益。 [2021 年英语（一）阅读]

compare to　　和……相比；把……比作　　

真 Equally, there is a sense that the travails of commuters in the South East, many of whom will face among the biggest rises, have received too much attention **compared to** those who must endure the relatively poor infrastructure of the Midlands and the North. 同样，人们也感觉到，与那些必须忍受相对较差的基础设施的中部和北部的人相比，东南部通勤者（他们当中很多人将面临最大幅度的票价上涨）的艰辛已经受到了太多关注。 [2021 年英语（一）阅读]

be good at　　善于，擅长　　

真 We're fairly **good at** judging people based on first impressions, thin slices of experience ranging from a glimpse of a photo to a five-minute interaction, and deliberation can be not only extraneous but intrusive. 我们很擅长根据第一印象和少得可怜的经验（从瞥一眼照片到五分钟的互动，应有尽有）来判断一个人，而深思熟虑可能不仅是无关紧要的，而且还可能会造成干扰。 [2021 年英语（二）阅读]

disagree with sb.　　不同意某人的观点；与某人有分歧

真 What do you say when you **disagree with** someone who has more power than you do? 当你与比你权力大的人意见不一致时，你会说什么？ [2021 年英语（二）阅读]

at/in/to the forefront of　　在……的最前沿；是……最重要的事　○○○

真 Zoos are **at the forefront of** conservation and constantly evolving to improve how they care for animals and protect each species in its natural habitat. 动物园走在保护动物的最前沿，它们不断改善照顾动物的方式，并保护其自然栖息地的每一个物种。

[2022 年英语（一）阅读]

拓 be in a leading position 处于领先地位

weigh up　　权衡；估量；称　○○○

真 As the latest crop of students pen their undergraduate application form and **weigh up** their options, it may be worth considering just how the point, purpose and value of a degree has changed and what Generation Z need to consider as they start the third stage of their educational journey. 当最新一批学生填写本科申请表并权衡他们的选择时，或许值得考虑学位的意义、目的和价值发生了怎样的变化，以及 Z 世代在开始他们教育旅程的第三阶段时需要考虑些什么。

[2022 年英语（一）阅读]

assist sb. in/with sth.　　帮助某人做某事　○○○

真 Fewer artists than scientists responded to the *Nature* poll; however, several respondents noted that artists do not simply **assist** scientists **with** their communication requirements. 在《自然》杂志的民意调查中，参与的艺术家比科学家少；然而，几位受访者指出，艺术家不仅仅是帮助科学家满足他们的交流需求。

[2022 年英语（一）阅读]

拓 help sb. with sth. 帮助某人做某事

in person　　本人；亲自　○○○

真 But when you can't connect **in person**, consider using technology. 但是当你不能亲自面对面交流时，可以考虑利用科技。

[2022 年英语（二）阅读]

constrain...from doing sth.　　限制……做某事　○○○

真 As countless boards and business owners will attest, **constraining** firms **from** firing poorly performing, high-earning managers is a handbrake on boosting productivity and overall performance. 正如无数董事会和企业主将会见证的那样，限制企业解雇业绩不佳的高收入经理人，是提高生产效率和整体业绩的一个手闸。

[2022 年英语（一）阅读]

拓 constraint on sth. 对某事物的限制或约束

discontent with　对……的不满

真 The percentage of UK graduates in non-graduate roles reflects public **discontent with** education. 英国大学毕业生从事不要求大学学历的工作的比例反映了公众对教育的不满。

[2022 年英语（一）阅读]

拓 be discontented with 对……不满意

hint at　暗示

真 Though plants lack brains, the firing of electrical signals in their stems and leaves nonetheless triggered responses that **hinted at** consciousness, researchers previously reported. 研究人员此前曾报告说，尽管植物没有大脑，但它们的茎和叶发出的电信号却能触发一些暗示有意识存在的反应。

[2022 年英语（一）完形填空]

be done with　完成；完全结束；与……断绝关系

真 It is unlikely that Generation Z will **be done with** education at 18 or 21; they will need to be constantly up-skilling throughout their career to stay employable. Z 世代不太可能在 18 或 21 岁完成受教育；他们将需要在整个职业生涯中不断提高技能，以保持受雇的资格。

[2022 年英语（一）阅读]

in the same camp　意见相同，志同道合

真 As a fellow environmentalist, animal-protection advocate and longtime vegetarian, I could properly be **in the same camp** as Emma Marris on the issue of zoos. 作为一名环保主义者、动物保护倡导者和长期素食者，在动物园问题上，我与艾玛·马里斯恰如其分地意见相同。

[2022 年英语（一）阅读]

本单元资源

something wrong with　……有问题；……出故障

例 Too many of us go through life without reaching success not because there's **something wrong with** us but because we've failed to define what success even means to us. 有太多的人终其一生都没有成功，这并非是因为我们有什么问题，而是我们甚至连成功对我们来说意味着什么都不清楚。

grow up　长大；成熟；逐渐发展

真 As we **grow up**, we learn to control our emotions so they are manageable and don't dictate our behaviours. 随着我们长大，我们学着去控制自己的情绪，好让情绪可控并且不会左右我们的行为。

[2016 年英语（二）阅读]

set up　设立，创建；组织，安排

真 The Nobels were, of course, themselves **set up** by a very rich individual who had decided what he wanted to do with his own money. 当然，诺贝尔奖本身是由一位非常富有的人设立的，他已经决定了如何处置自己的财产。

[2014 年英语（一）阅读]

slow down　（使）放松；（使）放慢；（使）减速

真 to **slow down** to the moment and live life happily 放慢脚步，把握当下，幸福生活

[2016 年英语（一）翻译]

be different from　与……不同

真 Parkrun **is different from** Olympic games in that it does not emphasize elitism. 公园跑与奥运会比赛的不同在于公园跑不强调精英主义。

[2017 年英语（二）阅读]

prevent...from　阻止……；防止……；阻碍……

真 Britain's town, it is true, are not **prevented from** applying, but they generally lack the resources to put together a bid to beat their bigger competitors. 的确，英国的小镇并没有被阻止申请，但它们通常缺乏资源来投标，以击败更大的竞争对手。　[2020 年英语（一）阅读]

by no means　绝不，一点也不

真 Up until a few decades ago, our visions of the future were largely—though **by no means** uniformly—glowingly positive. 直到几十年前，我们对未来的想象——尽管并不完全一致，但主要还是积极乐观的。 [2013 年英语（一）阅读]

think about 想一想；考虑，思考

真 **Think about** the present moment. 想想当下的情况。 [2015 年英语（二）阅读]

DAY 08

relieve of 缓解；使摆脱

词 relieve [rɪ'liːv] v. 解除；减轻，缓和

真 Studies from the US and Australia imply that taking a gap year helps **relieve** freshmen **of** pressures. 美国和澳大利亚的研究表明，间隔年有助于缓解大一新生的压力。 [2017 年英语（二）阅读]

take advantage of 利用

词 advantage [əd'vɑːntɪdʒ] n. 优势；利益

真 **take advantage of** college resources 利用大学资源 [2015 年英语（二）阅读]

拓 have the advantage of sb. 比某人强，占上风（尤指知其所不知）

scrape through 勉强通过（考试）；（在竞争、选举中）勉强获胜

拓 scrape [skreɪp] v. 擦净；削平；磨光；除掉；刮坏

例 She didn't study hard and just **scraped through** her final exams. 她没有努力学习，只是勉强通过了期末考试。

buy into 相信

真 You can get people to think it's nonsense at the same time that you **buy into** it. 你可以让别人以为这是一派胡言，同时自己深信不疑。 [2015 年英语（二）阅读]

pay a price for 为……付出代价

例 The American people are willing to **pay a price for** energy independence. 美国人民愿意为能源独立付出代价。

billions of 数以十亿计的；无数的，大量的

真 The Supreme Court's opinion Thursday overruled a pair of decades-old decisions that states said cost them **billions of** dollars in lost revenue annually. 最高法院周四的主张推翻了两项实施了几十年的裁决，各州表示这两项裁决每年会使其损失数十亿美元的收入。 [2019 年英语（一）阅读]

那些"没事"的逞强，最后变成了"真的"坚强。 **101** 》

| millions of | 数以百万计的；无数的，大量的 | |

真 **millions of** years 数百万年 [2013 年英语（一）阅读]

| beside the point | 无关紧要；离题，不相关 | |

真 But had Entergy kept its word, that debate would be **beside the point**. 但如果安特吉公司能信守承诺的话，争论也就毫无意义了。 [2012 年英语（一）阅读]

| at once | 立刻，马上 | |

真 to eat them **at once** 立刻把它们吃掉 [2019 年英语（一）阅读]

拓 right away 立刻，马上

| persuade sb. to do sth. | 说服某人做某事 | |

真 If that happens, passionate consumers would try to **persuade others to** boycott products, putting the reputation of the target company at risk. 如果上述情形发生的话，情绪激动的消费者会设法劝说其他消费者联合抵制目标企业的产品，从而危及它们的声誉。

[2011 年英语（一）阅读]

| a growing number of | 越来越多的 | |

真 **A growing number of** researchers and organisations are now thinking seriously about that question. 如今越来越多的研究人员和组织在认真思考这个问题。 [2013 年英语（一）阅读]

拓 increasingly more 越来越多的

| knock out | 否决；淘汰；击败；摧毁；使入睡；使不省人事 | |

真 On a five to three vote, the Supreme Court **knocked out** much of Arizona's immigration law Monday—a modest policy victory for the Obama Administration. 周一，最高法院以 5∶3 的表决结果否决了亚利桑那州的大部分移民法案——这对奥巴马政府而言是一次微弱的政策胜利。 [2013 年英语（一）阅读]

| be comparable to | 比得上；类似于；与……有可比性 | |

真 The author believes that exploring one's phone contents **is comparable to** getting into one's residence. 作者认为，查看一个人的手机内容就类似于进入一个人的住所。

[2015 年英语（一）阅读]

contrary to   与……相反，与……相悖

例 **Contrary to** what many believe, instead of marking the end of an era, it represents the start of a new one. 与许多人认为的相反，它不是一个时代结束的标志，而是象征着一个新时代的开始。

link A to B   使 A 与 B 相关联，将 A 与 B 联系起来

真 Facebook promised the European commission then that it would not **link** phone numbers **to** Facebook identities, but it broke the promise almost as soon as the deal went through. 脸书当时向欧盟委员会承诺不会将用户的手机号码与脸书账号进行关联，但是几乎就在收购获得批准的同时，脸书就违背了自己的承诺。   [2018 年英语（二）阅读]

protect...against/from   保护……免遭……

真 Hugging **protects** people who are under stress **from** the increased risk for colds that's usually associated with stress. 拥抱保护那些处于压力之下的人，使他们远离不断增加的患感冒的风险——感冒通常与压力有关。   [2017 年英语（一）完形填空]

plunge into   投身于；突然开始从事；经历，陷入（不好的事）

真 After *Pickwick*, Dickens **plunged into** a bleaker world. 《匹克威克外传》之后，狄更斯投身于一个更灰暗的世界。   [2017 年英语（一）阅读]

(be) immune to   对……有免疫力；不受……影响

真 Some Americans fear that immigrants living within the United States remain somehow **immune to** the nation's assimilative power. 一些美国人害怕居住在美国境内的移民不知为何仍对这个国家的同化有免疫力。   [2006 年英语（一）阅读]

be worse off   处境更糟；更加贫穷

真 Bob Liodice, the chief executive of the Association of National Advertisers, says consumers will **be worse off** if the industry cannot collect information about their preferences. 美国国家广告商协会的首席执行官鲍勃·雷奥戴斯说，如果该行业无法收集关于消费者喜好的信息，那么消费者面临的情况将更糟。   [2013 年英语（一）阅读]

拓 be badly off 处于困境的；境况不佳的；缺钱的；贫穷的

sign up (for)　　签约；报名（课程）；雇用

真 Reding invited corporations to **sign up for** gender balance goals of 40 percent female board membership. 雷丁邀请各家公司签订了一个性别均衡目标书，要求董事会保持 40% 的女性比例。

[2013 年英语（二）阅读]

cooperate with　　与……合作，与……协作

真 Among the children who had not been tricked, the majority were willing to **cooperate with** the tester in learning a new skill, demonstrating that they trusted his leadership. 没有被欺骗过的孩子大多数愿意与测试员合作学习一项新技能，这证明他们相信他的引导。

[2018 年英语（一）完形填空]

do away with　　终结；消除；谋杀

例 The company had to **do away with** free lunches in order to save money. 该公司为了节省开支，不得不取消免费午餐。

拓 get rid of 消除，去除

fall asleep　　入睡，睡着

例 As soon as the lights were dimmed, the baby **fell asleep**. 灯光一暗下来，小婴儿就睡着了。

make ends meet　　勉强维持生计；使收支相抵

例 I have to work at two jobs to **make ends meet**. 我不得不打两份工才能勉强维持生计。

in all　　总的来说；总计，总共

真 **In all**, the study concludes that whereas prosecutors should only evaluate a case based on its merits, they do seem to be influenced by a company's record in CSR. 总的来说，该研究得出结论，尽管检察官应该仅仅基于案件本身的情况进行评估，但是他们似乎还是受到了企业社会责任记录的影响。

[2016 年英语（一）阅读]

be capable of　　有能力……

真 Such behaviour is regarded as "all too human", with the underlying assumption that other animals would not **be capable of** this finely developed sense of grievance. 这种行为被认为是"人之常情"，因为人们潜在地认为其他动物没能进化出这种高度发达的怨愤情感。

[2005 年英语（一）阅读]

at odds with　　　与……有差异，与……相矛盾；与……有分歧

This top-down conception of the fashion business couldn't be more out of date or **at odds with** the feverish world described in *Overdressed*, Elizabeth Cline's three-year indictment of "fast fashion". 这种自上而下的时尚行业理念已经完全过时了，与伊丽莎白·克莱因在其《过度着装》一书中所描述的疯狂世界大相径庭，这本书是她耗时三年完成的对"快餐式时尚"的指控。　　　　　　　　　　　　　　　　　　　　　　[2013 年英语（一）阅读]

tell about　　　告诉（某人）有关……的情况；谈及

The police wanted Bob to **tell** them **about** his friends. 警察想让鲍勃告诉他们他朋友的情况。

be (stuck) in a rut　　　生活一成不变，墨守成规

rut [rʌt] *n.* 刻板乏味的生活；车辙

If you're in a period of change or just feeling stuck and **in a rut**, now may be a good time. 如果你正处于转变期，或只是觉得难以突破、生活一成不变，那么现在可能就是一个好时机。

[2016 年英语（一）阅读]

spend on　　　在……上花费

Researchers admit that their study does not answer the question of how much businesses ought to **spend on** CSR. 研究人员承认，他们的研究并不能解答企业应该在社会责任项目上投入多少的问题。

[2016 年英语（一）阅读]

at risk　　　有危险；冒风险

If that happens, passionate consumers would try to persuade others to boycott products, putting the reputation of the target company **at risk**. 如果上述情形发生的话，情绪激动的消费者会设法劝说其他消费者联合抵制目标企业的产品，从而危及它们的声誉。

[2011 年英语（一）阅读]

at the risk of doing sth. 冒可能做某事的危险 ‖ risk doing sth. 冒险做某事

at a...speed　　　以……的速度

Job opportunities are disappearing **at a** high **speed**. 工作机会正在快速消失。

[2013 年英语（二）阅读]

at a/the...rate of 以……速度

allow (...) to 允许 ◡◡◡

真 Elected leaders must be **allowed to** help supporters deal with bureaucratic problems without fear of prosecution for bribery. 民选领袖应该获准帮助支持者解决一些涉及官方的问题，而不必担心会遭到贿赂起诉。 [2017 年英语（一）阅读]

拓 permit to 允许

mislead...into doing sth. 误导……做某事 ◡◡◡

词 mislead [ˌmɪsˈliːd] v. 误导，引入歧途

真 The author is concerned that "moral licensing" may **mislead** us **into doing** worthless things. 作者担心"道德许可"可能会误导我们做毫无价值的事情。 [2019 年英语（二）阅读]

care about 关心；担心 ◇

真 **care about** needy workers 关心穷苦的工人 [2019 年英语（一）阅读]

look around 环顾，到处看 ◇

例 **look around** your space 看看你的四周

commit to 对……做出承诺；致力于 ◡◡◡

真 We need them to imagine the United States as a place where they can be productive for a while without **committing** themselves **to** staying forever. 我们需要他们把美国想象成这样一个地方：他们可以在一段时间内取得成果，而不需要承诺永久留下。 [2013 年英语（二）阅读]

at the time 在那时；在那段时间 ◡◡◡

真 Authorities may search through the possessions of suspects **at the time** of their arrest. 当局在逮捕嫌犯时可以搜查其财物。 [2015 年英语（一）阅读]

拓 at those days 那时，当时

trade with sb. 与某人进行贸易往来，与某人做生意 ◡◡◡

例 Many financial institutions refuse to **trade with him** after the scandal. 此次丑闻过后，许多金融机构都纷纷拒绝与他进行贸易往来。

拓 make a deal with 与……做生意；向……妥协

agree to 同意，应允，接受 ◇

真 Euro-zone members should **agree to** some fiscal and social harmonization: e.g., curbing

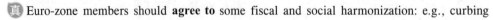

competition in corporate-tax rates or labour costs. 欧元区成员国应同意一定程度上的财政和社会协调：例如，遏制公司税率或人力成本的竞争。 [2011 年英语（二）阅读]

辨 **agree to** 指"同意，应允"，通常用于同意某件事情。如：They have not yet agreed to our requests but they are clearly weakening. 他们还没有同意我们的要求，但态度已明显软化。

agree with 表示"同意，赞同"，常常表示同某人意见一致，也可表示赞同某件事情。还表示"（气候、食物等）适合"之意。如：1) He agrees with me about the need for more hospitals. 关于多建一些医院一事，他同意我的意见。2) Too much meat doesn't agree with the girl. 那个女孩不适合吃太多肉。

agree on/upon 表示"就……取得一致意见"，指两方或多方就某个问题取得了一致的意见或达成了某种协议。如：We finally agreed on the date to negotiate. 我们终于就磋商的日期达成了一致意见。

move forward	向前移动；向前发展	

真 We still have a long way to go to get back to full employment, but at least we are now finally **moving forward** at a faster pace. 要恢复充分就业，我们还有很长的路要走，但至少我们现在终于在以更快的速度前进。 [2015 年英语（二）阅读]

be filled with	充满……	

真 a world without work would **be filled with** unease 一个没有工作的世界将充满焦虑不安 [2017 年英语（二）完形填空]

deliver...to	传达；交付	

真 To **deliver** results **to** its users quickly, then, Google has to maintain vast data centres round the world, packed with powerful computers. 为了快速向用户提供结果，谷歌必须在全球范围内维护庞大的数据中心，并配备功能强大的计算机。 [2011 年英语（二）翻译]

catch up (with sb.)	赶上（某人）；达到（与某人）相同的境界	

真 Students without experience can **catch up** after a few introductory courses. 没学过的学生在学习过一些入门课程之后就能赶上。 [2016 年英语（二）阅读]

拓 catch up on sth. 用额外时间做某事（以弥补所耽误的时间）‖ be caught up in sth. 被卷入或陷入某事物中 ‖ catch on (with) 受欢迎，变得流行 ‖ catch on 理解，懂

| **for a while** | 有段时间；暂时 | |

真 The world art market had already been losing momentum **for a while** after rising bewilderingly since 2003. 自 2003 年以来的迅猛增长之后，世界艺术品市场已经失去动力有一段时间了。

[2010 年英语（二）阅读]

拓 in a while 一段时间之内 ‖ for the moment 暂时

| **no doubt** | 无疑，毋庸置疑，很可能 | |

真 There is **no doubt** of the alternative—the corrupted landscapes of southern Portugal, Spain or Ireland. 不进行合理规划带来的后果是毋庸置疑的，就像葡萄牙南部、西班牙或爱尔兰的风景一样遭到破坏。

[2016 年英语（一）阅读]

拓 without doubt 无疑，毫无疑问

| **a host of** | 许多，大量；一大群 | |

词 host [həʊst] *n.* 许多，大量；主人；主持人 *v.* 主持，主办

真 Newton's laws of motion and Darwinian evolution each bind **a host of** different phenomena into a single explicatory framework. 牛顿的运动定律和达尔文的进化论分别将许多不同的现象归入一种单纯解释性的构架内。

[2012 年英语（一）翻译]

| **all the same** | 仍然，依然 | |

真 Not the 20% profit margins that were routine a few years ago, but profit **all the same**. 不是几年前惯常实现的 20% 的利润率，但依然有利润。

[2011 年英语（二）阅读]

| **carry out** | 实行，实施；实现 | |

例 a plan that you **carried out** 你实施的一个计划

| **trade up** | 卖次买好；（卖掉原有的以便）买更贵的东西；使熟悉某行 | |

真 Often they "**trade up**," leaving riskier, smaller firms for larger and more stable firms. 他们常常"追求工作升级"，离开风险较大、较小的公司，以便寻求更大、更稳定的公司。

[2011 年英语（二）阅读]

| **in respect of** | 关于，就……而言 | |

真 A parallel situation exists **in respect of** predatory mammals and fish-eating birds. 对于食肉的哺乳动物以及食鱼的鸟类来说，也存在类似的情况。

[2010 年英语（一）翻译]

be to do sth.　　打算做某事，准备做某事

🔴 It **was to ruin** lives in the quest for circulation and impact. 其真正目的是为了追求发行量和影响力而破坏人们的生活。　　[2015 年英语（一）阅读]

🔵 **be to do** 一般表示事先商定、安排或准备要做的事情。如：The students are to meet at the sports hall this afternoon. 今天下午学生们要在体育馆集合。

be going to 表示将要发生的事情或打算近期要进行的动作。如：Are you going to enter your name for the high jump? 你准备报名参加跳高比赛吗？

be about to 表示即将发生的动作，指最近就要发生的事情。如：The orchestra is tuning up and the concert is about to begin. 乐队正在调音，音乐会马上就开始。

the other day　　不久前的某一天，几天以前；有一天

🔴 Suppose you have found something wrong with the electronic dictionary that you bought from an online store **the other day**. 假设你发现前几天从一家网上商店购买的电子词典有问题。　　[2012 年英语（二）写作]

close off　　隔离；封锁

🔴 Factors such as the place and period in which we are reading, our gender, ethnicity, age and social class will encourage us towards certain interpretations but at the same time obscure or even **close off** others. 这些因素，诸如读者阅读的地点和时期，读者的性别、种族、年龄和社会阶层等，会促使读者以某种特定的解读方式来理解文本，但同时也会模糊甚至隔绝其他的解读方式。　　[2015 年英语（一）阅读]

pay out　　付巨款

🔴 Within weeks the world's two biggest auction houses, Sotheby's and Christie's, had to **pay out** nearly $200 million in guarantees to clients who had placed works for sale with them. 几周之内，世界上最大的两家拍卖行，苏富比拍卖行和佳士得拍卖行，必须向已经将作品交给他们出售的客户支付将近 2 亿美元的担保金。　　[2010 年英语（二）阅读]

🔶 **pay off** 全部偿还，还清；付清；带来好结果，行得通

pass down　　使世代相传，流传

🔴 Yet most ancestry testing only considers a single lineage, either the Y chromosome inherited through men in a father's line or mitochondrial DNA, which is **passed down** only from mothers. 但是多数血统鉴定只考虑单线谱系，或者是遗传自父亲的 Y 染色体，或者是仅由母亲遗传下来的线粒体 DNA。　　[2009 年英语（一）阅读]

有人陪你度过低谷固然好，没有的话，我在山顶等你。　**109** 》》

impinge on/upon　对……起作用或有影响

词 impinge [ɪmˈpɪndʒ] v. 对……有明显作用（或影响）；妨碍；侵犯

例 Are any of them allowing things to **impinge on** their focus and energy, without knowing how they could more productively identify the source of their distraction and how to deal with it? 他们中是否有人允许事情影响他们的注意力和精力，却又不知道如何更有效地识别其分心的根源以及如何应对呢？

talk to　与……交谈

真 **talk to** their fellow passengers 同其他乘客交谈　　　　[2015 年英语（二）完形填空]

拓 have a chat with 与……聊天，闲谈

as for　关于，至于

真 **As for** me, weighing myself every day caused me to shift my focus from being generally healthy and physically active to focusing occasionally on the scale. 就我而言，每天称自己的体重使我将关注点从身体总体健康、精力旺盛这方面转移到只关注体重秤。

[2019 年英语（二）完形填空]

have the last word　有最终决定权；有最后的发言权

真 It is not by chance that the *Funeral March* is not the last movement of the *Eroica Symphony*, but the second, so that suffering does not **have the last word**. 《葬礼进行曲》并不是《英雄交响曲》的最后一个乐章，而是第二乐章，这并非偶然，因为这样痛苦就不是最终的结局了。

[2014 年英语（一）翻译]

拓 have a word with 与……谈一谈 ‖ the last word (in) 最新（或时髦、先进等）的事物

happen to　碰巧，偶然发生

真 **happen to** love it 恰巧喜欢它　　　　[2011 年英语（一）翻译]

shut out　把……关在外面；排除

例 She closed her eyes tightly to **shut out** the nightmare images. 她紧闭双眼，仿佛这样就可驱走那噩梦般的情景。

hold true for　对……适用，适用于

真 Another surprise is that the findings **hold true for** both those with children and without, but

more so for nonparents. 另一个出人意料的是，这些发现对于有孩子和没孩子的人都适用，而对于没孩子的人更适用。 [2015 年英语（二）阅读]

move sb. toward 使某人获得……机会；推动某人…… ○○○

(真) Furthermore, these losses make us mature and eventually **move** us **toward** future opportunities for growth and happiness. 另外，这些痛失的东西使我们变得成熟，并最终给予我们收获成长和幸福的机会。 [2015 年英语（二）阅读]

in the course of 在……过程中，在……期间 ○○○

(例) Depending on the domain, it may also be useful to have a standardized set of topics that you want to make sure you cover **in the course of** your interview. 根据该领域的特点，准备一些访谈中必须涉及的标准化问题也有一定的帮助。

on the basis of... 根据，基于 ○○○

(真) **On the basis of** the precautionary principle, it could be argued that it is advisable to follow the FSA advice. 根据预防原则，遵循食品标准局的建议是明智的这件事可能引起争议。

[2020 年英语（一）完形填空]

make profits of 盈利 ○○○

(真) The Dutch giant Elsevier, which claims to publish 25% of the scientific papers produced in the world, **made profits of** more than £900m last year. 声称出版了全球 25% 科技论文的荷兰巨头爱思唯尔去年盈利超过 9 亿英镑。 [2020 年英语（一）阅读]

write down 写下，记下 ◇

(例) Therefore, **write down** all the things that you are putting off, and keep this list in clear sight, so that you are reminded of it. 因此，写下所有你要拖延的事情，并把清单放在视线范围之内，这样它就能时时刻刻提醒你了。

(拓) stick ... down 写下，记下 ‖ chalk up 记下，记录（成就、比赛得分等）

historical prejudice 历史偏见 ○○○

(真) It needs to put **historical prejudices** to one side and take some steps to address our urgent housing need. 首先需要撇开历史上的一些偏见，然后要采取一些措施来解决住房需求的燃眉之急。 [2014 年英语（二）阅读]

slacken off　　松懈，松劲；削减，减弱

真 Workers tended to be diligent for the first few days of the week in any case, before hitting a plateau and then **slackening off**. 在任何情况下，工人在一周的前几天往往都比较卖力，继而达到一个稳定水平，然后开始松懈。　　[2010 年英语（一）完形填空]

拓 slack up one's effort 松劲 ‖ die away 减弱

follow through　　坚持到底；自始至终

例 People talk a lot about standing up for beliefs and not compromising on values, but 99% of them never **follow through**. 人们经常说要坚持信仰，不要在价值观上妥协，但 99% 的人从未坚持到底。

拓 stay the course 坚持到底 ‖ follow through with sth. 把……进行到底

be tied to　　与……相关联，与……挂钩

真 In its latest survey of CEO pay, *The Wall Street Journal* finds that "a substantial part" of executive pay **is** now **tied to** performance. 《华尔街日报》最新的 CEO 薪酬调查发现，高管薪酬中的"很大一部分"目前是与绩效挂钩的。　　[2019 年英语（一）阅读]

in combination with　　与……联合，与……结合

真 During the Depression and the war, Americans had learned to live with less, and that restraint, **in combination with** the postwar confidence in the future, made small, efficient housing positively stylish. 在大萧条和战争期间，美国人早就学会了适应物资的匮乏，这种"节制精神"以及战后对未来生活的自信，使得小而空间利用率高的房子受到青睐。　　[2011 年英语（二）阅读]

trifle with　　轻视，随便对待；心不在焉地考虑或处理

词　trifle ['traɪfl] *n.* 无多大价值或重要性的事物、问题或活动

例　Don't **trifle with** me; give me a straight answer. 别拿我不当回事；给我一个直截了当的答复。

in time　　及时，适时

真　The pace of change in energy sources appears to be speeding up—perhaps just **in time** to have a meaningful effect in slowing climate change. 能源资源的变化速度似乎在加快——可能恰好在延缓气候变化方面有了积极影响。　　[2018 年英语（二）阅读]

拓　on time 按时

pick up　　改善；捡起，拾起；学会，获得；接载

真　**pick up** social signals 接收社交信号　　[2020 年英语（二）阅读]

in despair　　绝望地，失望地

词　despair [dɪ'speə(r)] *n.* 绝望 *v.* 失去全部希望

例　No one around us was looking pale or green, wringing their hands **in despair** at the possibility of the plane crashing. 我们周围没有一个人因为飞机有坠毁的可能而看上去面色苍白或者铁青，或是绝望地扭绞双手。

拓　despair of 对……失去全部希望，对……绝望

look on the bright side　　在困境中看到事物光明的一面

例　We should always **look on the bright side**. 不管什么时候我们都应该往好的方面看。

around the corner　　即将来临；很近；在附近

真　However, a true cashless society is probably not **around the corner**. 然而，真正的无现金社会可能不会马上到来。　　[2013 年英语（二）完形填空]

end up　　达到某种状态；到达或来到某处；最终成为；最后处于

真　Even when you win, you **end up** no better off. 即便你赢了，你也不会受益。　　[2019 年英语（一）阅读]

in turn　　　反过来；转而；依次，轮流　　

真 For a social epidemic to occur, however, each person so affected must then influence his or her own acquaintances, who must **in turn** influence theirs, and so on. 不过，想让一场社会潮流出现，每个受到影响的人随后都必须去影响自己的熟人，反过来这些熟人又必须接着影响他们的熟人，如此循环。 [2010 年英语（一）阅读]

拓 take turns 依次，轮流

fight against　　　争取克服，战胜……；对抗，与……作斗争　　

例 The new medicine keeps your brain working right, and also allows it to relax and helps to **fight against** mental fatigue. 新药不但可以帮助大脑正常工作，同时也能让大脑适时放松从而对抗思维疲劳。

lie with　　　取决于；是……的责任　　

例 In the last analysis, the responsibility for this failure must **lie with** the chief engineer. 追根究底，失败的责任在于总工程师。

lag behind　　　落后，落在后面　　

例 Modesty helps one to make progress, conceit makes one **lag behind**. 虚心使人进步，骄傲使人落后。

拓 forge ahead 前进 ‖ go ahead 前进

make an apology　　　道歉　　

真 Write a letter to your boss, Mr. Wang, telling him your decision, stating your reason(s), and **making an apology**. 给你的老板王先生写封信，告诉他你的决定，陈述你的理由，并道歉。

[2005 年英语（一）阅读]

拓 apologize [ə'pɒlədʒaɪz] v. 道歉

get through　　　（方案等）获得通过；到达；接通电话　　

真 have to **get through** the Senate 必须获得参议院的批准 [2018 年英语（一）阅读]

so far　　　到目前为止，迄今为止　　

真 We are thus led to distinguish, within the broad educational process which we have been **so far** considering, a more formal kind of education—that of direct tuition or schooling. 因此，

PART
01

在我们迄今所考虑的广义的教育过程中，我们必须区别出一种更为正规的教育，即直接教学或学校教育。 [2009 年英语（一）翻译]

throw off　　匆匆脱掉；摆脱，抛弃

例 I got time to **throw off** my disguise and dress me in my own clothes. 我有时间脱下我的伪装，穿上我自己的衣服。

at all times　　一直，总是

真 Parents don't have to be exquisitely present **at all times**. 父母并不需要总是在孩子周围。
[2017 年英语（二）阅读]

on the contrary　　相反，反之

真 **On the contrary**, constraints on improving productivity explain why education isn't developing more quickly there than it is. 相反，生产力的提高受到限制则解释了为什么教育没有比现在发展得更快。 [2009 年英语（一）阅读]

with/in regard to　　关于，对于

真 **With regard to** mass sport, the author holds that governments should invest in public sports facilities. 对于大众体育，作者认为政府应该在公共体育设施方面进行投资。
[2017 年英语（二）阅读]

in the making　　在形成中，在成长中

例 If you want to see the country's future **in the making**, you really should visit. 如果你想要看到该国正在形成的未来，你就要实地去访问它。

some of　　有些，一些

真 The building has housed **some of** the nation's most significant diplomats and politicians. 一些美国最重要的外交官和政治家曾在这座大楼里工作。 [2018 年英语（一）阅读]

to be sure　　诚然，的确

真 **To be sure**, the future is not all rosy. 诚然，未来并不完全是美好的。 [2013 年英语（一）阅读]

as a result of　　由于；作为……的结果，因此

真 **As a result of** President Bush's reform, retired people may have less secured payments. 由于布什总统的改革，退休人员的担保付款可能会减少。 [2017 年英语（一）阅读]

by way of　经由，通过

例 Einstein brought this vision to fruition **by way of** a successful mathematical theory. 爱因斯坦以成功的数学理论的形式把这一预见变成了科学硕果。

a pile of/piles of　一堆；很多

词 pile [paɪl] *n.* 堆；摞；叠

真 For one trial, each participant was shown **a pile of** pens that the researcher claimed were from a previous experiment. 在一次试验中，研究人员给每位参与者都出示了一堆圆珠笔，并声称这些圆珠笔来自早先的试验。 [2018 年英语（二）完形填空]

be puzzled by　被……迷惑；因……而感到迷惑不解

词 puzzle ['pʌzl] *v.* 使困惑；让……伤脑筋

例 It was not only these odd sights that astounded her, for she **was** even more **puzzled by** what she heard. 令她吃惊的不仅是这些新奇的景象，人们的言谈更使她茫然不知所云。

拓 puzzle over 对……苦苦思索（以便理解）‖ confuse [kən'fjuːz] *v.* 使困惑

have an effect on　影响，对……产生影响

真 All of which, of course, **have** a positive **effect on** happiness levels. 当然，所有这些都会对幸福程度产生积极的影响。 [2016 年英语（二）阅读]

in a sense　在某种意义上

真 It is this implicit or explicit reference to nature that fully justifies the use of the word *garden*, though **in a** "liberated" **sense**, to describe these synthetic constructions. 正是由于这种对自然界或含蓄或明确的参照，才充分证明了用"花园"一词来描述这些人为的建造是合理的，虽然这个词在这里是一种灵活的用法。 [2013 年英语（一）翻译]

waste time doing sth.　浪费时间做某事

例 He suggests that we should not **waste time worrying** what other people think about us. 他暗示说我们不应该浪费时间去担心他人对我们的看法。

in some ways　在某些方面；在某种程度上

真 **In some ways**, this quest for commonalities defines science. 在某些方面，科学就是对共性的探索。 [2012 年英语（一）翻译]

拓 in a way 在某种程度上；有点儿

first and foremost   首先；最重要的

真 Most wives want their husbands to be, **first and foremost**, conversational partners, but few husbands share this expectation of their wives. 大多数妻子希望她们的丈夫首先是可以聊天的伴侣，但很少有丈夫对妻子有这样的期望。 [2010 年英语（二）阅读]

have a break   休息一下

真 It gives parents time to have a shower, do housework or simply **have a break** from their child. 这样能够让父母腾出时间去洗澡、做家务或者只是单纯地和孩子分开一会儿休息一下。 [2017 年英语（二）阅读]

come up with   提出，想出

真 In their recent work, however, some researchers have **come up with** the finding that influentials have far less impact on social epidemics than is generally supposed. 然而，在最近的研究中，一些研究人员有了新的发现，影响力人士对社会流行风潮的影响力并没有通常认为的那么大。 [2010 年英语（一）阅读]

give in   屈服；让步；投降

例 never **give in** to any of life's difficulties 决不向生活中的任何困难屈服

拓 surrender [sə'rendə(r)] v. 投降；（被迫）放弃，交出

all at once   突然；一起，同时

例 The best ideas you'll ever have in your life will not strike you **all at once**. 你一生中最棒的想法不会突然出现在你的脑海。

拓 all of a sudden 突然

set aside   留出，拨出

真 If the bills become law, state boards and commissions will be required to **set aside** 50 percent of board seats for women by 2022. 如果该法案成为法律，各州的董事会和委员会将被要求在 2022 年之前为女性留出 50% 的董事会席位。 [2020 年英语（一）阅读]

a waste of   浪费……

真 Many jobs are boring, degrading, unhealthy, and **a waste of** human potential. 许多工作枯燥无聊、有失体面、损害身心健康，还浪费人的潜能。 [2017 年英语（二）完形填空]

define as 定义为，解释为

真 The concept of sustainable development has been **defined as** profitable. 可持续发展的概念被定义为有利可图。 [2016 年英语（一）阅读]

as usual 像往常一样，照例

真 Lead your life **as usual**. 像往常一样过日子。 [2015 年英语（一）阅读]

in effect 实际上，事实上；生效

真 **In effect**, the U.S. can import food, or it can import the workers who pick it. 实际上，美国可以进口食物，也可以引进收割食物的劳动者。 [2019 年英语（二）阅读]

be busy with 忙于

例 Mr. Lee **is busy with** the affairs of the street committee all day long; you can hardly ever find him at home. 李先生成天忙着街道的事儿，家里见不到他的人影儿。

intrude on 侵犯；打扰；干涉

词 intrude [ɪnˈtruːd] *v.* 侵入；打扰

真 On the overturned provisions the majority held the Congress had deliberately "occupied the field", and Arizona had thus **intruded on** the federal's privileged powers. 对于被否决的条款，大多数人认为是国会已故意"占领该领域"，亚利桑那州因此侵犯了联邦法案的优先权。 [2013 年英语（一）阅读]

end up with 以……结束，以……告终

真 Constant health scares just **end up with** no one listening. 持续的健康恐慌最终会导致无人倾听。 [2020 年英语（一）完形填空]

originate from 源于，起源于，来自

词 originate [əˈrɪdʒɪneɪt] *v.* 起源，发源；引起

真 The group in question are a particular people **originated from** central Europe. 论文中所讨论的人群来自中欧的一个特定民族。 [2008 年英语（一）完形填空]

be responsible for 对……负责；是……的原因

真 Customers **were** generally **responsible for** paying the sales tax to the state themselves if they weren't charged it, but most didn't realize they owed it and few paid. 如果消费者没有被征收销售税，他们通常要自己承担向政府缴纳销售税的责任，但大多数人没有意识到他们

应该缴纳销售税，只有少数人缴纳了。 [2019 年英语（一）阅读]

拓 **be liable for** 有……责任或义务 ‖ **answer for** 对……负责；因……而受罚

look out | 注意，留心，当心

例 **look out** for spelling mistakes 留心拼写错误

silver lining | 一线希望（或慰藉）

真 No one tries harder than the jobless to find **silver linings** in this national economic disaster. 在这场国家经济灾难中，要找到一线希望，失业者要付出比常人更多的努力。 [2012 年英语（二）阅读]

拓 **a flash of hope** 一线希望，一丝希望

a range of | 一系列

词 range [reɪndʒ] *n.* 成套或成系列的东西；种类；范围；幅度

真 For years, studies have found that first-generation college students—those who do not have a parent with a college degree—lag other students on **a range of** education achievement factors. 多年前，许多研究发现"初代"大学生——那些父母没上过大学的大学生——在一系列教育成就方面都要低于其他学生。 [2015 年英语（二）阅读]

拓 **in/within range (of sth.)** 在……范围内 ‖ **out of range (of sth.)** 超出……的范围

be harmful to | 对……有害

真 Our imitation of behaviors **is harmful to** our networks of friends. 我们的行为模仿对我们的朋友圈是有害的。 [2012 年英语（一）阅读]

拓 **be beneficial/good to** 对……有益 ‖ **be bad to** 对……有害

all the time | 始终，一直

真 Waiting lists increase **all the time** and we are simply not building enough new homes. 排队买房的名单一直在增加，现在建的新房供不应求。 [2014 年英语（二）阅读]

拓 **from beginning to end** 始终，自始至终 ‖ **from start to finish** 自始至终 ‖ **all along** 一直，自始至终

all day long | 整天；全天

真 Now office workers unthinkingly sip bottled water **all day long**. 现在人们在办公室整天都会不假思索地喝着瓶装水。 [2010 年英语（二）阅读]

拓 **the whole day** 整天 ‖ **all day** 整天

be used to do　被用来做

真 As this new science of habit has emerged, controversies have erupted when the tactics have **been used to sell** questionable beauty creams or unhealthy foods. 随着这门新的习惯科学的出现，当这种策略被用来销售有问题的美容霜或不健康食品时，就引发了争议。

[2010 年英语（二）阅读]

辨 used to do sth. 指"过去经常做某事"，主语通常是人。如：She used to go traveling. 她过去经常去旅游。

be used to do sth. 表示"被用于做某事"，主语通常是物。如：The pen is used to take notes. 笔是用来做笔记的。

used to (doing) sth. 意为"习惯于（做）某事"，相当于 be accustomed to doing sth.，主语通常是人。该结构中的 to 是介词，后面跟名词、代词或动名词。be 可以用 become，get 等来代替。如：Now he is used to living in the city. 现在他习惯于生活在这个城市。

stick to　坚持

词 stick [stɪk] v. 插入，刺穿；粘牢；放置

真 Whichever approach, the key is to determine your length of focus time and **stick to** it. 不论是采取哪种办法，关键在于判定你能集中注意力的时间，并且保持专注。[2018 年英语（二）阅读]

far off　远离

真 Sometimes storms blew the vessels **far off** their course, and often calm brought unbearably long delay. 有时候，暴风雨使得船只严重偏离航线，而经常性的风平浪静又令他们陷入长时间的滞留状态，令人难以忍受。

[2015 年英语（一）阅读]

拓 far away from 远离，离……远

at the bottom　在底部；在底端

真 This seems a justification for neglect of those in need, and a rationalization of exploitation, of the superiority of those at the top and the inferiority of those **at the bottom**. 这种说法似乎为忽视那些需要帮助的人找到了借口，使剥削合理化，令上层人优越、底层人卑微。

[2011 年英语（一）翻译]

拓 at the top 在顶端 ‖ at bottom 其实，实际上；基本上

part and parcel of...　……的主要部分或重要部分

真 If the study of law is beginning to establish itself as **part and parcel of** a general education, its aims and methods should appeal directly to journalism educators. 如果法律学习逐渐被认为是通识教育的一个重要组成部分，那么它的目标和方法会很快吸引新闻教育工作者。

[2007 年英语（一）翻译]

be famous for　　因……而著名

真 Pyle **was famous for** covering the ethical side of the war. 派尔以报道战争的伦理方面而闻名。　　　　　　　　　　　　　　　　　　　　　　[2012 年英语（二）完形填空]

拓 be famous as 作为……而出名

discourage...from doing sth.　　阻止……做某事

词 discourage [dɪsˈkʌrɪdʒ] v. 设法阻止；使丧失信心

真 When asked what they want to do, they should be **discouraged from saying** "I have no idea."
当问他们将来想做什么时，尽量不要让他们回答说"我不知道"。　　[2007 年英语（一）阅读]

拓 stop...from doing sth. 阻止……做某事

new vision　　新愿景；新视野

真 We need to create a **new vision** for public health where all of society works together to get healthy and live longer. 我们需要为公共卫生创造一个新的愿景，让全社会共同努力，实现健康和长寿。　　　　　　　　　　　　　　　　　　[2011 年英语（二）阅读]

so...that　　如此……以至于……

真 His analysis should therefore end any self-contentedness among those who may believe that the global position of English is **so** stable **that** the young generations of the United Kingdom do not need additional language capabilities. 有些人可能会认为英语在世界上的地位很稳定，以至于英国的年轻人不需要掌握其他语言，他的分析应该能就此结束这些人的自满。

[2017 年英语（一）翻译]

miss the point　　没有抓住重点

例 You must have **missed the point** because the teacher only let us write an abstract. 你一定没有抓住重点，因为老师只让我们写一个摘要。

without permission　　未经许可

例 Never take something **without permission**, even if you know that your friend will be okay with it. 在没有得到允许的情况下不要拿朋友的东西，即使你知道朋友不会介意。

拓 authorize [ˈɔːθəraɪz] v. 批准；授权

in terms of　　依据；在……方面

真 Moreover, the integration of the European community will oblige television companies to cooperate more closely **in terms of** both production and distribution. 欧洲共同体的形成也将迫使电视公司在制作和播送方面更加密切地合作。　　[2005 年英语（一）翻译]

拓 when it comes to 当提到；就……而论

marvel at　　对……感到惊奇；大为赞叹

词 marvel ['mɑːvl] *v.* 感到惊奇；大为赞叹

真 To read such books today is to **marvel at** the fact that their learned contents were once deemed suitable for publication in general-circulation dailies. 今天读这样的书，就是要惊叹于这样一个事实：他们博大精深的内容曾经被认为适合在公众发行的日报上发表。
　　[2010 年英语（一）阅读]

拓 be surprised at 对……感到吃惊或诧异

stay away from　　远离；外出

真 **stay away from** commercial advertisers 远离商业广告主　　[2012 年英语（一）阅读]

in fact　　事实上，实际上

真 **In fact**, "becoming more efficient" is part of the problem. 事实上，"变得更加有效率"也是问题的一部分。　　[2016 年英语（二）阅读]

at bottom　　实际上

真 Universal history, the history of what man has accomplished in this world, is **at bottom** the History of the Great Men who have worked here. 世界史，即人类在这个世界的成就史，说到底是一部伟人的历史。　　[2012 年英语（二）阅读]

拓 be at the bottom of sth. ……是某事物的起因或根源 ‖ from the bottom of one's heart 深情地；忠实地；诚恳地

hold onto　　持有；紧紧抓住；保持住

真 In France, shareholders who **hold onto** a company investment for at least two years can sometimes earn more voting rights in a company. 在法国，持有公司投资至少两年的股东有时可以在该公司获得更多的投票权。　　[2019 年英语（一）阅读]

communicate with 与……沟通

真 try to **communicate with** you 试着和你交流 [2018 年英语（二）阅读]

be amazed at 对……感到惊讶；对……感到害怕

例 You'll **be amazed at** how some people react to a simple "Hello" or a big smile from a passing runner. 你会惊叹于那些人对来自路过的跑步者的一句简单的"你好"或者一个微笑是如何反应的。

拓 be surprised at 惊奇，惊讶于

with time 随着时间的推移

例 **With time**, all of the rooftop tiles will fade to the same color. 随着时间的流逝，所有屋顶的瓦片又将慢慢变成同样的颜色。

enable...to 使……能够做

真 Half a century of town and country planning has **enabled** it **to** retain an enviable rural coherence. 半个世纪的城乡规划使它得以保持令人羡慕的持续性。 [2016 年英语（一）阅读]

face up to 面对

例 We should not only inform the world of our achievements, but also of our efforts to **face up to** problems. 我们不仅要向世界展示我们所取得的成就，还要体现我们面对问题所付出的努力。

seek to 追求；争取

真 Astronomy and Hawaiian culture both **seek to** answer big questions about who we are, where we come from and where we are going. 天文学和夏威夷文化都在寻求关于"我们是谁、从哪里来、要到哪里去"这些重大问题的答案。 [2017 年英语（一）阅读]

at a rate 以……的速度

真 A report last year pointed out that the costs both of subscriptions and of these "article preparation costs" had been steadily rising **at a rate** above inflation. 去年的一份报告指出，订阅费用和这些"文章准备费用"一直在以高于通货膨胀率的速度稳步上升。

[2020 年英语（一）阅读]

scoop up　　占据；得到；铲起；兜接；舀上来

真 Writing in *The New Republic*, Alice Lee notes that increasing the number of opportunities for board membership without increasing the pool of qualified women to serve on such boards has led to a "golden skirt" phenomenon, where the same elite women **scoop up** multiple seats on a variety of boards. 艾丽丝·李在《新共和》杂志上撰文指出，在不增加合格女性董事人数的情况下，增加成为董事会成员的机会，导致了一种"金裙"现象，即同一位精英女性在不同董事会占据多个席位。 [2020 年英语（一）阅读]

arouse controversy　　引起争议

真 He helped popularize the idea that some diseases not previously thought to have a bacterial cause were actually infections, which **aroused** much **controversy** when it was first suggested. 他曾倡导了如下观点，即以前人们认为跟细菌无关的一些疾病其实也是传染病。这种观点首次提出时引起了很大的争议。 [2008 年英语（一）完形填空]

with respect to　　关于；就……而言；在……方面

例 Our responsibility is to make sure that we create a law that, regardless of the technology, includes a set of legal guarantees that consumers have **with respect to** their information. 我们的职责是确保新增一条法律，无关技术层面，确保用户享有关于其个人信息的一整套法律保护。

拓 in/with regard to 关于；至于

occur to　　被想到，被想起

真 If a relevant and important idea **occurs to** you now, work it into the draft. 假如你此刻突然想到了一个相关且重要的观点，那么把它写进初稿。 [2008 年英语（一）阅读]

拓 call to mind （使）想起，想到

in contact with　　与……有联系

真 However, the Justices said that Arizona police would be allowed to verify the legal status of people who come **in contact with** law enforcement. 然而，法官们说，亚利桑那州的警察将被允许去确认那些涉及法律执行的人的法律地位。 [2013 年英语（一）阅读]

拓 in connection with 与……有关，有……相连

be forced to　　被迫……

真 Those **forced to** exercise their smiling muscles reacted more enthusiastically to funny cartoons than did those whose mouths were contracted in a frown, suggesting that expressions may influence emotions. 那些被强迫锻炼笑肌的人比那些蹙眉绷嘴者对滑稽的漫画反应更加热烈，这说明表情可以影响情绪。

[2011 年英语（一）完形填空]

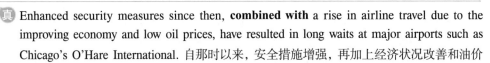

combine with　　与……结合

真 Enhanced security measures since then, **combined with** a rise in airline travel due to the improving economy and low oil prices, have resulted in long waits at major airports such as Chicago's O'Hare International. 自那时以来，安全措施增强，再加上经济状况改善和油价低廉导致航空旅行增加，造成芝加哥奥黑尔国际机场等主要机场的等待时间延长。

[2017 年英语（一）阅读]

拓 integrate with 使与……结合

extract...from　　从……拔出；从……提取、摘录；从……中获得

真 He hired a dentist to transplant nine teeth into his jaw—having **extracted** them **from** the mouths of his slaves. 他聘请了一名牙医，在他的下颚里植入了 9 颗牙，而这 9 颗牙都是从他的奴隶的嘴里拔出来的。

[2008 年英语（一）阅读]

拓 pull out 拔出，抽出

by and large　　大体上，总的来说

真 And if you need to predict human height in the near future to design a piece of equipment, Gordon says that **by and large**, "you could use today's data and feel fairly confident." 戈登说，如果你需要预测人类在不远的将来身高如何以便设计一种装备的话，基本上"你可以十分自信地采用目前的数据"。

[2008 年英语（一）阅读]

拓 in summary 总之；概括地说

formal education　　正规教育

真 The relationship between **formal education** and economic growth in poor countries is widely misunderstood by economists and politicians alike. 经济学家及政治家普遍误解了贫穷国家中正规教育与经济发展之间的关系。

[2009 年英语（一）阅读]

be suited for　　适合做……，适合于……

真 The earliest forms of art, like painting and music, **are** those best **suited for** expressing joy. 早期的艺术形式，如绘画和音乐，是最适合描写欢乐的。

[2006 年英语（一）阅读]

and so on/forth　等等

真 His concern is mainly with the humanities: literature, languages, philosophy **and so on**. 他主要关注的是人文学科，如文学、语言、哲学等。 [2011 年英语（一）阅读]

pay rise/raise　加薪，涨工资

真 Everybody loves a fat **pay rise**. Yet pleasure at your own can vanish if you learn that a colleague has been given a bigger one. 人人都喜欢大幅加薪。但假如得知你的同事工资涨幅比你还大，你加薪后那种快乐的心情就会消失无踪。 [2005 年英语（一）阅读]

拓 salary increase 涨薪

本单元资源

because of 因为

真 The growing frequency of wildfires is a national concern **because of** its impact on federal tax dollars. 鉴于其对联邦税收的影响，全国都在关注越来越频发的森林大火。

[2017 年英语（二）阅读]

look forward to 盼望，期待

真 You might even be tempted to assume that humanity has little future to **look forward to**. 你甚至可能倾向于设想人类的未来希望渺茫。

[2013 年英语（一）阅读]

in print 已出版，已刊印；在销售中

词 print [prɪnt] *n.* 出版业；出版界；印刷字体 *v.* 印刷；打印；刊登

例 I wonder if that book is still **in print**. 我想知道那本书是不是还在出版。

in the past 在过去

真 **In the past**, workers with average skills, doing an average job, could earn an average lifestyle. 过去，一个掌握普通技能、从事普通工作的人可以过上普通的生活。 [2013 年英语（二）阅读]

attend to 处理；对付；注意；照料

例 As Nilekani suggests, with expanding wealth, India eventually will be able to **attend to** environmental issues. 正如奈利卡尼所说，随着财富的增长，印度最终将有能力解决环境问题。

at any rate 无论如何

真 **At any rate**, this change will ultimately be acclaimed by an ever-growing number of both domestic and international consumers. 无论如何，这一变化最终将受到越来越多国内外消费者的欢迎。

[2010 年英语（一）阅读]

shut down 停工，关闭

例 Many people know to lock or **shut down** the computer when leaving for the day, and perhaps even when going to lunch, but they might step out to discuss something with a coworker without thinking about it. 许多人都知道在下班的时候锁定或者关闭电脑，甚至在出去吃

午饭的时候也记得，但是他们可能在暂时离开座位和同事谈论事情的时候，把开着的电脑忘在脑后。

consist of 包括；由……组成

真 But they show comprehension to **consist** not just **of** passive assimilation but of active engagement in inference and problem-solving. 但是这些阅读方式也表明理解不仅仅是被动地吸收信息，也包括主动推理和解决问题。 [2015 年英语（一）阅读]

拓 be made up of 由……所组成 ‖ be composed of 由……组成 ‖ consist in 以……为主要组成部分

return to 回到；恢复到

真 The housing sector needs to accept that we are very unlikely to ever **return to** era of large-scale public grants. 住房部门必须承认，我们不太可能再回到大规模公共补贴的时代。

[2014 年英语（二）阅读]

mend one's ways 培养好习惯；改进生活方式

例 It seems that he is **mending his ways**. 看起来他在改进生活方式。

拓 fall/get into the habit of doing sth. 养成做某事的习惯 ‖ be in the habit of doing sth. 有做某事的习惯

approach to 通往……的方法；接近

真 Only Ukip, sensing its chance, has sided with those pleading for a more considered **approach to** using green land. 只有独立党察觉到了自己的机会，站在了那些恳求更慎重地利用绿地的人一边。 [2016 年英语（一）阅读]

accuse of 谴责，控告

词 accuse [əˈkjuːz] v. 谴责，控告

真 We need to be careful not to **accuse** opponents **of** bad arguments too quickly. 我们需要小心，不要过早地指责对手的错误论点。 [2019 年英语（一）阅读]

in practice 在实践中；实际上

真 Bryjolfsson and McAfee discussed the predictability of machine behavior **in practice**. 布林约尔弗森和麦凯菲讨论了机器行为在实践中的可预测性。 [2014 年英语（二）阅读]

拓 put into practice 实行，实施；落实

exempt from 豁免，免除

词 exempt [ɪg'zempt] v. 免除；豁免 a. 被免除的；获豁免的

真 The court's ruling is based on the assumption that public officials are **exempt from** conviction on the charge of favoritism. 法院的裁决是基于这样一个假设：公职人员可免于因徇私舞弊而被定罪。 [2017 年英语（一）阅读]

check on 检查；核实

真 The phrase "to sign on" most probably means to **check on** the availability of jobs at the jobcentre. "签到"一词很可能是指查看就业中心是否有工作。 [2014 年英语（一）阅读]

in theory 理论上

例 **In theory**, everyone agrees that we need to strengthen and open up these institutions. 在理论上，每个人都同意我们需要加强和开放这些组织机构。

make a difference 有影响，有关系

真 Their clever designs and lightweight composites certainly **make a difference**. 他们巧妙的设计和轻质的复合材料肯定会不同凡响。 [2010 年英语（二）阅读]

拓 make no difference 没有影响

be limited to 限于

真 When this practice first started decades ago, it **was** usually **limited to** freshmen, to give them a second chance to take a class in their first year if they struggled in their transition to college-level courses. 在几十年前这一做法刚开始时，通常仅限于大一新生，如果他们在向大学水平课程过渡的过程中遇到困难，可以在第一年再给他们一次上课的机会。 [2019 年英语（一）阅读]

rule out 不考虑；排除；排斥

真 The biotech companies would like judges to **rule out** gene patenting. 生物技术公司希望法官排除基因专利。 [2012 年英语（二）阅读]

make sure 确保

真 After a spouse has been selected, each family investigates the other to **make sure** its child is marrying into a good family. 在选定了结婚对象之后，双方家庭就会调查了解彼此的情况，以确保他们的孩子与一户好人家联姻。 [2016 年英语（一）完形填空]

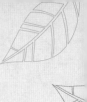

| **strive for** | 努力；力争 | |

例 You should do the best that you can **strive for** the best grade that you can possible get. 你应该尽你所能争取最好的成绩。

拓 strive to do sth. 努力做某事

| **go about** | 着手做；传开；从事 | |

真 Peretti says the *Times* (*The New York Times*) shouldn't waste time getting out of the print business, but only if they **go about** doing it the right way. 佩雷蒂指出，除非以正确的方式着手，否则《纽约时报》不应该浪费时间去脱离印刷出版行业。　　[2016 年英语（一）阅读]

| **thin out** | 使变得稀或少 | |

真 The state's proposed Forest Carbon Plan aims to double efforts to **thin out** young trees and clear brush in parts of the forest. 该州提出的森林碳排放计划旨在加倍努力减少部分森林的幼树并清除灌木丛。　　[2019 年英语（二）阅读]

拓 thin down 使……变薄、细、稀等；变瘦，变苗条

| **on behalf of sb.** | 做某人的代表或代言人；为某人之利益 | |

真 The right compensation design can provide incentives for executives to think **on behalf of** all stakeholders. 正确的薪酬设计可以激励高管代表所有利益相关者进行思考。

[2019 年英语（一）阅读]

拓 on sb.'s behalf 代表某人；为了某人

| **be key to** | 是……的关键 | |

真 "Thinking about long-term consequences **is key to** reducing the possible negative effects of curiosity," Hsee says. 克里斯多夫·奚称："考虑长期后果是减少好奇心可能带来的负面影响的关键所在。"　　[2018 年英语（二）阅读]

| **run counter to** | 违反；与……背道而驰 | |

真 I don't like quotas either; they **run counter to** my belief in meritocracy, governance by the capable. 我也不喜欢定额，这种做法与我任人唯贤的精英管理理念相悖。

[2013 年英语（二）阅读]

| **help (to) do** | 帮助做某事；有助于做某事 | |

真 **help to develop** projects aimed directly at solving global problems 有助于开展那些直接致力于解决全球问题的研究项目。　　[2013 年英语（一）阅读]

now that 既然；由于

真 **Now that** you have developed a topic into a tentative thesis, you can assemble your notes and begin to flesh out whatever outline you have made. 既然你已经把一个主题发展成一个试验性的论文，你可以整理你的笔记，开始充实你所列的任何提纲了。 　　[2008 年英语（一）阅读]

major in 主修（大专院校的）科目

词 major ['meɪdʒə(r)] *n.* 主修科目，专业 *v.* 主修

真 **major in** business 主修商业 　　[2008 年英语（一）阅读]

exert influence on 对……施加影响

例 Its objective was to **exert influence on** both the US as well as the foreign media. 它的目的是对美国和外国媒体施加影响。

separate from 与……分离

真 That would make their rulings more likely to be seen as **separate from** politics and, as a result, convincing as law. 这将使他们的裁决更有可能被视为独立于政治之外，并因此像法律一样令人信服。 　　[2012 年英语（一）完形填空]

on a scale 在……规模上

真 The interviewers had rated applicants **on a scale** of one to five. 这些面试官为申请者的打分分为 1~5 五个等级。 　　[2013 年英语（一）完形填空]

拓 scale down 缩减 ‖ scale up 增加

answer to 回答，应答；……的答案

真 *Overdressed* is the fashion world's **answer to** consumer-activist bestsellers like Michael Pollan's *The Omnivore's Dilemma*. 《过度着装》是时装界在与诸如迈克尔·波伦的《杂食者的困境》这样的消费者维权派畅销书遥相呼应。 　　[2013 年英语（一）阅读]

drop out 退学；脱离

真 won't **drop out** of high school 不会高中辍学 　　[2016 年英语（二）阅读]

be considered as 被认为 / 看作是……

真 Only gradually was the by-product of the institution noted, and only more gradually still **was** this effect **considered as** a directive factor in the conduct of the institution. 人们只能逐渐地

注意到这种机构附带产生的影响；而人们把这种影响视为机构运作的指导性因素的过程则更加缓慢。

[2009 年英语（一）翻译]

take responsibility for 对……负责

真 It tells the fashion industry that it must **take responsibility for** the signal it sends women about the social tape-measure they must use to determine their individual worth. 这告诉时尚行业，它会向女性传达一种关于衡量个人价值的社会标准的信号，对此它必须承担责任。

[2016 年英语（一）阅读]

in the workplace 在工作场所

真 It would have been inconceivable to have imagined a ban on smoking **in the workplace** or in pubs. 想象一下在工作场所或酒吧里禁止吸烟是不可思议的。 [2011 年英语（二）阅读]

in an effort to 企图（努力想）；试图要

真 Behavioral scientists tested students' willingness to expose themselves to unpleasant stimuli **in an effort to** satisfy curiosity. 行为科学家们测试了学生们为了满足好奇心而让自己体验不舒服的刺激的意愿。

[2018 年英语（二）完形填空]

in consequence 因此；结果

例 **In consequence**, people know less of their neighbors than ever before. 因此，人们对邻居的了解比以往任何时候都少。

derive from 源出，来自；得到，获取

真 Elegance, he believed, did not **derive from** abundance. 他认为优雅并非来源于复杂装饰。

[2011 年英语（二）阅读]

try out 尝试

真 The "threatened" tag gave the federal government flexibility to **try out** new, potentially less confrontational conservations approaches. "受到威胁"这样一个标签可以让联邦政府灵活地去尝试新的、潜在对抗性更小的保护措施。 [2016 年英语（二）阅读]

to a certain degree/extent 在某种程度上

例 Succeeding in social media requires allowing customer control of the message, at least **to a certain degree**. 想在社会媒体上取得成功，要求在一定程度上允许客人对信息有控制权。

拓 to some degree/extent 在某种程度上

believe in 相信；信仰；肯定……的价值或正确性

(真) They were helping sustain the quality of something they **believe in**. 他们在帮助维持他们信任的产品的质量。 [2016 年英语（一）阅读]

(拓) believe it or not 信不信由你

(辨) believe 表示"相信（事物的真实性或人的诚实）"。如：I believe my friend. 我相信我的朋友。

believe in 既可以指"相信"，还可以表示"信仰；相信……的存在"，较 believe 程度更深。如：He said that he believed in peace. 他说他信仰和平。

get back to 重新回到；恢复

(真) We still have a long way to go to **get back to** full employment. 要恢复充分就业我们还有很长的路要走。 [2015 年英语（二）阅读]

convince of 使确信；使明白

(真) If you're not **convinced of** the inherent value in taking a year off to explore interests, then consider its financial impact on future academic choices. 如果你不相信花一年时间去探索兴趣的内在价值，那么考虑一下它对未来学术选择的经济影响。 [2015 年英语（二）阅读]

prohibit...from doing sth. 禁止……做某事

(真) The Supreme Court will work out whether, during an arrest, it is legitimate to **prohibit** suspects **from** using their mobile phones. 最高法院将决定，在逮捕期间禁止嫌疑人使用手机是否合法。 [2015 年英语（一）阅读]

a sequence of 一系列，一连串

(词) sequence ['siːkwəns] *n.* 次序，顺序

(真) Parks feature, particularly in the earlier works, such as John Hilliard's very funny *Across the Park*, in which a long-haired stroller is variously smiled at by a pretty girl and unwittingly assaulted in **a sequence of** images that turn out to be different parts of the same photograph. 公园景象可以作为创作主题，这种主题在早期作品中尤其常见，比如约翰·希利亚德的《穿过公园》。这是一个非常有趣的作品：一位美女朝着一个长发流浪者露出各种笑容，然而又出其不意地对他发起了攻击，而这些都被同一张照片记录了下来。 [2014 年英语（二）阅读]

(拓) in sequence 按顺序 ‖ out of sequence 没有按正确的顺序

anything but　决不；根本不

例 She's meant to be really nice but she was **anything but** nice when I met her. 她本应该十分友善，但我见到她时，她一点也不友好。

in an instant　瞬间；马上

词 instant ['ɪnstənt] *n.* 瞬间；片刻；某一时刻 *a.* 立即的；即食的

真 Our mental health doesn't really go anywhere; like the sun behind a cloud, it can be temporarily hidden from view, but it is fully capable of being restored **in an instant**. 心理健康并没有消失；就像乌云背后的太阳，它可能暂时被遮住而看不到了，但是它完全能够立刻重焕光芒。　　　　　　　　　　　　　　　　　　[2016 年英语（一）翻译]

guilty of　犯了……罪；对……感到内疚

真 More journalists may be found **guilty of** phone hacking. 可能会有更多的记者被认定犯有电话窃听罪。　　　　　　　　　　　　　　　　　　　　　　[2015 年英语（一）阅读]

拓 commit a crime 犯罪

speak of　谈到；论及

真 These gardens **speak of** various other fundamental urges, beyond that of decoration and creative expression. 这些花园除了用来装饰和表达创造力之外，还道出了人类其他的一些根本需求。　　　　　　　　　　　　　　　　　　[2013 年英语（一）翻译]

拓 mention ['menʃn] *v.* 提及，说起

stress the importance of　强调……的重要性

真 The birthday phenomenon found among soccer players is mentioned to **stress the importance of** professional training. 提到足球运动员的生日现象是为了强调职业训练的重要性。

[2017 年英语（一）阅读]

regard...as　将……视为；认为……是

词 regard [rɪ'gɑːd] *v.* 注意，留意；看待，认为

真 Slavery was **regarded as** a peculiar institution. 奴隶制被认为是一种特殊的制度。

[2008 年英语（一）阅读]

hunt for 搜寻，寻找

例 It means phone users no longer have to **hunt for** the right charger. 这意味着使用手机的人不再需要四处寻找合适的充电器。

in general 通常；基本上

例 She said these firms, **in general**, adopt the labor standards where they operate, and in Africa, those standards are very low. 她说这些公司通常都会采用当地的劳工标准，而在非洲，这些标准都很低。

stay up 熬夜，不去睡；处于原位不动

例 to **stay up** all night 熬通宵

crop up 突然出现

例 The best business opportunity often **crops up** at the point when investors are most nervous and markets are most volatile. 最佳商机总是在投资者们最紧张、市场最不稳定的情况下突然出现。

cover up 掩盖；掩藏

真 People with higher self-esteem tended to **cover up** their depressions. 自尊心强的人常常会掩盖他们的抑郁。
[2014 年英语（二）阅读]

involve in （使）参与；（使）陷入；涉及

真 Collectors were no longer actively **involved in** art-market auctions. 收藏者们不再积极参与艺术品市场的拍卖。
[2010 年英语（二）阅读]

拓 become/get involved in 与……有关联 ‖ be involved with sb. 与某人有密切关系的

care for 关照

真 people **caring for** infants 照顾婴儿的人
[2010 年英语（二）完形填空]

ward off 避开；挡开

例 Whether you worry every day or once in a while, these strategies can help you **ward off** your worries. 不论你是否每天都忧虑还是偶尔忧虑，这些策略都将有助于缓解你的忧虑。

refer to 提到，说到，涉及；向……查询信息

（真）So, what Kennedy was **referring to** was that while GDP has been the most common method for measuring the economic activity of nations, as a measure, it is no longer enough. 所以，肯尼迪所指的就是，尽管国内生产总值是衡量一个国家经济活动最常用的方法，但作为衡量手段，它已经不再足够。

[2017 年英语（一）阅读]

a succession of 一连串，一系列

（词）succession [sək'seʃn] *n.* 一连串的事物；一系列；连续；继承（权）

（真）The art market had witnessed **a succession of** victories. 艺术品市场已经见证了一连串的胜利。

[2010 年英语（二）阅读]

（拓）in succession 连续（的）

no longer 不再

（真）at a rate that the people could **no longer** ignore 以人们再也无法忽视的速度

[2020 年英语（一）翻译]

race against/with 与……赛跑

（真）We need to reframe **race against** the machine as race with the machine. 我们需要将"同机器赛跑"改为"同机器共同进步"。

[2014 年英语（二）阅读]

to a great extent 在很大程度上

（真）Art collection as a fashion had lost its appeal **to a great extent**. 艺术品作为一种时尚在很大程度上失去了它的吸引力。

[2010 年英语（二）阅读]

out of fashion 过时的

（真）Works of art in general had gone **out of fashion**. 艺术品基本上都已经过时。

[2010 年英语（二）阅读]

worth doing sth. 应该做某事；值得做某事

（真）Before explaining the connection to the Obamacare, it is **worth making** an important distinction. 在解释与奥巴马医改的联系之前，有必要做一个重要的区分。

[2015 年英语（二）阅读]

（拓）worthwhile [ˌwɜːθ'waɪl] *a.* 值得的

in decline　　　　下降；衰退

词 decline [dɪ'klaɪn] *v./n.* 下降；衰退

真 Art Market **in Decline** 衰退的艺术品市场　　　　　　　　　　[2010 年英语（二）阅读]

judge from　　　　根据……推断

词 judge [dʒʌdʒ] *v.* 判断；评判；裁判；评价

真 **Judging from** the context, the phrase "wreaking havoc" most probably means causing damage. 根据上下文可以推断，词组 "wreaking havoc" 的意思很可能是"产生危害"。

[2010 年英语（二）阅读]

in public　　　　在公共场合；公开地；公然

真 Men tend to talk more **in public** than women. 在公共场合，男性比女性话语更多。

[2010 年英语（二）阅读]

cut out　　　　停止使用或消耗；戒除；删掉；剪下

例 To be fair, the FSA says it is not telling people to **cut out** roast foods entirely, but to reduce their lifetime intake. 公平地说，英国食品标准局并不是要人们完全不吃烤的食物，而是要减少他们一生的摄入量。

[2020 年英语（一）完形填空]

discriminate against　　　　歧视；区别对待；排斥

真 But it has already sparked significant controversy, with the United States trade representative opening an investigation into whether the tax **discriminates against** American companies, which in turn could lead to trade sanctions against France. 但它已经引发了巨大的争议，随着美国贸易代表开始调查该税是否歧视美国公司，这件事可能导致美国转而对法国进行贸易制裁。

[2020 年英语（一）阅读]

put in place　　　　正在实施；落实到位

真 Instead, the digital services tax is part of a much larger trend, with countries over the past few years proposing or **putting in place** an alphabet soup of new international tax provisions. 随着各国在过去几年提出或实施了零零散散的一些新的国际税收规定，数字服务税反而只是一个更大趋势的一部分。

[2020 年英语（一）阅读]

have a bone to pick with...　　　　对……有意见，对……不满；找……算账

真 If you **have a bone to pick with** someone in your workplace, you may try to stay tight-lipped

around them. 如果你对职场中的某位同事有意见，或许你应尽量对他们"守口如瓶"。

[2020 年英语（二）阅读]

| **pull off** | 做成（某件难事）；停靠路边 |

真 This one may be a bit more difficult to **pull off**, but it can go a long way to achieving results. 这一点可能有点儿难以实现，但它对取得成果大有帮助。 [2020 年英语（二）阅读]

| **sweep through** | 掠过，扫过；迅速传遍于 |

真 This very fact embodied the new ways of thinking that **swept through** Europe during most of the 17th century. 这一事实体现了在 17 世纪的大部分时间里席卷欧洲的新思维方式。

[2020 年英语（一）翻译]

| **interact with** | 与……相互作用；和……交往 |

真 While that may well be true, researchers have also recently found that **interacting with** strangers actually brings a boost in mood and feelings of belonging that we didn't expect. 虽然这很有可能是真的，但研究人员最近也发现，与陌生人互动实际上会出乎意料地改善我们的情绪和增强我们的归属感。 [2021 年英语（二）翻译]

| **due to** | 因为；归功于 | |

真 Ferraro suggests the results may transfer to other parts of Asia, **due to** commonalities such as the importance of growing rice and market access. 费拉罗认为，由于种植水稻的重要性和市场准入等共性，这些结果可能会传到亚洲其他地区。 [2021 年英语（一）阅读]

| **plan to do sth.** | 计划或打算做某事 |

真 "Reskilling" is something that sounds like a buzzword but is actually a requirement if we **plan to** have a future in which a lot of would-be workers do not get left behind. "重新培训"听起来像是一个流行词，但如果我们想要拥有一个不让很多潜在员工落在后面的未来，"重新培训"实际上是一个必要条件。 [2021 年英语（二）阅读]

| **admit...to/into** | 许可……进入；接受某人（入院或入学） |

真 High growth rates increased the chances for academic innovation; they also weakened the forms and processes by which teachers and students are **admitted into** a community of scholars during periods of stability or slow growth. 高增长率增加了学术创新的几率；它们也弱化了教师和学生在经济停滞期或低增长阶段进入学术圈的形式和流程。

[2021 年英语（一）翻译]

intend to　　　　打算……；想要……　　　

真 In his study about Indonesia, Ferraro **intends to** find out the relation of CCTs to its forest loss. 在对印度尼西亚的研究中，费拉罗打算找出有条件现金援助与该国森林减少的关系。

[2021 年英语（一）阅读]

拓 be intended to 打算

at best　　　　　至多，在最好的情况下　　　

真 Efforts in Canada and elsewhere have been arguably languid **at best**, and have given us a situation where we frequently hear of employers begging for workers, even at times and in regions where unemployment is high. 加拿大和其他地方的努力充其量可以说是毫无成效的，也给我们呈现了这样的局面：我们经常听到雇主苦苦寻求工人，即使在失业率高的时候和地区也是如此。

[2021 年英语（二）阅读]

point of view　　　观点，看法，立场　　　

真 Remind the person that this is your **point of view**, and then invite critique. 提醒对方这是你的观点，然后邀请对方进行评论。

[2021 年英语（二）阅读]

in a row　　　　　连续　　　　　　　　　

真 Last year marked the third year **in a row** that Indonesia's bleak rate of deforestation has slowed in pace. 去年是印度尼西亚惨淡的森林砍伐率连续第三年放缓的一年。

[2021 年英语（一）阅读]

start up　　　　开始；发动；突然站起；突然出现　　

真 That seems to be the case in Sweden: When forced to furlough 90 per cent of their cabin staff, Scandinavian Airlines decided to **start up** a short retraining program that reskilled the laid-off workers to support hospital staff. 瑞典的情况似乎就是如此：当被迫暂时解雇 90% 的空乘人员时，斯堪的纳维亚航空公司决定启动一个短期再培训项目，让下岗的员工学习新技能，以支援医护人员。

[2021 年英语（二）阅读]

close down	关闭，倒闭；停止播送

真 a "buy and kill" tactic to simply **close them down** 一种只是为了把它们关闭的"买了就杀"的策略　　　　　　　　　　　　　　　　　　　[2021 年英语（二）阅读]

give rise to	引起，使发生，造成

真 The growth of higher education manifests itself in at least three quite different ways, and these in turn have **given rise to** different sets of problems. 高等教育的发展至少以三种截然不同的方式表现出来，而这些反过来又引发了不同的问题。　　[2021 年英语（一）翻译]

take action to do sth.	采取行动做某事

真 Congress needs to **take action to** ensure net neutrality.（美国）国会需要采取行动确保网络中立。　　　　　　　　　　　　　　　　　　[2021 年英语（一）阅读]

dozens of	几十个；很多

真 **dozens of** countries worldwide 世界上的很多国家　　　[2021 年英语（一）阅读]

stay on	继续停留；保持

真 Their teams of engineers **stayed on**, making them two of the many "acqui-hires" that the biggest companies have used to feed their great hunger for tech talent. 它们的工程师团队留在了微软，这使得它们成了众多"人才并购"中的两个，而"人才并购"一直用来满足大公司对科技人才的巨大需求。　　　　　　　　　　　[2021 年英语（二）阅读]

lay out	安排；摆放；清晰地表达

真 I have reasons to think that won't work. I'd like to **lay out** my reasoning. 我有理由认为这行不通。我想说说我的理由。　　　　　　　　　　　　[2021 年英语（二）阅读]

PART
01

DAY
11

本单元资源

DAY
11

| tend to | 常常；倾向于 | |

真 People **tend to** underestimate the time it takes to travel a familiar route. 人们往往低估了走熟悉路线所需的时间。 [2015 年英语（二）翻译]

| be likely to | 有可能 | |

真 While eye contact may be a sign of connection or trust in friendly situations, it's more likely to be associated with dominance or intimidation in adversarial situations. 虽然眼神交流在友好的氛围下可能是一种心有灵犀或信任的表现，但在敌对的情况下，它更可能与支配或恐吓联系在一起。 [2020 年英语（一）阅读]

| lie down | 躺下 | |

真 The first draft will appear on the page only if you stop avoiding the inevitable and sit, stand up, or **lie down** to write. 要想让初稿呈现在纸上，你就要动笔去写，哪怕你是坐着、站着还是躺着写都行，只要你不再试图逃避这件不可避免的事情。 [2008 年英语（一）阅读]

| stem from | 起源于；由……造成 | |

真 Marriage break-up **stems from** sex inequalities. 婚姻的破裂源于性别的不平等。 [2010 年英语（二）阅读]

拓 from stem to stern 从头到尾

| introduction to... | ……的简介；……的入门 | |

词 introduction [ˌɪntrəˈdʌkʃn] *n.* 介绍；序言；入门

真 The author will most probably focus on a brief **introduction to** the political scientist Andrew Hacker. 作者最有可能会关注政治科学家安德鲁·海克的简介。 [2010 年英语（二）阅读]

| be rooted in | 根植于，扎根于 | |

词 root [ruːt] *v.* 生根成长；使深深扎根 *n.* 根；根部；根源；根基

真 The drive to discover **is** deeply **rooted in** humans. 探索的动力深深植根于人类。 [2018 年英语（二）完形填空]

拓 take/strike root 生根，扎根；建立，确立

看了太多的晚霞，不如潮起潮落。 **141** 》》》

belong to 属于

真 We need them to feel that home can be both here and there and that they can **belong to** two nations honorably. 我们需要他们感到，家可以在这里，也可以在那里，他们可以光荣地属于两个国家。 [2013 年英语（二）阅读]

immune from 不受……的影响；（对某事物）免除，豁免

真 When there is rapid improvement in the price and performance of technology, jobs that were once thought to be **immune from** automation suddenly become threatened. 当技术的价格大幅度降低且性能迅速提高时，曾经被认为不受自动化影响的工作突然受到威胁。 [2014 年英语（二）阅读]

prior to （在时间上）在……前面

词 prior ['praɪə(r)] *a.* 先前的；较早的

真 The practice of selecting so-called elite jurors **prior to** 1968 showed the inadaptability of anti-discrimination laws. 1968 年以前选拔所谓的精英陪审团的做法表明反歧视法有不当之处。 [2010 年英语（二）阅读]

short of 缺乏；不足；除……以外

真 In a 2012 survey, 71 percent of tree-fruit growers and almost 80 percent of raisin and berry growers said they were **short of** labor. 在 2012 年的一项调查中，71% 的果树种植者和近 80% 的葡萄干和浆果种植者表示，他们缺乏劳动力。 [2019 年英语（二）阅读]

be supposed to do sth. 被期望或被要求（按规则、惯例等）做某事

词 suppose [sə'pəʊz] *v.* 认为，以为；假定属实

真 They **were supposed to** perform domestic duties. 她们被认为应该操持家务。 [2010 年英语（二）阅读]

ought to 应该

真 All countries **ought to** enjoy equal taxing rights. 所有国家都应享有平等的征税权利。 [2020 年英语（一）阅读]

conform to 符合，遵守；与……相符或一致

真 States ought to **conform to** the federal court in reforming the jury system. 在陪审团制度的改

革中，各州应该与联邦法院协调一致。 [2010 年英语（二）阅读]

拓 conform with 与……相符或一致 ‖ observe [əbˈzɜːv] *v.* 遵守；看到

center around/on/upon 集中在；以……为中心 ◯◯◯

真 In discussing the U.S. jury system, the text **centers on** its tradition and development. 本文在讨论陪审团制度时，主要以它的传统和发展为中心。 [2010 年英语（二）阅读]

recall doing sth. 回想起做某事 ◯◯◯

词 recall [rɪˈkɔːl] *n.* 回忆；记起；召回

真 Ning **recalls spending** a confusing year in the late 1990s selling insurance. 宁回忆起 20 世纪 90 年代后期销售保险时那困惑的一年。 [2010 年英语（二）翻译]

拓 beyond/past recall 想不起来的；不能取消的

be desperate for 非常渴望；极需要 ◯◯◯

词 desperate [ˈdespərət] *a.* 极度渴望的；绝望的；孤注一掷的

真 He'd been through the dot-com boom and burst and, **desperate for** a job, signed on with a Boulder agency. 那时他刚刚经历了网络泡沫的膨胀和破灭，由于极需得到一份工作，也就与博德代理公司签了约。 [2011 年英语（一）翻译]

拓 be desperate to do sth. 极想做某事，强烈渴望做某事

stare at 凝视；盯住 ◯◯

例 We **stared at** each other for a while when we first met. 我们初次遇见时彼此凝视了一会儿。

turn the corner 转危为安；渡过难关；拐弯 ◯◯◯

真 Everyone said, "Just wait, you'll **turn the corner**, give it some time." 每个人都说："只要耐心等待，你会渡过难关的。" [2010 年英语（二）翻译]

in due course 在适当的时候；及时地；顺次 ◯◯◯

真 Write a letter to your American colleague to welcome him/her to visit China **in due course**. 给你的美国同事写封信，欢迎他或她在适当的时候访问中国。 [2010 年英语（二）写作]

base on 以……为根据；基于 ◯◯◯

真 According to research from Princeton University, people assess your competence, trustworthiness, and likeability in just a tenth of a second, solely **based on** the way you look.

根据普林斯顿大学的研究，人们仅仅根据你的外貌，仅在十分之一秒内就能评估出你的能力、可信度和受喜爱程度。

[2016 年英语（一）阅读]

| **at least** | 至少 | |

真 Today's CEO, **at least** for major American firms, must have many more skills than simply being able to "run the company." 如今的首席执行官，相比于仅仅能"经营公司"，他们还必须拥有更多的技能，至少对于美国的大公司来说是如此。

[2020 年英语（二）阅读]

拓 at most 至多

| **carry on** | 继续；参加 | |

例 If we **carry on** like this, bird flu and swine flu will be just the beginning of a century of viral outbreaks. 如果我们继续这么做，禽流感和猪流感将只是病毒大爆发世纪的开场而已。

拓 carry on with (doing) sth. 继续（做）某事

| **linger on** | 继续存留；缓慢消失；持续看；苟延残喘 | |

例 The letter itself is written on a school child's lined paper, as her eyes run down the page they **linger on** the date, July, 2005 and the dappling of yellow blotches. 信是写在一张学生用的横格纸上的，她浏览着，眼睛停留在信的日期（2005 年 7 月）和大块黄色的斑点上。

| **set in** | 开始；来临 | |

例 I must get those trees planted before the cold weather **sets in**. 我得在天气转冷之前把这些树种上。

| **log in/on** | 登录；注册 | |

真 Google and Microsoft are among companies that already have these "single sign-on" systems that make it possible for users to **log in** just once but use many different services. 谷歌和微软公司已经同众多公司一道加入了"单次登录"系统，该系统允许其用户仅登录一次便可享受多项不同的服务。

[2011 年英语（二）完形填空]

拓 log off/out 退出；注销系统

| **in vain** | 徒然；无效 | |

例 Our efforts were not **in vain**; it yields our desired outcome. 我们的努力没有白费；我们得到了想要的结果。

拓 to no avail/without avail 没有成果，徒劳无功

| mix up | 混合；掺和 |

真 The dual aim was **mixed up**: The stress on success over taking part was intimidating for newcomers. 这两个目标搅和在了一起：相较于只是参与其中，要在比赛中胜出的压力使新人望而却步。 [2007 年英语（二）阅读]

DAY 11

| in return | 作为回报 |

真 Demanding too much of air travelers or providing too little security **in return** undermines public support for the process. 对航空旅客要求过多或相应为其提供的安全保障过少，反过来会削弱公众对安保程序的支持。 [2017 年英语（一）阅读]

| in/by contrast | 相比之下 |

真 Cargo aircraft, **in contrast**, might be easier to reschedule, as might routine military flight. 相比之下，货机和常规的军用飞机或许更容易协调一些。 [2010 年英语（二）阅读]

拓 in contrast to 与……截然不同

| with caution | 谨慎地；小心地 |

词 caution ['kɔːʃn] *n.* 谨慎；警告，告诫

真 But for all the reasons there are to celebrate the computer, we must also act **with caution**. 然而，即使我们有无数理由可以赞美电脑，我们也要小心谨慎。 [2012 年英语（一）阅读]

拓 cautious ['kɔːʃəs] *a.* 谨慎的

| with delight | 欣然地 |

词 delight [dɪ'laɪt] *n.* 高兴，快乐，愉快

例 "I'm thinking, why not do the party here?" she said **with delight**. 她欣然地说："我在想，为什么不在这里开派对呢？"

拓 to the delight of 令……高兴的是 ‖ take (great) delight in (doing) sth. 以（做）某事为乐

| according to | 根据 |

真 **according to** a University of Oxford study 根据牛津大学的一项研究 [2018 年英语（一）阅读]

| fail to | 未能 |

真 Official retrospections continue as to why London 2012 **failed to** "inspire a generation." 官方依旧在反省 2012 年伦敦奥运会为何没有"激励一代人"。 [2017 年英语（二）阅读]

be accustomed to 习惯于

真 By offering on-trend items at dirt-cheap prices, Cline argues, these brands have hijacked fashion cycles, shaking an industry long **accustomed to** a seasonal pace. 克莱因指出，这些品牌以极为低廉的价格提供时尚产品，洗劫了时尚流行周期，在一个长久以来习惯以季节为周期的行业引起了震动。 [2013 年英语（一）阅读]

拓 accustom sb./sth./oneself to sth. 使某人或某事物或自己习惯于某事物

threaten to 威胁要……

真 The recession **threatened to** remove the advertising and readers that had not already fled to the Internet. 经济衰退给报业带来了巨大威胁，它带走了广告和那些尚未转向网络的读者。 [2011 年英语（二）阅读]

拓 threaten sb. with sth. 用某事物威胁某人

complain about 抱怨

真 **complain about** the new awards 抱怨新设立的奖项 [2014 年英语（一）阅读]

compare with 与……相比较

真 The data of an individual there gains its value only when it is **compared with** the data of countless millions more. 个人数据只有在与无数人的数据相比较时，才能获得自身价值。 [2018 年英语（一）阅读]

辨 compare...to... 指 "把……比作……"，常用来表达异类事物的比喻。如：Her beautiful face is compared to a flower. 她美丽的脸庞被比喻成一朵花。

compare...with... 指 "把……和……比较"，常用于同类相比。如：A captain is often compared with an explorer. 人们经常拿探险家和船长来作比较。

depend on 依赖于；取决于

真 the everyday services we **depend on** for our well-being and for growth 我们提升幸福感和推动发展所依赖的日常服务 [2017 年英语（一）阅读]

infer from 从……推断出；从……得出结论

例 The meaning of some new words can be **inferred from** the context. 有些生词的意思可以从上下文推断出来。

拓 conclude [kən'kluːd] v. 推断

be to blame　该受责备；应该负责

真 We have no one else **to blame** for our present condition except ourselves. 对于我们目前的处境，除了我们自己，不应该怪其他任何人。　[2011 年英语（一）翻译]

拓 lay/put the blame (for sth.) on sb. 把某事归咎于某人

lose interest in　对……失去兴趣

真 Readers have **lost** their **interest in** car and film reviews. 读者对汽车、电影评论类报纸丧失了兴趣。　[2011 年英语（二）阅读]

拓 retain/have interest in 对……保持或有兴趣

associate with　与……有关；和……联系在一起

真 Britain's Labor Party, as its name implies, has long been **associated with** trade unionism. 英国工党，顾名思义，与工会制度的关系由来已久。　[2012 年英语（一）阅读]

have an influence upon/on　对……有影响

例 And nobody will deny the fact that the attitude of the teachers does **have** an important **influence upon** the molding of the psychological foundation for pupils. 没有人会否认教师的态度对塑造小学生的心理基础有重要影响这一事实。

be related to　与……有关

真 Last year a federal task-force urged reform for patents **related to** genetic tests. 去年，一个联邦工作小组敦促在基因检测专利方面进行改革。　[2012 年英语（二）阅读]

be reliant on　依赖于

词 reliant [rɪˈlaɪənt] a. 依赖的，依靠的

真 Elegance of architectural design **was** not **reliant on** abundant decoration. 建筑设计的优雅不依赖于繁复的装饰。　[2011 年英语（二）阅读]

take...into consideration　考虑到

真 This scale **took** numerous factors **into consideration**. 测评过程考虑到了很多因素。

[2013 年英语（一）完形填空]

be faced with　面临着

真 The EU **is faced with** so many problems that even its supporters begin to feel concerned. 欧盟面临着许多问题，以至于其支持者甚至也开始担忧。　[2011 年英语（二）阅读]

begin to do sth. 开始做某事

真 We might then **begin to** solve our immigration challenges. 之后，我们再开始着手解决移民带来的挑战。 [2013 年英语（二）阅读]

be available to 对……来说是容易得到的

真 This can make them feel happier, which lets them **be** more **available to** their child the rest of the time. 这可以让他们感觉更加快乐，而感觉更加快乐会让他们在其余的时间里更多地陪伴孩子。 [2017 年英语（二）阅读]

seem to 似乎；看起来

真 Firms **seem to** invest more in places where most people are relatively happy, rather than in places with happiness inequality. 公司似乎在大多数人相对快乐的地方投资更多，而在快乐指数不均衡的地方则投资较少。 [2016 年英语（二）完形填空]

impose on 将……强加于；赢得……的欢心

词 impose [ɪm'pəʊz] v. 强加；对……课税

真 Last Thursday, the French Senate passed a digital services tax, which would **impose** an entirely new tax **on** large multinationals that provide digital services to consumers or users in France. 上周四，法国参议院通过了一项数字服务税，将对在法国向消费者或用户提供数字服务的大型跨国公司征收一项全新的税。 [2020 年英语（一）阅读]

introduce...to... 介绍……给……，向……介绍……

真 Cigarette-style warnings should be **introduced to** children about the dangers of a poor diet. 应当用香烟式的警告提醒儿童不良饮食的危险。 [2011 年英语（二）阅读]

set an example for 为……树立榜样

真 Parents should **set good examples for** their children by keeping a healthy diet at home. 父母应该为孩子树立健康饮食的好榜样。 [2011 年英语（二）阅读]

sense of responsibility 责任感

真 The government should strengthen the **sense of responsibility** among businesses. 政府应该致力于加强企业的责任感。 [2011 年英语（二）阅读]

take a toll on　给……造成重大伤亡（或损失）；损害

（真）Many everyday tasks **take a** surprising **toll on** the environment. 很多日常工作对环境造成了意想不到的危害。　[2011 年英语（二）翻译]

make improvement　进行改善

（真）However, Google and other big tech providers monitor their efficiency closely and **make improvements**. 然而，谷歌和其他几家高技术提供商正严密监视它们的能源利用效率并不断改善。　[2011 年英语（二）翻译]

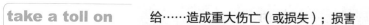

DAY
11

on the road to　在……过程中；在去……的旅途中

（真）Monitoring is the first step **on the road to** reduction. 监控是减少排放的第一步。
　[2011 年英语（二）翻译]

（拓）on one's/the way 在来（或去）的行进中；在路上

suggestion on　对……的意见

（真）Write him/her a letter to give him/her **suggestions on** how to get prepared for university life. 给他或她写一封信，就如何为大学生活做准备提出建议。　[2011 年英语（二）写作]

be/get prepared for　为……做好准备

（真）Studies show that students who take a gap year **are** generally better **prepared for** and perform better in college than those who do not. 研究表明，和那些直接上大学的人相比，休整一年的学生通常做了更充分的准备，在进入大学之后学业更加优秀。　[2017 年英语（二）阅读]

（拓）prepare for 为……做准备

at the end of　在……结束时；在……尽头

（真）**at the end of** the 19th century 在 19 世纪末　[2011 年英语（一）完形填空]

by this means　用这种方法

（例）Only **by this means** can your spoken English make greater progress. 只有这样，你的英语口语才能取得更大的进步。

be angry at　对……发怒；因……生气

（例）If someone **is angry at** you, don't fall for the being angry too. 如果有人对你发怒，不要以怒还怒。

be fatal to　　　　对……是致命的

例 Once you become famous, the public cannot tolerate any spot on you. Though some spot may be common to average people, it may **be fatal to** celebrities. 一旦你出名了，大众就容不得你的任何一个污点，哪怕有些对于平常人来讲是很正常的，对于名人来讲却是致命的。

distract one's attention　　　　转移某人的注意力

词 distract [dɪ'strækt] *vt.* 转移，分心

真 The exercise shows that mothers' use of devices **distracts children's attention**. 实验表明，妈妈使用电子设备会分散孩子的注意力。　　　　　　　　[2017 年英语（二）阅读]

interfere in　　　　干涉，干预

例 Such an argument presupposes that government does not **interfere in** markets and production. 这种说法是建立在预先假设政府不会干预市场和生产的基础上的。

拓 meddle in 干预，干涉

be distinct from　　　　与……不同

例 Jamaican Reggae **is** totally **distinct from** North American jazz and blues. 牙买加雷鬼音乐与北美的爵士乐和蓝调截然不同。

a sort of　　　　一种；有点儿

真 At Harvard, Mr Menand notes, "the great books are read because they have been read"—they form **a sort of** social glue. 梅南德先生指出，在哈佛大学，"学生阅读这些伟大的作品就是因为前人一直在读"——这些作品本身就形成了一种社会黏着力。

[2011 年英语（一）阅读]

at first glance　　　　乍一看，初看；第一眼就……

真 **At first glance** this might seem like a strength that grants the ability to make judgments which are unbiased by external factors. 乍看之下这是优势，使人能够做出不受外界因素影响而带有偏见的决定。　　　　　　　　[2013 年英语（一）完形填空]

拓 at first sight 乍一看，初看起来

deprive...of　　　　剥夺，使失去

真 For several decades America's colleges and universities have produced graduates who don't know the content and character of liberal education and are thus **deprived of** its benefits. 几十年来美国的高等院校培养出的毕业生对于通识教育的内容和特性知之甚少，因此也就失去了从中受益的机会。 [2014 年英语（一）阅读]

make compromises　做出让步

词 compromise ['kɒmprəmaɪz] *n.* 妥协；和解；折中方案

真 The astronomy community is **making compromises** to change its use of Mauna Kea. 天文学界正在做出让步，改变对莫纳克亚山的使用。 [2017 年英语（一）阅读]

live off　靠……生活

真 And there are the townsfolk who largely **live off** the tourists who come, not to see the plays, but to look at Anne Hathaway's Cottage, Shakespeare's birthplace and the other sights. 另一边则是主要依靠游客谋生的小镇居民，那些游客来这儿不是为了看戏，而是为了看安妮·海瑟薇的小屋、莎士比亚的出生地以及其他景点。 [2006 年英语（一）阅读]

be/become skeptical of/about　对……表示怀疑的

词 skeptical ['skeptɪkl] *a.* 怀疑的；不可知论的

真 You could argue that art **became** more **skeptical of** happiness because modern times have seen so much misery. 你可能会争辩说：艺术对快乐产生了怀疑是因为当今时代见证了如此多的苦难。 [2006 年英语（一）阅读]

拓 be suspicious of 对……表示怀疑

gain/get/have control over　控制住；镇压

真 The better you understand the cultural context, the more **control** you can **have over** your impact. 你对文化环境理解得越深刻，你就越能掌控你的影响。 [2016 年英语（一）阅读]

in store　将要发生；就要出现；准备着

真 The Hawthorne experiments had another surprise **in store**. 霍桑实验还有一个令人意想不到的发现。 [2010 年英语（一）完形填空]

come in　定期收取（钱）；进入；流行；参与（讨论、安排或任务）

真 In many rich countries average wages in the state sector are higher than in the private one. But the real gains **come in** benefits and work practices. 在很多富裕国家，公共部门的平均工资比私有部门高，但真正的收入来自各项福利和工作制度。 [2012 年英语（一）阅读]

between jobs　暂时赋闲在家，待业中　

真 The financial crisis has made it more acceptable to be **between jobs** or to leave a bad one. 金融危机让人们更容易接受待业或辞掉一份不好的工作。 [2011 年英语（一）阅读]

pass through　通过；经过市镇等（逗留但不长久）；经历（一段时间）　

真 During childbirth, larger babies have more difficulty **passing through** the birth canal. 分娩过程中，较大的婴儿更难通过产道。 [2012 年英语（一）阅读]

on the rise　在增加，在上涨　

例 Diversity is **on the rise**, which is a good phenomenon for the whole society. 多样性在增加，这对整个社会来说是个好现象。

be open to　易受到……的；对……开放的；愿意接受的　

真 Newly published discovery claims and credible discoveries that appear to be important and convincing will always **be open to** challenge and potential modification or refutation by future researchers. 新发表的科学发现声明和可信的科学发现看起来非常重要且令人信服，但却始终会受到之后研究人员的质疑，甚至可能会被修正乃至反驳。 [2012 年英语（一）阅读]

within reason　合理的，理智的　

真 In Europe, where forestry is ecologically more advanced, the noncommercial tree species are recognized as members of native forest community, to be preserved as such, **within reason**. 在林业生态更为发达的欧洲，没有商业价值的树种被看成是当地森林群落的成员，同样受到了合理的保护。 [2010 年英语（一）阅读]

click on　点击　

真 By watching what people search for, **click on** and say online, companies can aim "behavioral" ads at those most likely to buy. 通过监测人们在网上搜索、点击和发布的内容，公司可以将"行为"广告投放给最可能购物的人群。 [2013 年英语（一）阅读]

of course　当然　

真 In the popular imagination, **of course**, guilt still gets a bad rap. 当然，在大众眼中，内疚仍旧备受诟病。 [2019 年英语（一）阅读]

in the process of   在……的过程中

真 Notions of evidence and fact, of basic rights and public interest are at work **in the process of** journalistic judgment and production just as in courts of law. 证据和事实、基本权利和公共利益的概念被用于新闻评判和制造新闻的过程中，这与在法庭上是一样的。

[2007 年英语（一）阅读]

DAY
11

DAY 12

本单元资源

be located in   坐落于

例 They analysed common traits in these habitats and found that they **were** mostly **located in** forests that were at least 100 years old. 根据对这些栖息地的共同特征的分析，研究发现它们都位于至少拥有 100 年历史的古老森林里。

in no time   立即，马上

例 Without hesitating, John started chatting her up, and **in no time**, John had her cracking up. 不带一丝犹豫，约翰开始与她搭讪，很快，约翰逗得她哈哈大笑。

拓 at once 立刻，马上

conclude from   从……中得出结论；从……推断出

真 We can **conclude from** the last paragraph that IQ scores and SAT results are highly correlated. 从最后一段我们可以得出结论：智商分数和 SAT 成绩高度相关。 [2007 年英语（一）阅读]

move away   离去；搬家

例 It would be helpful to families that find keeping in touch more difficult as their children grow up and **move away**. 这对那些发现随着孩子长大离开、保持联系变得更加困难的家庭很有帮助。

live by   履行；以……谋生

真 Either Entergy never really intended to **live by** those commitments, or it simply didn't foresee what would happen next. 要么安特吉从未真正打算去履行这些承诺，要么它根本没有预见到接下来会发生什么。 [2012 年英语（一）阅读]

拓 fulfill [fʊlˈfɪl] v. 履行；实现；满足 ‖ fulfill a promise 履行承诺

encounter with   与……突然的或意外的（尤指敌对的）相遇

词 encounter [ɪnˈkaʊntə(r)] n. 突然的或意外的（尤指敌对的）相遇

例 When he was a child, Warren Buffett had an awe-inspiring **encounter with** Sidney Weinberg, Goldman Sachs's legendary leader, sparking a lifelong affection for the bank. 在沃伦·巴菲特还是个孩子的时候，他便与高盛历史上的传奇领袖西德尼·温伯格有了一次令他心生敬畏的相遇，这一相遇激起了巴菲特对高盛银行一生的钟爱。

cut corners 走捷径；省钱（或人力、时间等）

例 Do not **cut corners** and follow instructions to the letter, if you want to be successful. 如果你想要成功，就不要图省事，要严格按照说明去做。

for free 免费地；义务地；无偿地

真 With the content of papers secured **for free**, the publisher needs only to find a market for its journal. 在免费获得论文内容的情况下，出版商只需要为其期刊找到市场。

[2020 年英语（一）阅读]

拓 free of charge 免费

meet one's need 满足某人的需求

例 The decoration style of this apartment just **meets your needs**. 这套公寓的装修风格正好满足你的需要。

get in 进入；到达；收获，收集

例 to **get in** the water 进入水中

get ahead 取得进步；获得成功；走在前面

真 I was living in so much frustration that that was my escape, to go to school, and **get ahead** and do better. 我一直生活得如此挫败，以至于上学、取得进步、努力做得更好成为我逃避的方式。

[2008 年英语（一）阅读]

in any case 无论如何；总之

真 It might be poetic, philosophical, sensual, or mathematical, but **in any case** it must, in my view, have something to do with the soul of the human being. 它可能是诗意的、哲学的、感性的，或是精细的，但无论如何，在我看来，音乐都一定与人类的灵魂有某种关联。

[2014 年英语（一）阅读]

拓 in any event 无论如何；不管怎样

bring/get...under control 控制，抑制

真 Cartwright seems to suggest that visualizing bad dreams helps **bring** them **under control**. 卡特赖特似乎在说明想象噩梦有助于控制噩梦。

[2005 年英语（一）阅读]

拓 be in control (of sth.) 指挥、管理或支配（某事物）

in agreement with　与……一致；同意 ○○○

例 The researchers found, **in agreement with** previous studies, that both men and women identified angry expressions most quickly. 研究人员发现，与之前的研究结果相一致，男性和女性最快辨别出的表情都是愤怒。

wear away　磨损；（因重复使用而）变薄，变光滑；磨薄；磨光 ○○○

例 This pair of leather shoes is starting to **wear away**; I need to buy a new one. 这双皮鞋开始磨损了，我需要买一双新的。

by means of　用某种方式；借助于

真 **by means of** careful searching 通过仔细搜索　　　　　　　　[2014 年英语（一）阅读]

be resistant to　抗拒，抵制 ○○○

真 Writing for the National Immigration Forum, Gregory Rodriguez reports that today's immigration **is** neither at unprecedented levels nor **resistant to** assimilation. 格雷戈里·罗德里格斯在给国家移民论坛的报告中提到，如今的移民既没有达到一个空前的水平，也没有表现出对这种同化的抵制。　　　　　　　　[2006 年英语（一）阅读]

in light of　鉴于，由于，考虑到；根据，按照 ○○○

例 **In light of** experts' remarks, we rejected her team application for this project. 鉴于专家们的意见，我们拒绝了她的团队对这个项目的申请。

拓 in view of 鉴于，考虑到

cut back　减少，削减，缩减；剪枝；修剪 ○○○

例 The company is heading for a crisis, with cash-starved financial sector forced to **cut back** on vital financial payment. 资金紧张的财政部门不得不削减主要的财政支出，这家公司眼看就要陷入危机。

in a manner　以……方式；在一定程度上 ○○○

真 On the other, it links these concepts to everyday realities **in a manner** which is parallel to the links journalists forge on a daily basis as they cover and comment on the news. 另一方面，法律以一种方式把这些观念同日常实际联系起来，这种联系方式类似于新闻记者在报道和评论新闻时基于日常规则所形成的方式。　　　　　　　　[2007 年英语（一）翻译]

take pains
尽力，煞费苦心，千方百计

例 If you want to succeed in this field, you must **take pains**. 如果你要在这个领域中取得成功，就得下一番苦心。

put/place/set a premium on
重视，珍视

真 To combat the trap of **putting a premium on** being busy, Gal Newport, author of *Deep Work: Rules for Focused Success in a Districted World*, recommends building a habit of "deep work"—the ability to focus without distraction. 为了避免陷入鼓励忙碌的陷阱，《深度工作：在容易分心的世界保持专注的法则》一书的作者盖尔·纽波特推荐养成一种"深度工作"的习惯—— 一种不会分心的专注能力。 [2018 年英语（二）阅读]

push aside
推开，推向一边；排除，避免

例 Lichen is the staple of their winter diet, and they must **push aside** the snow to reach it. 地衣是它们冬季食物的主食，它们必须把雪推开才能吃到地衣。

take apart
拆开，拆卸；分辨

例 Back then, when her parents left home, Sue would **take apart** the television and reassemble it before they returned. 换做以前，当她的父母离开家时，苏就会拆开电视机，并在她父母回来之前重新组装。

sit up
熬夜；端坐；使……坐起身来

例 Once they get together, they will **sit up** talking and drinking. 一旦聚在一起，他们就会饮酒谈天，直至深夜。

拓 stay up late 熬夜，睡得很晚

bad debt
坏账；死账；呆账

真 Today they argue that market prices overstate losses, because they largely reflect the temporary illiquidity of markets, not the likely extent of **bad debts**. 现在，他们认为市场价格夸大了损失，因为市价主要反映了市场暂时的流动性不足，而非坏账可能达到的程度。 [2010 年英语（一）阅读]

拓 get into debt 负债，欠债 ‖ out of debt 不欠债；还清债务

resign from
辞职；退去

词 resign [rɪ'zaɪn] *v.* 辞职，辞去

例 In this economic crisis, they wish Tim could reconsider his decision to **resign from** the board of directors. 在此次经济危机中，他们希望蒂姆可以重新考虑辞去董事会职务的决定。

拓 quit [kwɪt] *v.* 辞职

detach from　　拆下；脱离；使分开

词 detach [dɪ'tætʃ] *v.* 拆卸；（使）分开，脱离

例 If you think it's not beautiful, you can **detach** the hood **from** the jacket. 如果您觉得不美观，可以把风帽从夹克上拆下来。

cut across　　与……不符；走捷径，抄近路

真 They **cut across** the insistence by top American universities that liberal-arts education and professional education should be kept separate, taught in different schools. 它们有悖于顶级美国大学主张文科教育和职业教育应分学院教导的传统观点。　　　　　[2011 年英语（一）阅读]

speak for　　代表……讲话；为……辩护

例 At Dan's high school graduation, he was invited to **speak for** the students. 在丹的高中毕业典礼上，他受邀代表学生讲话。

elite school　　精英学校

词 elite [eɪ'liːt] *n.* 精英

例 The educational experience for students in **elite schools** is designed to ensure students meet rigorous academic standards. 精英学校学生的教育体验旨在确保学生达到严格的学术标准。

拓 selective school 精英学校

be liable to　　易于……的；有……倾向的；应负有责任，应遵守……

词 liable ['laɪəbl] *a.* 可能受……影响的；有可能的；有责任的

例 Your ideas will **be liable to** misrepresentation by the others if you do not clarify exactly what you think. 如果你不确切地澄清你的想法，你的意见有可能被其他人曲解。

拓 be apt to 易于，倾向于

break away (from)　　脱离，逃跑，离开

例 Our company must **break away from** convention and adopt as many advanced techniques as possible to achieve the greatest progress of the company in a short period of time. 我们公司必须打破常规，尽量采用先进技术，在较短时期内，实现公司的最大进步。

let...in 让……进入，放……进来；嵌入

例 In tourist season, when the number of tourists reaches the peak, the scenic area staff will not **let** other tourists **in**. 在旅游旺季，当游客人数达到高峰时，景区工作人员不会让其他游客进入。

拓 enter ['entə(r)] *v.* 进入

at the thought of 一想到……（就）

例 Not only has our school given me an extraordinary honour, but the months of fear and sleepless I've experienced **at the thought of** participating in such an important competition on behalf of the school have made me lose weight. 这不仅是因为我们学校给了我这个非凡的荣誉，而且是因为数月以来，每当想到要代表学校参加如此重要的比赛，我就会心生焦虑、失眠，体重也减轻了。

be wrapped up in 注意力完全集中于……；与……难解难分

例 They **are** so **wrapped up in** the proceedings that they don't notice me. 他们都特别专注于进程，以至于根本不会注意到我。

box office 票房；售票处

真 They all seem to look alike (though they come from all over)—lean, pointed, dedicated faces, wearing jeans and sandals, eating their buns and bedding down for the night on the flagstones outside the theatre to buy the 20 seats and 80 standing-room tickets held for the sleepers and sold to them when the **box office** opens at 10:30 a.m. 尽管他们来自天南海北，但看起来都一个样：瘦削，棱角分明，面容专注，身着牛仔裤和凉鞋，吃着自带的干果面包，晚上睡在剧院外的石板上，为了赶在票房上午 10:30 开门的时候买到为这些露宿者准备的 20 张坐票和 80 张站票。

[2006 年英语（一）阅读]

be crucial to 对……来说至关重要

词 crucial ['kruːʃl] *a.* 极其重要的

真 But acknowledging fire's inevitable presence in human life **is** an attitude **crucial to** developing the laws, policies, and practices that make it as safe as possible, she says. 但是承认火不可避免地存在于人类生活中的这样一种态度对于制定使其尽可能安全的法律、政策和惯例来说至关重要，她说道。

[2017 年英语（二）阅读]

拓 be vital to 对……来说至关重要

stick up for　　捍卫，维护

例 After so much suffering, she learned how to **stick up for** herself and her family. 在经历了这么多苦难之后，她学会了如何捍卫自己和她的家人。

by mistake　　错误地；无意地

例 take her neighbour's clothes **by mistake** 错收了邻居家的衣服

拓 wrongly ['rɒŋli] *ad.* 错误地

not have a leg to stand on　　（论点等）站不住脚；对行为无合理的解释

例 He did **not have a leg to stand on** because when the police arrived, he had a knife and $300 in his pocket. 当警察到时，他口袋里有一把刀和 300 美元，他真是有口难辩。

fall behind　　落后，跟不上；拖欠

例 **fall behind** schedule 进度落后

拓 lag behind 落后，拖欠

take care　　小心，留心

例 **Take care** not to stain my dress, because I will wear it to my friend's wedding tomorrow. 小心别弄脏我的礼服，因为明天我要去参加朋友的婚礼。

拓 be careful 小心，当心

for ever　　永远；永恒地；总是

例 John was so in love he was sure that he and his wife could be together **for ever**. 约翰如此爱他的妻子，以至于他确信他们能永远在一起。

so as to　　以便，为了

真 Bottled water, chewing gum and skin moisturizers are mentioned in Paragraph 5 **so as to** reveal their impact on people's habits. 文章第 5 段提到瓶装水、口香糖和润肤霜是为了揭示它们对人们习惯的影响。

[2010 年英语（二）阅读]

fall apart　　破裂，破碎；散开

例 Their marriage finally **fell apart**. 他们的婚姻终于破裂了。

拓 fall to pieces 破碎；倒塌

in the world　　在世界上；到底，究竟

真 As a linguist, he acknowledges that all varieties of human language, including non-standard ones like Black English, can be powerfully expressive—there exists no language or dialect **in the world** that cannot convey complex ideas. 作为一名语言学家，他认为各种各样的人类语言，包括像黑人英语这样的非标准语言，都具有强大的表现力——世上没有传达不了复杂思想的语言或方言。

[2005 年英语（一）阅读]

as regards sb./sth.　　关于，至于某人或某事物

例 **As regards** the education of adults, this school's method seems to me full of wisdom. 关于成人教育，在我看来，这所学校的方法充满了智慧。

for sure　　肯定地，有把握地

真 the one thing we know **for sure** 我们确定的一件事情

[2013 年英语（二）阅读]

(just) in case　　以防（万一）

例 His family wanted to be here earlier tomorrow morning **in case** the tourist guide had forgotten to deal with this matter. 他的家人想明天早上早点来，以防导游忘了处理这件事。

拓 in case of sth. 若发生某事，假如

date back to　　追溯到；始于

真 Studies **dating back to** the 1930s indicate that laughter relaxes muscles, decreasing muscle tone for up to 45 minutes after the laugh dies down. 追溯到20世纪30年代的多项研究表明，笑使肌肉放松，在笑停止后，肌肉张力低于正常水平的时间长达45分钟之久。

[2011 年英语（二）完形填空]

put forth　　提出；生出，长出

例 Think about what the world would be like, if these ideas had never been **put forth**. 想想看假如这些观念不曾被提出，我们的世界会是什么样子。

tie down　　束缚，约束

例 The enfant terrible of the business world attributes his success to hard-work, lack of personal distractions and extensive use of binding employment contracts: I like to **tie down** my best employees. 这名商界怪才将他的成功归因于三点：一是勤奋努力，二是一心工作，三是广泛采用约束力大的雇佣合同：我喜欢把最优秀的员工牢牢拴住。

on thin ice　　如履薄冰，处境危险　　○○○

例 This kind of love, always in fear, treading **on thin ice**. 这种爱总让人战战兢兢，如履薄冰。

be stuck in　　困住，陷于；卡住　　○○○

真 For all the possibilities of our new culture machines, most people **are** still **stuck in** download mode. 尽管这些新的文化机器为我们提供了各种可能的用途，但大多数人还是深陷于下载模式之中。　　[2012 年英语（一）阅读]

be fascinated with　　痴迷于……，对……着迷　　○○○

词 fascinate ['fæsɪneɪt] v. 使（某人）着迷、神魂颠倒或极感兴趣

例 If you look back into history, you will certainly **be fascinated with** many quaint customs and cultures. 如果你回顾历史，你肯定会被许多奇异的风俗习惯所吸引。

switch off　　关掉，切断（电源）　　○○○

例 So you may **switch off** your cellphone and computer once in a while, put aside your troubles, give yourself a hug, and give yourself a vacation, then you will feel more relaxed. 因此不妨偶尔关掉你的手机和电脑，把烦恼暂时放在一边，给自己一个拥抱，给自己放个假，这样你会感觉更加轻松。

spell out　　讲清楚，详细解释；拼出（某字）　　○○○

真 Please **spell out** their argument fully and charitably. 请完整并友善地阐明他们的观点。

[2019 年英语（一）阅读]

virtual currency　　虚拟货币　　○○○

词 virtual ['vɜːtʃuəl] a. 虚拟的；事实上的 ‖ currency ['kʌrənsi] n. 货币；通货

例 Online Game **virtual currency** is limited to the scope of the virtual services provided by the exchange issuing enterprise itself. 网络游戏虚拟货币的适用范围仅限于兑换发行企业自身所提供的虚拟服务。

move up　　（使）升级，提升　　○○○

例 It will take hard work and a little bit of help and luck, if you want to **move up** this year. 如果你想要今年晋升，就必须努力工作，再加上别人的协助和一点点运气。

tear apart
拆散；撕开

词 tear [teə(r)] v. 撕，扯；撕碎

例 Facing the current situation of the company, the first two solutions are unrealistic and need to be **tore apart** to solve the crisis. 面对公司目前的处境，前两种方案不切实际，需要拆分方案以解决此次危机。

be soft on
对……有同情心，对……心肠软

例 In order to maintain the peace of the country, we must not **be soft on** criminals. 为了维护国家安宁，我们对犯罪分子绝对不能手软。

keep up
持续不停；使……不能睡觉；维持，保持；保养，维修

例 Let's hope the sunny weather **keeps up** for next week's sports meeting. 但愿下周运动会时还是这样的好天气。

in the eyes of
在……看来；在……心目中

例 Almost all go back to the village, a bit richer and more important **in the eyes of** their fellow villagers. 几乎所有人都会回到村庄，在回去之后，他们在村民的眼里显得更富有、更重要。

fasten...to/onto
把……固定住，把……系上

例 The little girl **fastened** a red flower **to** her dress. 这个小女孩把一朵红花别在了自己的裙子上。

set about (doing) sth.
着手做某事

例 Mr. Lee built a facility just off the main road and **set about** building his client base. 李先生在主路旁创建了这家医院并着手打造自己的客户群。

reach a consensus
达成共识

真 In response to these many unilateral measures, the Organization for Economic Cooperation and Development (OECD) is currently working with 131 countries to **reach a consensus** by the end of 2020 on an international solution. 为了应对这些单边措施，经济合作与发展组织目前正与 131 个国家商讨，希望能在 2020 年年底之前就国际解决方案达成共识。

[2020 年英语（一）阅读]

shift from...to...　从……转为……

真 One study found that people responded best to comments that **shifted from** negative **to** positive, possibly because it suggested they had won somebody over. 一项研究发现，人们对从消极到积极的评价反应最好可能是因为这表明他们赢得了某人的支持。

[2020 年英语（二）阅读]

fail at　在……方面失败

真 Every time we **fail at** something, we can choose to look for the lesson we're meant to learn. 每当我们在某件事上失败时，我们可以选择去寻找我们理应去吸取的教训。

[2020 年英语（二）翻译]

a version of　……的一个版本

真 The robot rats were quite minimalist, resembling **a** chunkier **version of** a computer mouse with wheels to move around and colourful markings. 这些机器鼠的设计极其简单，类似电脑鼠标的矮胖版，有轮子可以移动，还有五颜六色的标记。 [2020 年英语（二）阅读]

sit out/through　（在剧院等）一直坐到（演出等）结束

例 She does not think she could **sit through** the film again, because it was so harrowing. 她觉得自己无法把那部电影再重温一遍，因为故事太让人痛心了。

work up　引起，激起；(to) 渐渐达到；发展到

例 If you want to earn more money, you must **work up** the enthusiasm or courage to do your job. 如果你想赚到更多的钱，就必须鼓起热情或勇气去做你的工作。

less than　少于，不到

真 work **less than** 35 hours 工作少于 35 个小时　　　　　[2015 年英语（二）阅读]
拓 more than 多于，超过

decorate...with...　用……装饰……

真 Completed in 1875, the State Department's south wing was the first to be occupied, with its elegant four-story library, Diplomatic Reception Room, and Secretary's office **decorated with** carved wood, Oriental rugs, and stenciled wall patterns. 国务院大楼的南翼于 1875 年建成，并第一个被投入使用，它拥有设计优雅的四层图书馆、外交接待室，以及装饰着木雕工艺、东方地毯和镂花墙的部长办公室。

[2018 年英语（一）阅读]

take in 了解；理解；吸收；欺骗；让……进入

真 The sightseers can **take in** everything and get out of town by nightfall. 游客们可以在夜幕降临前游遍所有景点，然后离开城镇。 [2006 年英语（一）阅读]

拓 take out 取出；去掉；把……带出去

arrive on the job 到岗

真 One survey found that bureaucratic delays led the average H-2A worker to **arrive on the job** 22 days late. 一项调查发现，官僚机制所导致的拖延使得持 H-2A 签证的普通工人到岗工作的时间推迟 22 天。 [2019 年英语（二）阅读]

be equal to 相等，相同；胜任；合适

真 In several of the studies, when stressed-out female rats had their ovaries removed, their chemical responses became **equal to** those of the males. 一些研究发现，当处于极度焦虑状态的雌鼠的卵巢被切除后，它们体内的化学反应就会与雄鼠相同。 [2008 年英语（一）阅读]

part with 放弃

真 For one thing, the South could not afford to **part with** its slaves. 一方面，美国南方无法承受放弃奴隶。 [2008 年英语（一）阅读]

get out 离开，出去；泄露

真 This poor Mike really needs to **get out** of the past and find himself again. 可怜的迈克真的需要忘记过去，找回自我。 [2006 年英语（一）阅读]

side effect 副作用

真 Scholars, policymakers, and critics of all stripes have debated the social implications of these changes, but few have looked at the **side effect**. 来自各领域的学者、政策制定者和批评家都对这些变化的社会意义进行了讨论，但是很少有人看到这一变化的副作用。

[2007 年英语（一）阅读]

either...or... 或者……或者……；不是……就是……

真 Malti and others have shown that cooperation and sharing can result from **either** sympathy **or** guilt. 马尔蒂和其他人已经表明合作与分享可能源自同情或内疚。 [2019 年英语（二）阅读]

on the side　额外；作为兼职

例 One of his clients was a stockbroker who happened to have a little farm **on the side**. 他的一个客户是股票经纪人，碰巧另外有个小农场。

drop by　下降了

真 The cost of solar panels has **dropped by** 80 percent and the cost of wind turbines by close to one-third in the past eight years. 在过去八年的时间里，太阳能电池板的价格降低了80%，风力发电机的价格下降了约三分之一。　　　　　　　　　　[2018 年英语（二）阅读]

拓 fall by 下降了……

be proficient in　精通

真 The children of immigrants tend to **be** bilingual and **proficient in** English. 移民者的孩子往往能够说两种语言并且精通英语。　　　　　　　　　　　　　　　　[2006 年英语（一）阅读]

be equivalent to　等于，相当于

真 In a society that so persistently celebrates procreation, is it any wonder that admitting you regret having children **is equivalent to** admitting you support kitten-killing? 在一个一直歌颂生育的社会中，承认后悔生育孩子就相当于承认自己支持残杀幼猫，这有什么奇怪的吗？

[2011 年英语（一）阅读]

to the point　中肯，扼要；切题；到……的程度

真 It is difficult **to the point** of impossibility for the average reader under the age of forty to imagine a time when high-quality arts criticism could be found in most big-city newspapers. 对于 40 岁以下的普通读者而言，很难想象曾有一个时代，那时大多数大城市的报纸上都能读到高品质的艺术评论。　　　　　　　　　　　　　　[2010 年英语（一）阅读]

本单元资源

in the small hours 下半夜，凌晨

例 To complete the study, he went to sleep **in the small hours** for several weeks. 为了完成该项研究，他已连续数周凌晨入睡。

sooner or later 早晚，迟早

例 In the new financial year, John works hard every day and he will catch up with other colleagues in the company **sooner or later**. 新财年里，约翰每天坚持不懈地努力，他迟早会赶上公司其他同事。

more or less 或多或少

例 The writer said that he hoped he would write **more or less** like himself. 那位作家说他希望自己能或多或少地写一些像自己的东西。

have faith in 信任，相信

例 After all, if we do not feel worthy of love, how on earth will we **have faith in** ourselves to handle anything that life throws our way? 毕竟，如果我们觉得自己都不值得爱，我们怎么能相信自己能够处理生活抛给我们的难题呢？

at the cost of 以……为代价

例 In this case, you must finish your report **at the cost of** your nap time. 目前这种情况，你必须牺牲自己的午休时间来完成这次报告。

vote for 为……投票

真 If everything was going so well, then why did over 17 million people **vote for** Brexit, despite the warnings about what it could do to their country's economic prospects? 如果一切进展顺利的话，那么为什么有超过 1700 万人投票选择脱欧，甚至不顾此举可能会对国家经济前景带来影响的警示呢？

[2017 年英语（一）阅读]

拓 vote for 投票赞成 ‖ vote against 投票反对 ‖ vote with one's feet 用脚投票（用去或不去某处表明想法）

by hand 用手；（信件）亲手交付，由专人递送

例 We search for fossils in the high Arctic, moving hundreds of tons of rock **by hand** in wet, freezing conditions. 我们在北极高纬度地区寻找化石，在潮湿、冰冻的条件下用手搬运数百吨岩石。

take effect
实施，实行；起作用；产生预期或要求的结果；见效

例 The laws don't **take effect** until the end of the year. 这项法规要到年底才生效。

be liable for
对……负有责任；必须按法律做（某事）

例 In contrast, unmarried intimate partners **are** not **liable for** each other's debts. 相比之下，未结婚的亲密伴侣对彼此的债务没有责任。

bed down
安排过夜

例 On those nights when these backpackers could find no inn to take them in, they **bedded down** in the fields. 那几天晚上，这些驴友们找不到可以投宿的客栈，便只好露宿野外。

snatch at
伸手抓；抢取；抓取

例 In later work, we will **snatch at** every opportunity to improve our work. 在后期的工作中，我们会抓住一切机会改进我们的工作。

pour into
不断地涌入

真 They spend the night (some of them four or five nights) **pouring** cash **into** the hotels and restaurants. 他们要过夜（有些人甚至会住四五夜），所以就把大量的钱消费在了小镇的旅馆和饭店里。

[2006 年英语（一）阅读]

every so often
偶尔，不时

例 **Every so often** he is going to come back. 他会偶尔回来的。

拓 every now and then 偶尔，不时 ‖ occasionally [əˈkeɪʒnəli] ad. 偶然；偶尔

cut up
切碎；割伤，打伤；使伤心，使难受

例 **cut up** the wood 把木头切碎

scream at
对……大喊大叫

真 You lose your patience and either **scream at** your kids or say something that was too harsh and does nobody any good. 你失去耐心，对着孩子大喊大叫，或者说一些过于刻薄但又对谁都没什么好处的话。

[2020 年英语（二）完形填空]

start over 重新开始

真 You wish that you could turn back the clock and **start over**. 你希望可以让时间倒回去，重新来过。 [2020 年英语 (二) 完形填空]

stick by 坚持忠于；遵守，坚持 (协议、原则等)

例 I will **stick by** my decision. 我会坚持我的决定。

拓 be loyal to 忠于

strive to 争取，力图

真 The most successful monarchies **strive to** abandon or hide their old aristocratic ways. 最成功的王室成员努力抛弃或隐藏其原有的贵族生活方式。 [2015 年英语 (一) 阅读]

拓 endeavour to 努力，尽力

come off 实现，成功，奏效

例 The plan didn't **come off**. 计划没有成功。

拓 work [wɜːk] v. 应验，实现

make a complaint 投诉

词 complaint [kəm'pleɪnt] n. 投诉；抱怨，埋怨

真 Write an e-mail to the customer service center to **make a complaint** and demand a prompt solution. 向客户服务中心发送电子邮件，投诉并要求立即解决。 [2012 年英语 (二) 写作]

talk over 详细探讨；坦诚交谈

例 Frank often **talks** things **over** with his father. 弗兰克有事总和他的父亲坦诚地谈一谈。

fill in/out 填充，填写

例 Please **fill in** some of the details of the accident. 请把事故的情况填得详细一些。

拓 make out 开具，填写 (表格或文件)

take away 解除，消除；带回食用；拿走；抓走

例 The doctor gave me two pills to **take away** the pain. 医生给了我两片止痛片。

拓 take away from 减少；贬低

| **be tolerant of** | 容忍，对……持包容态度 | |

例 We need to **be tolerant of** different points of view. 我们需要对不同的观点持包容态度。

拓 bear with 对……有耐心；忍耐

| **straight away** | 立即，马上 | |

例 She headed back home **straight away**. 她马上向家里走去。

拓 right away 立即，马上 ‖ immediately [ɪˈmiːdiətli] *adv.* 立即，马上 ‖ straight off/out 毫不犹豫，立即

| **not in the least** | 绝对不；一点也不 | |

例 They were **not in the least** worried about the situation then. 他们完全不担心当时的情况。

| **rush through** | 快速通过成为官方政策；匆促生产；赶制 | |

真 After a bruising encounter with Congress, America's Financial Accounting Standards Board (FASB) **rushed through** rule changes. 在与国会的交锋遭受挫败之后，美国财务会计标准委员会（FASB）匆忙通过了对准则的修改。 [2010 年英语（一）阅读]

| **come down to** | 降至；（问题、决定等）归结为 | |

真 Since then it may have **come down to** $50 billion. 自那以后，它（艺术品市场的价值）可能降至 500 亿美元。 [2010 年英语（二）阅读]

| **out of condition** | 不能使用；（由于缺乏锻炼而）身体状况不佳 | |

例 The TV is **out of condition**. 这台电视坏了，不能使用。

拓 in good condition 处于良好的状态 ‖ on no condition 一点也不；决不

| **package deal** | （政府或机构制订的）一揽子协议（或提议） | |

词 package [ˈpækɪdʒ] *n.* 包裹 *v.* 将……包装（供出售等）

真 There has to be coordination of programs. What's needed is a **package deal**. 各个项目间必须协同运作。我们需要的是一揽子方案。 [2006 年英语（一）完形填空]

| **suitable for/to** | 适于；合适 | |

真 To read such books today is to marvel at the fact that their learned contents were once deemed **suitable for** publication in general-circulation dailies. 如果今天再来读这些书籍的话，就会不禁惊诧于这样的事实：这些学术性的内容竟然曾被认为适合刊登在面向广大读者发行的日报上。 [2010 年英语（一）阅读]

keep one's eyes/ears open　留神看 / 找

真 Enjoy the beauty of the world around and **keep the eyes open** to see the possibilities before you. 享受周围世界的美好，留心发现眼前的机会。　　　　　　　　[2015 年英语（一）阅读]

prejudice against　对……的偏见

词 prejudice ['predʒudɪs] *n.* 偏见

真 The author holds that George Osborne's preference reveals a strong **prejudice against** urban areas. 作者认为，乔治·奥斯本的偏好揭示了他对城市地区的强烈偏见。[2016 年英语（一）阅读]

root cause　根本原因

真 These issues all have **root causes** in human behavior: all require behavioral change and social innovations, as well as technological development. 导致所有这些问题的根本原因都在于人类的行为，这些问题都要求人们在行为上做出转变，对社会进行变革，同时发展技术。

[2013 年英语（一）阅读]

dress up　盛装打扮；装扮；伪装

例 **dress up** for dinner 盛装赴宴

as far as sb. be concerned　就某人而言；依某人看；在某人看来

例 **As far as I'm concerned**, you did a great job. 在我看来，你做得很棒。

pay back　偿还；报复

例 I will **pay back** all my debts next year. 明年我会把欠款还清。

bond with sb.　增强或建立与某人的信任关系

真 They may have **bonded** more **with** the social robot because it displayed behaviours like communal exploring and playing. 它们可能更喜欢社交机器人，因为它表现出了集体探索和玩耍的行为。　　　　　　　　[2020 年英语（二）阅读]

hand in　交（作业）；提出（辞职）；递交（辞呈）

例 I have already **handed in** my paper. 我已经把论文交上去了。

拓 turn in 上交；归还

come under	遭受（压力）；受到（袭击）；是……的目标；归入，编入

例 The headmaster **came under** heavy pressure to resign. 校长背负着巨大的辞职压力。

drive away	赶走；使想离开

真 It would be a shame to raise prices too much because it would **drive away** the young people who are Stratford's most attractive clientele. 涨价太多可能会令他们感到遗憾，因为这将会赶走对斯特拉福镇最着迷的年轻客户。 [2006 年英语（一）阅读]

拓 expel [ɪk'spel] *v.* 把……开除；驱逐出境 ‖ banish ['bænɪʃ] *v.* 放逐；流放；驱逐出境；赶走

be in the grip of sth.	受制于某事物

词 grip [grɪp] *n.* 紧抓，紧握

例 They **were in the grip of** fate and had no volition of their own. 他们被命运掌控，毫无自主选择的余地。

stop over (at/in)	中途停留（尤指乘飞机旅行时）

例 I **stopped over in** Japan on the way to America. 在去美国的途中我在日本稍作了停留。

拓 stop off (at/in) 中途稍作停留（做某事）

for the time being	目前，暂时

例 I am staying at my cousin's house **for the time being**. 我暂时寄宿在堂姐家里。

拓 for the moment 暂时；目前 ‖ temporarily ['temprərəli] *ad.* 暂时

feel like (doing) sth.	想要（做）某事物

真 The most loyal customers would still get the product they favor, the idea goes, and they'd **feel like** they were helping sustain the quality of something they believe in. 这种理念认为，最忠实的消费者始终都会购买他们喜欢的产品，他们会觉得自己是在帮助维持他们所信任的某种东西的品质。 [2016 年英语（一）阅读]

have an advantage over	胜过；优于

真 David Graddol concludes that monoglot English graduates face a bleak economic future as qualified multilingual youngsters from other countries are proving to **have a** competitive **advantage over** their British counterparts in global companies and organisations. 戴维·格兰多推断，只会英语这一种语言的毕业生将面临暗淡的经济前景，因为事实证明，在跨国

公司和组织机构中，来自其他国家的掌握多种语言的年轻人比英国年轻人更具竞争优势。

[2017 年英语（一）翻译]

拓 excel [ɪk'sel] *v.* 突出；胜过他人 ‖ surpass [sə'pɑːs] *v.* 超过；胜过

---

go out　　　　被公布；出门；退潮；发布；熄灭；出局；过时

例 Word **went out** that the director had resigned. 经理已经辞职的消息公布了。

---

time after time　　　多次，反复，不断地

例 We succumbed to the pressure **time after time**. 我们一次又一次地屈服于压力。

---

attuned to　　　熟悉……；适应……；与……调合或一致

词 attuned [ə'tjuːnd] *a.* 熟悉

真 Rats and other animals need to be highly **attuned to** social signals from others so they can identify friends to cooperate with and enemies to avoid. 老鼠和其他动物需要高度适应来自其他动物的社交信号，这样它们才能识别出是需要合作的朋友，还是需要避开的敌人。

[2020 年英语（二）阅读]

---

behind the scenes　　在幕后；在后台；秘密地

真 Bankers have been blaming themselves for their troubles in public. **Behind the scenes**, they have been taking aim at someone else: the accounting standard-setters. 在公开场合，银行家们一直将他们的问题归咎于自身。而私下他们却一直将矛头对准其他人：会计准则的制定者们。

[2010 年英语（一）阅读]

拓 on the scene 在场 ‖ in secret 秘密地；私下地

---

in memory of　　　作为对……的纪念；纪念

例 The tombstone is erected **in memory of** a great scientist. 墓碑是为纪念一位伟大的科学家而建的。

拓 to the memory of 作为对……的纪念；纪念

---

take cover　　　躲避（炮火、轰炸或坏天气）

例 **Take cover** as quickly as you can, below ground if possible, and stay there until instructed to do otherwise. 要迅速寻找掩体，如有可能，躲入地底下，然后待在那里，直到听到新的指示，否则不要出来。

in search of	寻找	

例 He has had to travel the country **in search of** his grandfather. 他不得不走遍全国寻找他的祖父。

tear into	怒斥，强烈批评	

例 He failed the exam. I **tore into** him. 他考试没及格，我把他狠狠地数落了一顿。

around the world	世界各地	

真 Yet the link between feeling good and spending money on others can be seen among rich and poor people **around the world**, and scarcity enhances the pleasure of most things for most people. 但在世界上，不管是在穷人还是富人中，都能看到感觉幸福和为别人花钱这两件事之间是有联系的，而稀缺性提高了大多数人对大多数事物的乐趣。 [2014 年英语（二）阅读]

sit back	袖手旁观；在一旁闲着	

例 This time they didn't **sit back**. 这一次他们没有袖手旁观。

take after	（在外表、举止方面）像（某家庭成员）；追赶，跟踪	

例 Your daughter **takes after** you. 你女儿长得像你。

do justice to	给……以公正的评价；公平对待；恰当处理	

例 We can't **do justice to** such a complex situation in just a few pages. 我们不可能仅用几页就将这么复杂的形势恰如其分地描述出来。

distinguish...from	区别……和……	

真 Quinn and her colleagues conducted a test to see if rats can **distinguish** a friendly rat **from** a hostile one. 奎因和她的同事进行了一项测试以查看老鼠是否能区分友好的老鼠和不友好的老鼠。 [2020 年英语（二）阅读]

wish for	期望得到	

例 I **wish for** a big room. 我想要一个大房间。

walk up	沿……走去；向上走	

例 You will find the building on your left as you **walk up** the street. 沿这条街走，在你的左边你会发现那个建筑。

wash up	洗脸，洗手；洗餐具；将……冲到岸边

例 She went to the bathroom to **wash up**. 她去洗手间去洗漱。

no other than	只有；除……外没有

例 That basket-woman was **no other than** her stepmother. 那个拿筐子的女人不是别人，正是她的继母。

拓 other than 除……以外；不同于

on record	在唱片上；有记录的；有记载的

真 Contrary to the descriptions **on record**, no systematic evidence was found that levels of productivity were related to changes in lighting. 与实验记录的描述相反，没有系统的证据表明生产力水平与照明的变化有关。 [2010 年英语（一）完形填空]

win over	说服；把……争取过来

真 But to **win over** these young workers, manufacturers have to clear another major hurdle 但是要想把年轻工人争取过来，制造商们还需要清除另外一个主要障碍。[2017 年英语（二）阅读]

go into	进入；参加；撞到；仔细检查或调查；开始某动作

真 Indeed, the Flatiron students might not **go into** IT at all. 的确，Flatiron 学校的学生可能根本不会进入 IT 行业。 [2016 年英语（二）阅读]

count for...	对……来说重要，有价值

真 If the district finds homework to be unimportant to its students' academic achievement, it should move to reduce or eliminate the assignments, not make them **count for** almost nothing. 如果学区觉得家庭作业对于学生的学业不怎么重要，应该减少或免去家庭作业，而不是让它几乎毫无价值。 [2012 年英语（二）阅读]

take steps to do sth.	采取步骤做某事

例 Americans should **take steps to protect** their digital privacy. 美国人应该采取措施以保护他们数字化的隐私。 [2015 年英语（一）阅读]

spring up	出现；涌现；萌芽

例 When some existing obstacles are removed, new ones **spring up**. 当现有的一些障碍被清除，新的障碍又会出现。

abide by 恪守；遵守；服从

真 The company provoked justified outrage in Vermont last week when it announced it was reneging on a longstanding commitment to **abide by** the state's strict nuclear regulations. 上周，该公司在佛蒙特州激起了正当的愤慨，当时该公司宣布放弃遵守该州严格的核法规的长期承诺。 [2012 年英语（一）阅读]

couple...with... 把……与……连接起来

真 This success, **coupled with** later research showing that memory itself is not genetically determined, led Ericsson to conclude that the act of memorizing is more of a cognitive exercise than an intuitive one. 这次（实验的）成功以及后来的研究都表明，记忆力本身并不是由遗传决定的。由此，埃里克松推断出：与其说记忆行为是一种直觉行为，不如说它是一种认知行为。 [2007 年英语（一）阅读]

in quest of 追求；寻求

词 quest [kwest] *n.* 寻找，寻求；搜索；追求

真 The fourth edition of the *Diagnostic and Statistical Manual of Mental Disorders* says "pathological gambling" involves persistent, recurring and uncontrollable pursuit less of money than of the thrill of taking risks **in quest of** a windfall. 第四版《心理障碍诊断统计手册》指出，"病态嗜赌症"是一种持续的、反复的、无法控制的追求，这种追求与其说是为了钱，不如说是追求意外之财而去冒险的兴奋感。 [2016 年英语（二）阅读]

search through 仔细搜索

真 California has asked the justices to refrain from a sweeping ruling, particularly one that upsets the old assumptions that authorities may **search through** the possessions of suspects at the time of their arrest. 加利福尼亚州已经要求法官们避免做出以偏概全的裁决，尤其是有一项裁决推翻了当局在逮捕嫌犯时可以搜查其财物的传统设想。 [2015 年英语（一）阅读]

tell the truth 说实话

例 Lying comes easily to them and they find it almost difficult to **tell the truth**. 说谎对他们来说很容易，他们发现说实话却很困难。

waste away 日渐衰弱；日益消瘦

例 People may grow thin and **waste away** gradually once they have cancer. 一旦患上癌症，人们可能会变得消瘦，并逐渐衰弱下去。

the advent of ……的出现；……的到来

真 Even after **the advent of** widespread social media, a pyramid of production remains, with a small number of people uploading material, a slightly larger group commenting on or modifying that content, and a huge percentage remaining content to just consume. 甚至在社交媒体广泛出现之后，仍然存在金字塔式的生产结构，即只有小部分人上传信息，稍多的人对此信息进行评论或修改，而绝大部分人仅仅满足于消费这些信息。

[2012 年英语（一）阅读]

vote down 否决；投票击败

真 However, the mechanisms proposed were unwieldy and the Bill was **voted down** following the change in government later that year. 然而，所提出的机制运转不畅，该法案在那年后来政府换届后被否决了。

[2022 年英语（一）阅读]

warn of 警告；提醒

真 At a time when Thomas Piketty and other economists are **warning of** rising inequality and the increasing power of inherited wealth, it is bizarre that wealthy aristocratic families should still be the symbolic heart of modern democratic states. 在托马斯·皮凯蒂和其他经济学家提醒人们注意不平等的加剧和因世袭财富而不断扩大的权力时，奇怪的是这些富裕的世族竟仍然是现代民主国家的核心象征。

[2015 年英语（一）阅读]

at the height of 在……最高峰；在鼎盛时期

真 As much of Mexico City shut down **at the height of** a panic, cases began to crop up in New York City. 随着墨西哥城在恐慌最严重的时候关闭，纽约市开始出现病例。

[2010 年英语（二）完形填空]

fall for 迷恋；信以为真；上当

例 He says that men tend to **fall for** pretty faces, while women are highly attracted to men with fat wallets. 他说男性更容易对漂亮女性心动，而女性更容易被经济实力雄厚的男性所吸引。

拓 be infatuated with 迷恋

DAY 13

a series of
一系列；一连串

真 Glasgow's year as European capital of culture can certainly be seen as one of **a complex series of** factors that have turned the city into the powerhouse of art, music and theatre. 格拉斯哥作为欧洲文化之都的这一年当然可以被看作是一系列使这座城市成为艺术、音乐和戏剧中心的复杂因素之一。

[2020 年英语（一）阅读]

above all
最重要的是；首先；尤其 ◇

真 **Above all**, even in dense forest, you should be able to spot gaps in the tree line due to roads, train tracks, and other paths people carve through the woods. 最重要的是，即使在茂密的森林里，你也应该能够发现树木间的缝隙，因为有一些小的道路、火车轨道和人们在树林中开辟的其他道路。

[2019 年英语（一）完形填空]

train of thought
思路；思绪；一连串的思想或思路

真 He asserted, also, that his power to follow a long and purely abstract **train of thought** was very limited, for which reason he felt certain that he never could have succeeded with mathematics. 他还断言，自己在深入理解冗长且完全抽象的思维方面的能力是有限的，因此他认定自己在数学方面根本不可能有大的作为。

[2008 年英语（一）翻译]

agree on
对……达成一致；同意；对……取得一致意见

真 But most find it difficult to **agree on** what a "general education" should look like. 但是大多数人发现，对于"通识教育"的界定人们很难达成共识。 [2011 年英语（一）阅读]

拓 agree upon 对……取得一致意见；达成协议

on the board
在董事会；在布告栏上；在那块木板上

词 board [bɔːd] *n.* 董事会；布告；板

真 But the researchers believe that outside directors have an easier time of avoiding a blow to their reputations if they leave a firm before bad news breaks, even if a review of history shows they were **on the board** at the time any wrongdoing occurred. 但是研究人员相信，外部董事如果在坏消息传开之前就离开公司，就能较为轻松地避免声誉受损，即便在审查过往记录时发现公司当年出现违法行为时他们尚且在任。 [2011 年英语（二）阅读]

拓 on board 在船（或火车、飞机）上 ‖ across the board 全面的；全体的

a string of　一连串；一系列 ⟡⟡⟡

词 string [strɪŋ] *n.* 一连串的事物；绳子；成列或成行的人

真 As a News Feature article in *Nature* discusses, **a string of** lucrative awards for researchers have joined the Nobel Prizes in recent years. 正如《自然》杂志上的一篇新闻特写文章所讨论的那样，近年来，一系列为研究人员颁发的奖金丰厚的奖项加入了诺贝尔奖的行列。

[2014 年英语（一）阅读]

DAY
13

with ease　轻易地，不费力地，容易地 ⟡⟡⟡

真 With or without permission, they straddle laws, jurisdictions and identities **with ease**. 不管有没有得到允许，他们都能轻易跨越法律、司法和身份的限制。

[2013 年英语（二）阅读]

拓 in a breeze 轻而易举地

fill up　填补；装满 ⟡⟡

例 Unconsciously and unintentionally we **fill up** the gaps and supplement the dream-images. 我们会不自觉地填补梦境中未被想起的空白和增补梦的意象。

go forth　出发，向前 ⟡⟡⟡

真 It was the purpose and responsibility of great minds to **go forth** and seek out the truth, which they believed to be founded in knowledge. 那些伟大的人物的目标和责任就是出发去寻找真理，他们坚信，真理是建立在知识之上的。

[2020 年英语（一）翻译]

(be) removed from　有区别；不同；遥远；关系远 ⟡⟡⟡

真 We **are** even farther **removed from** the unfocused newspaper reviews published in England between the turn of the 20th century and the eve of World War II, at a time when newsprint was dirt-cheap and stylish arts criticism was considered an ornament to the publications in which it appeared. 20 世纪初到二战前夕，英国报纸上的评论主题自由，而我们现在距离这样的评论甚至越来越远了；当时，新闻用纸相当低廉，高雅的文艺评论被认为能够为刊登它们的报刊增光添彩。

[2010 年英语（一）阅读]

拓 be different from 与……不同

in addition to　加之，除……之外 ◇

真 This will help to grow your internal network, **in addition to** being a nice break in the work day. 这除了能让你在工作日得到一次很好的休息之外，还将有助于扩大你的内部关系网。

[2020 年英语（二）阅读]

by chance 偶然地；意外地；非有意地

例 discovered **by chance** a long lost antique vase 偶然发现一个丢失已久的古董花瓶

拓 by accident 偶然；意外地

offer up 提供；奉献；祭献

真 The lesson is not that you should make your personal life an open book, but rather, when given the option to **offer up** details about yourself or painstakingly conceal them, you should just be honest. 这并不是说你应该把自己的个人生活变成人尽皆知的事，而是说，当你可以选择是提供关于你自己的细节或是煞费苦心地隐藏它们时，你只需诚实面对。

[2020 年英语（二）阅读]

urge...to 敦促，怂恿，激励

例 The government and insurance industry have been **urged to** collaborate to calm public fears. 该国政府和保险业被督促携手合作，以平息公众的恐慌。

拓 egg on 怂恿

sit on 成为……的成员；拖延，压着不办

例 How many people **sit on** the commission? 该委员会有多少成员？

seek out 找到；找出

例 Children **seek out** regularities and rules in acquiring language. 儿童在学习语言过程中会找出各种规律和规则。

opt to do sth. 选择做某事

真 More Americans are **opting to** work well into retirement, a growing trend that threatens to upend the old workforce model. 越来越多的美国人选择工作到退休，这一日益增长的趋势可能会颠覆旧的劳动力模式。

[2022 年英语（二）阅读]

拓 choose to do sth. 选择做某事

settle down 过更安定或宁静的生活；定居；使安静下来

真 Even more surprising is that more than half of "unretirees"—those who plan to work in retirement or went back to work after retiring—said they would be employed in their later years even if they had enough money to **settle down**, the survey showed. 调查显示，更令人

惊讶的是，超过一半的"不退休人士"——计划在退休后继续工作或退休后重返工作岗位的人，声称即使他们有足够的钱过安稳的生活，也会在晚年继续工作。

[2022 年英语（二）阅读]

team up (with) 　（与某人）一起工作（尤指为一共同目标）；合作　　◯◯◯

真 It is advised in Paragraph 5 that those with one degree should **team up with** high-paid postgraduates. 第 5 段建议只有一个学位的人与收入高的研究生合作。[2022 年英语（一）阅读]

hunt down 　对……穷追到底　　◯◯◯

真 Were it not for opportunities to observe these beautiful, wild creatures close to home, many more people would be driven by their fascination to travel to wild areas to seek out, disturb and even **hunt** them **down**. 如果不是有机会在家附近观察到这些美丽的野生动物，更多的人会被它们的魅力驱使着去野外寻找和打扰它们，甚至对它们穷追到底。[2022 年英语（一）阅读]

analogous to 　类似于，类同于　　◯◯◯

真 Beginning in 2006, some scientists have argued that plants possess neuron-like cells that interact with hormones and neurotransmitters, forming "a plant nervous system, **analogous to** that in animals," said lead study author Lincoln Taiz. 从 2006 年开始，一些科学家认为植物拥有与激素和神经递质相互作用的神经元样细胞，形成了"一个植物神经系统，类似于动物的神经系统，"该研究的主要作者林肯·塔伊兹说。　　[2022 年英语（一）完形填空]

拓 similar to 类似于

enroll in　　加入；注册，登记

真 Mr. Roth has three community-college students **enrolled in** a work-placement program, with a starting wage of \$13 an hour that rises to \$17 after two years. 罗斯先生让三名社区大学的学生加入了实习项目，给他们的时薪最开始是 13 美元，两年后涨到了 17 美元。

[2017 年英语（二）阅读]

watch out (for)　　小心，当心；提防

例 The art market works through snobbery and sleight of hand, but here it becomes a bit like a TV shopping channel—**watch out**, the dead-eyed determination to shift product is showing. 惊艳的才华和灵巧的双手创造了艺术作品，但是在这里，它变得有点儿像电视购物——小心，不要让盲目的购买决定改变产品本身的意义。

拓 be careful 当心

engage in　　参加；从事

真 "There is one and only one social responsibility of business," wrote Milton Friedman, a Nobel prize-winning economist, "That is, to use its resources and **engage in** activities designed to increase its profits." 曾获得过诺贝尔奖的经济学家米尔顿·弗里德曼写道："企业有且仅有一种社会责任，那就是运用它的资源，致力于旨在增加自身利润的活动。"

[2016 年英语（一）阅读]

on impulse　　一时冲动，心血来潮

词 impulse ['ɪmpʌls] *n.* 冲动；脉冲；刺激 *v.* 推动

例 A new study in the journal shows that people who enjoy a traditional Thanksgiving meal are less likely to buy things **on impulse**. 该期刊中的一项研究表明，那些喜欢传统感恩节美食的人不太可能冲动购物。

拓 out of impulse 一时冲动

for the most part　　大多数情况下；主要地；多半

真 Yet **for the most part**, the animal kingdom moves through the world downloading. 然而，在很大程度上，动物界基本活在被动消费的世界中。 [2012 年英语（一）阅读]

拓 in most cases 大部分情况下 ‖ in most situations 在大多数情况下

a/the majority of 　大多数；大部分

真 "I think that, for **the majority of** scientific papers nowadays, statistical review is more essential than expert review," he says. "我认为，对于现今大多数科技论文而言，统计数据审核比专家审核更加重要。"他说。 [2015 年英语（一）阅读]

拓 at large 大多数

in order to 　为了；以便

真 **In order to** "change lives for the better" and reduce "dependency," George Osborne, Chancellor of the Exchequer, introduced the "upfront work search" scheme. 为了"让生活变得更美好"，同时降低"依赖性"，财政大臣乔治·奥斯本提出了一个"求职先于补助"计划。 [2014 年英语（一）阅读]

stand by 　站在旁边；袖手旁观；支持；坚持

真 the stranger **standing by** you 站在你身边的陌生人 [2015 年英语（二）完形填空]

switch on 　开启；接通

例 Just **switch on** the environmentally friendly votive, leave it in direct sunlight and—like those solar yard spike-lights—it continually does its thing. 只需打开环保采光，将其置于阳光直射处，就像那些太阳灯一样，它就会一直工作。

by far 　到目前为止

例 That's the best way, **by far**, to become a better, more confident writer. 目前为止，那是成为一个更好、更自信的作家的最好方法。

拓 up to this point 迄今为止

superior to 　优于；比……优越

真 He adds humbly that perhaps he was "**superior to** the common run of men in noticing things which easily escape attention, and in observing them carefully." 他谦虚地补充道：或许自己"在注意到容易被忽略的事物，并对其加以仔细观察方面优于常人"。[2008 年英语（一）翻译]

on the surface 　在表面上；外表上

真 How do archaeologists know where to find what they are looking for when there is nothing visible **on the surface** of the ground? 当地表上看不到任何东西的时候，考古学家是如何知道他们要找的东西在哪的呢？ [2014 年英语（一）阅读]

draw out　　取出；拟订；拉长；导致

真 The bargain is very pure: Employee puts in hours of physical or mental labor and employee **draws out** life-sustaining moola. 这种交易非常纯粹：员工花费体力或脑力劳动以获得维持生计的金钱。

[2015 年英语（二）阅读]

the bulk of　　大部分的；大多数的；主要的

真 Rested in the Pacific Ocean, Mauna Kea's peak rises above **the bulk of** our planet's dense atmosphere, where conditions allow telescopes to obtain images of unsurpassed clarity. 莫纳克亚山坐落在太平洋上，其峰顶穿越了地球上大部分稠密的大气层，那里的条件使得望远镜可以获得无比清晰的图像。

[2017 年英语（一）阅读]

exclude...from　　把……排除在外

真 You are now **excluded from** the work environment that offers purpose and structure in your life. 现在，你被排除在工作环境之外，而正是那份工作为你提供生活的目标和架构。

[2014 年英语（一）阅读]

set a threshold for　　给……设定门槛

真 A designer is most likely to be rejected by CFW for **setting a** high age **threshold for** models. 一位设计师遭到哥本哈根时装周拒绝，很可能是因为其对模特设定过高的年龄门槛。

[2016 年英语（一）阅读]

拓 on the threshold of 即将开始

designate...as...　　指定……为……；委任……为……

真 They had pushed the agency to **designate** the bird **as** "endangered", a status that gives federal officials greater regulatory power to crack down on threats. 他们曾敦促该机构将该鸟类划归为"濒危物种"，这样就可以赋予联邦官员更多的管制权力去减少威胁。

[2016 年英语（二）阅读]

real estate　　房地产；不动产

真 While more families buck an older-generation proclivity to leave kids in the dark about **real estate** decisions. 然而，越来越多的家庭反对老一辈人让孩子们对房产决策一无所知的倾向。

[2019 年英语（二）阅读]

at the mercy of　在……的支配下

例 The actors are afraid of letting themselves be **at the mercy of** the film director and producer, who have more control over the movie's final editing. 演员们都很怕将自己置于电影导演和制片人的制约之下，因为他们对影片的最终剪辑拥有更多的控制权。

to the core　彻底的，十足的；直至核心

词 core [kɔː(r)] *n.* 核心；要点；果心

例 She is an innovator and entrepreneur **to the core**, and this role suits her perfectly. 她是彻彻底底的革新者和企业家，这个头衔非常适合她。

拓 top to bottom 从上到下；彻底的 ‖ thorough ['θʌrə] *a.* 彻底的；完全的

take part in　参加

例 Most of the parents thought their children would fall behind if they did not **take part in** such activities. 大多数家长认为如果他们的孩子不参加这些活动，就会落后于别人。

be aware of　明白，知道；察觉到；意识到

真 We **are aware of** and take responsibility for the impact the fashion industry has on body ideals, especially on young people. 我们清楚时尚行业对于理想身材的影响，特别是对年轻人，我们对此负有责任。　[2016 英语（一）阅读]

拓 be unaware of 不知道，没有察觉到

burn out　不再热衷；烧坏；烧尽

真 Then his marriage failed, his career **burned out** and his drinking became serious. 接着他的婚姻破裂了，他对事业倦怠了，酗酒也更严重了。　[2013 年英语（二）阅读]

back and forth　反复地，来回地

真 Pairs of opponents hit the ball **back and forth** until one winner emerges from all who entered. 每组对手来回击球，直至所有参赛的人中出现了一个获胜者。　[2019 英语（一）阅读]

拓 to and fro 往复的，来来回回的

get the best of　战胜，击败；对……占有优势

真 There is only one way...to **get the best of** an argument—and that is to avoid it. 在争论中唯一的获胜方式就是避免争论。　[2019 英语（一）阅读]

DAY 14

in conflict 不一致；有矛盾

例 This is important since some principles may be **in conflict**. 这非常重要，因为有些原则可能相互冲突。

confine...to... 将……限制在……以内

真 **Confine** your comment **to** matters you understand. 发表评论时不要超出自己所了解的事情的范围。 [2014 英语（二）阅读]

count on 指望；依靠，期待

真 Even as we humans **count on** forests to soak up a good share of the carbon dioxide we produce, we are threatening their ability to do so. 当我们人类正指望森林吸收我们制造的大量二氧化碳时，我们也在对森林吸收二氧化碳的能力造成威胁。 [2019 英语（二）阅读]

the same as 与……一样，与……一致

真 The drive to discover is deeply rooted in humans, much **the same as** the basic drives for food or shelter. 探索的欲望深深扎根于人类，就如同人类对食物和住所的基本需求一样。

[2018 英语（二）完形填空]

come to 来到，到达；达到；结果是

真 It is surely a good thing that the money and attention **come to** science rather than go elsewhere. 财富和注意力流向科学领域而不是其他地方是一件好事。 [2014 英语（一）阅读]

over time 随着时间的流逝

真 Parents need to remind their children that their needs and desires may change **over time**. 家长需要提醒孩子他们的需求和心愿可能会随着时间而改变。 [2019 英语（二）阅读]

show up 出席，到场；露出，显出

真 First two hours, now three hours—this is how far in advance authorities are recommending people **show up** to catch a domestic flight. 最初是两个小时，现在是三个小时——这是管理部门建议搭乘国内航班的旅客提前到达机场的时间。 [2017 英语（一）阅读]

restore one's bearings 找回方向

真 You may be surprised how quickly identifying a distinctive rock or tree can **restore your bearings**. 你可能会惊喜地发现，辨别一块特别的岩石或树会很快地帮你找回方向。

[2019 英语（一）完形填空]

suffer from
患病；遭受；忍受，忍耐

真 The kind of paper that purports to show that people who eat more than one kilo of broccoli a week were 1.17 times more likely than those who eat less to **suffer** late in life **from** pernicious anaemia. 这类论文旨在说明，每周吃超过一公斤西兰花的人晚年患重症贫血的可能性是吃西兰花少的人的 1.17 倍。

[2019 年英语 (一) 阅读]

拓 have trouble with 与……有纠纷；有……的病痛

come in handy
有用处

真 This is where supermarkets and their anonymity **come in handy**. 这就是超市和它的匿名性发挥作用的地方了。

[2013 年英语 (二) 阅读]

make money
赚钱；盈利；发财致富

真 the pressure to **make money** 赚钱的压力

[2014 年英语 (一) 阅读]

拓 earn money 赚钱

call forth
唤起，引起；振作，鼓起

真 In most of the homeless gardens of New York City the actual cultivation of plants is unfeasible, yet even so the compositions often seem to represent attempts to **call forth** the spirit of plant and animal life. 要在纽约大多数无家可归者的花园里面培育植物，是很难实现的，但即便如此，这些花园的布局似乎体现了人们唤起植物与动物生命力的尝试。

[2013 年英语 (一) 阅读]

there and then
当场，当即

真 When you start a conversation from **there and then** move outwards, you will find all of a sudden that the conversation becomes a lot easier. 当你以此作为交谈的开始，然后向外延伸，你会发现突然之间你们的交谈变得容易多了。

[2018 年英语 (二) 阅读]

on the whole
总的来说

真 People are, **on the whole**, poor at considering background information when making individual decisions. 总的来说，人们在做个人决定的时候对于背景信息的考虑不太周全。

[2013 年英语 (一) 完形填空]

拓 all things considered 从整体来看

for one thing   首先；一方面

真 **For one thing**, conversations about wildfires need to be more inclusive. 首先，对于森林野火的探讨应该将更多的因素考虑进来。 [2017 年英语（二）阅读]

拓 at the beginning 首先；从一开始；起初；从头开始

start with   以……作为开始

真 To take this approach to the New Englanders normally means to **start with** the Puritans' theological innovations and their distinctive ideas about the church. 以这种方法看待新英格兰人通常意味着要从这些清教徒的神学变革和他们关于教堂的独特的理念入手。

[2009 年英语（一）阅读]

拓 begin with 从……开始

be characterized by   以……为特征

真 He argued that human evolution **was characterized by** a struggle he called the "survival of the fittest," in which weaker races and societies must eventually be replaced by stronger, more advanced races and societies. 他认为人类进化是以他称为"适者生存"的斗争为特征的，其中较弱的种族和社会最终一定被更强、更高级的种族和社会所取代。[2009 年英语（一）阅读]

拓 be distinguished by 具有……的特性；以……为特征

cut off   切断，使隔绝；切下；打断，停止

真 Foreign bureaus have been savagely **cut off**. 驻外分社被无情地撤掉。 [2011 年英语（二）阅读]

拓 keep apart 分离；隔开

a variety of   各种各样的……；种种

真 To find their sites, archaeologists today rely heavily on systematic survey methods and **a variety of** high-technology tools and techniques. 为了找到它们的遗址，今天的考古学家在很大程度上依靠系统的调查方法以及各种各样的高科技工具和技术。[2014 年英语（一）阅读]

get ready   准备好

真 Many see that the country is **getting ready** to build lots of new power plants to meet our energy needs. 许多人看到，国家正在准备建造许多新的发电厂来满足我们的能源需求。

[2005 年英语（一）阅读]

拓 be up for 准备好

flesh out　充实（某事物）；增加细节或详情　○○○

词 flesh [fleʃ] *v.* 充实 *n.* 肉

真 Now that you have developed a topic into a tentative thesis, you can assemble your notes and begin to **flesh out** whatever outline you have made. 既然你已经把一个话题发展成一个试探性的论题，你就可以整理笔记，开始充实你之前列好的提纲。　[2008 年英语（一）阅读]

far from　远非，远离　○○○

真 And it (Fundamental Physics Prize) is **far from** the only one of its type. 而且这种类型的奖项可不是只有基础物理学奖。　[2014 年英语（一）阅读]

as often as　像……一样频繁；每当　○○○

真 The defining term of intelligence in humans still seems to be the IQ score, even though IQ tests are not given **as often as** they used to be. 虽然智商测试不像过去用得那样多了，但对人类智力进行定义的仍然是智商测试分数。　[2017 年英语（一）阅读]

embark on/upon　从事；着手，开始工作　○○○

真 Although more than half of Harvard undergraduates end up in law, medicine or business, future doctors and lawyers must study a non-specialist liberal-arts degree before **embarking on** a professional qualification. 尽管一半以上的哈佛本科生最终主修法律、医学或者商业，但在开始专业资格学习之前，这些未来的医生和律师必须要获得一个非专业的文科学位。　[2011 年英语（一）阅读]

拓 set about 着手；开始做……

at the expense of　以……为代价；由……付费，由……承担费用　○○○

真 Furthermore, the highest CEO salaries are paid to outside candidates, not to the cozy insider picks, another sign that high CEO pay is not some kind of depredation **at the expense of** the rest of the company. 此外，最高的首席执行官薪水都是支付给外部候选人的，而不是内部轻松挑选出的候选人，这是表明给首席执行官高薪并不是以牺牲公司其他员工利益为代价的另一个标志。　[2020 年英语（二）阅读]

拓 at the price of 以……的价格；以……的代价

in action　起作用；在行动　○○○

真 Rosenberg, the recipient of a Pulitzer Prize, offers a host of examples of the social cure **in**

action. 普利策奖获得者罗森伯格提供了许多实践中的社会治愈方法的例子。

[2012 年英语（一）阅读]

close to　　接近于；在附近

It has not gotten anywhere **close to** that, and one big reason is sticker shock: Passengers must pay \$85 every five years to process their background checks. 实际人数远未达到这一目标，一大原因在于标价冲击波。乘客每五年须缴纳 85 美元才能进行背景调查。

[2017 年英语（一）阅读]

lead up to　　导致；使话题（渐渐）转向

Instead of including that paragraph, she added one that described Lengel's crabbed response to the girls so that she could **lead up to** the A & P "policy" he enforces. 她没有把那段话写进去，而是新增了一段描写兰格尔对女孩们的粗暴回应，进而引出兰格尔推行的 A&P "政策"。

[2008 年英语（一）阅读]

together with　　和；连同

These tools can help you win every argument—not in the unhelpful sense of beating your opponents but in the better sense of learning about the issues that divide people, learning why they disagree with us and learning to talk and work **together with** them. 这些工具可以帮助你赢得每一场辩论——不是在毫无帮助的意义上击败你的对手，而是在更好的意义上了解使人们产生分歧的问题，了解他们为什么跟我们意见不太一致，并学会与他们交流和合作。

[2019 年英语（一）阅读]

stay with　　陪着；和；粘附

"We wake up from dreams happy or depressed, and those feelings can **stay with** us all day," says Stanford sleep researcher Dr. William Dement. 斯坦福睡眠研究员威廉·德门特博士说："我们从梦中醒来，有时高兴，有时沮丧，这些情绪会伴随我们一整天。"

[2005 年英语（一）阅读]

that is (to say)　　也就是说；即；换言之

Many of us lose time by engaging in unnecessary actions; **that is to say**, we procrastinate when it comes to the more important things we need to do right now. 我们当中的许多人通过把时间花在不必要的事情上而浪费了时间；也就是说，我们拖延了那部分原本需要花在当下更重要的事情上的时间。

take (...) into account　把……加以考虑，把……考虑进去

真 Dr. Myers and Dr. Worm argue that their work gives a correct baseline, which future management efforts must **take into account**. 迈尔斯博士和沃尔姆博士称，他们的研究工作提供了一个正确的基准数据，这一数据将是未来的管理层所必须考虑的。

[2006 年英语（一）阅读]

拓 take ... into consideration 考虑；考虑到；顾及

throw into　使进入（某一状态）；扔进

真 Gap year experiences can lessen the blow when it comes to adjusting to college and being **thrown into** a brand new environment. 空档年的经历会减少学生适应大学和身处一个全新环境时遭受的打击。

[2017 年英语（二）阅读]

all but　除……之外全部都；几乎，差一点

真 **All but** two pieces sold, fetching more than £70 million, a record for a sale by a single artist. 所有作品中只有两件没有售出，销售额超过了 7000 万英镑，创造了单个艺术家的拍卖纪录。

[2010 年英语（二）阅读]

earn one's living　谋生，挣钱维持生计

真 Teaching has traditionally been the method whereby many intellectuals **earn their living**. 教书在传统上是很多知识分子谋生的手段。

[2006 年英语（一）阅读]

拓 make a living/seek a livelihood/earn a living 谋生

treat to　款待，招待

真 You won't be eating out a lot, but save your pennies and once every few months **treat** yourself **to** a set lunch at a good restaurant. 你不总是外出就餐，但你会把钱攒起来，每隔几个月就去一家高档的餐厅好好款待一下自己。

[2010 年英语（二）阅读]

beyond dispute　无可争议；无疑地

词 dispute [dɪ'spjuːt] n. 辩论；争吵；意见不同

例 That the internet has considerably changed our life is now **beyond dispute**. 互联网已经极大地改变了我们的生活，这是无可争议的。

拓 beyond doubt 毫无疑问；确凿无疑 ‖ rest assured 放心；确信无疑

slip in　　悄悄溜进去

真 Skin moisturizers are advertised as part of morning beauty rituals, **slipped in** between hair brushing and putting on makeup. 广告宣称早上化妆要抹保湿霜，这让润肤霜的使用悄悄地成为梳头和上妆之间的必要程序。 [2013 年英语（二）阅读]

saturate...with　　使充满

真 In the early days, too, longlines would have been more **saturated with** fish. 而且，早些年的多钩长线渔网本可以挂住更多的鱼。 [2006 年英语（一）阅读]

cope with　　（成功地）应付，（妥善地）处理

真 "It's just that they have so much more to **cope with**," says Dr. Yehuda. 耶胡达医生说："只是她们（女性）要应付的事情太多。" [2013 年英语（二）阅读]

crack down (on)　　严厉打击；镇压

例 In January-April fixed-asset investment rose by 30.5%—the fastest rate since 2004, when the authorities **cracked down** sharply to curb excessive investments. 从一月到四月，固定资产投资增长了 30.5%，这是自 2004 年以来政府采取措施严厉打击过度投资后出现的最大涨幅。

live in　　住在

真 Today we **live in** a world where GPS systems, digital maps, and other navigation apps are available on our smart phones. 现在我们生活在一个智能手机上装有全球定位系统、数字地图和其他各种导航应用程序的世界。 [2019 英语（一）完形填空]

stay put　　安于现状；留在原处不动

真 The norms of culture in Western civil services suit those who want to **stay put** but is bad for high achievers. 西方公务员的文化模式适合那些希望安于现状的人，但对取得卓越成就的人来说却不利。 [2012 英语（一）阅读]

be fond of　　喜欢，喜爱；爱好

例 He **is** very **fond of** Chinese classical literature and has spent some time reading Tang poetry. 他很喜欢中国古典文学，花了一段时间去读唐诗。

to be fair　　公平；公正；公平地说

真 The purpose of editing the *News of the World* was not to promote reader understanding, **to be fair** in what was written or to betray any common humanity. 编辑《世界新闻报》的目的不

是为了提升读者的理解能力，不是为了在报道中追求公平，也不是为了揭露共有的人性。

[2015 年英语（一）阅读]

even if/though 即使，虽然

真 **Even if** families don't sit down to eat together as frequently as before, millions of Britons will nonetheless have got a share this weekend of one of the nation's great traditions: the Sunday roast. 即使一家人不再像以前那样频繁地坐在一起吃饭，数百万英国人这个周末仍然可以分享英国的一大传统：周日烤肉。

[2020 年英语（一）阅读]

DAY
14

go through 详细检查；经历，遭受

真 The court has ruled that police don't violate the Fourth Amendment when they **go through** the wallet or pocketbook of an arrestee without a warrant. 最高法院已经裁定，警方在没有搜查令的情况下搜查被捕者的钱包或皮夹并没有违反宪法第四条修正案。

[2015 年英语（一）阅读]

straight up   直率的；真实的；（酒）不加冰块的   ◯◯◯

真 When Liam McGee departed as president of Bank of America in August, his explanation was surprisingly **straight up**. 利亚姆·麦吉 8 月份辞掉美国银行总裁的职位时，他的理由直白得出人意料。   [2011 年英语（一）阅读]

in business   经商；在经营；在商界   ◯◯◯

真 But his primary task is not to think about the moral code, which governs his activity, any more than a businessman is expected to dedicate his energies to an exploration of rules of conduct **in business**. 但是，他的首要任务并不是考虑支配自己行动的道德规范，就如同人们不能指望商人将他的精力投入到探索行业行为规范当中一样。   [2006 年英语（一）阅读]

dream up   虚构，凭空想出   ◯◯◯

真 In previous eras of drastic technological change, entrepreneurs smoothed the transition by **dreaming up** ways to combine labor and machines. 在以往技术迅猛革新的时代，企业家们依靠构想将人工与机器相结合实现了平稳过渡。   [2018 年英语（一）阅读]

be at a standstill   处于停顿状态   ◯◯◯

真 Retail sales of food and drink in Europe's largest markets **are at a standstill**, leaving European grocery retailers hungry for opportunities to grow. 在欧洲最大的市场里，食品和饮料的零售已陷入停滞状态，这让欧洲的食品杂货零售商极度渴求新的发展机遇。

[2010 年英语（一）阅读]

拓 bring to a standstill 使处于停顿状态

touch on/upon   关系到，涉及   ◯◯◯

真 As Hagel notes, Brynjolfsson and McAfee indeed **touched on** his point in their book. 正如哈格尔所指出的，布林约尔弗森和安德鲁·麦凯菲的确也在书中谈到了他的观点。

[2014 年英语（二）阅读]

拓 make reference to 提到，谈及

as to   至于，关于   ◯◯◯

真 Official retrospections continue **as to** why London 2012 failed to "inspire a generation." 官方依旧在反省 2012 年伦敦奥运会为何没有"激发一代人"。   [2017 年英语（二）阅读]

lump together　把……合在一起（考虑）　

真 Databases used by some companies don't rely on data collected systematically but rather **lump together** information from different research projects. 一些公司数据库中的数据并非系统性地采集而得，而是将不同研究项目的信息混杂在一起。　　[2009 年英语（一）阅读]

put up　提供；建造；举起；提高；提名；暂住　

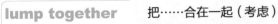

真 Among the most popular: paternity and kinship testing, which adopted children can use to find their biological relatives and families can use to track down kids **put up** for adoption. 其中，最受欢迎的是亲子和亲族鉴定。利用这种鉴定，被领养的孩子可以找到有血缘关系的亲属，而家人则借此追查被收养孩子的下落。　　[2009 年英语（一）阅读]

bring together　集合；使……团结起来　

真 But the market generates interest far beyond its size because it **brings together** great wealth, enormous egos, greed, passion and controversy in a way matched by few other industries. 但市场产生的利益远远超过其规模，因为它汇集了巨大的财富、极度的自负、贪婪、激情和争议，这是其他行业所无法比拟的。　　[2010 年英语（二）阅读]

拓 come together 集合

in keeping with　和……一致，与……协调　

真 But **in keeping with** our examination of southern intellectual life, we may consider the original Puritans as carriers of European culture, adjusting to New World circumstances. 但是为了与我们对美国南部思想生活的研究保持一致，我们可以将最初的清教徒们视作欧洲文化的传承者，他们适应了新大陆的环境。　　[2009 年英语（一）阅读]

burst into　闯入；情绪的突然发作　

真 The room **burst into** laughter; the man looked puzzled and hurt. 全屋人爆发出一阵笑声；那个人看上去既困惑又伤心。　　[2010 年英语（二）阅读]

拓 break into 闯入；破门而入

no more than　不过，仅仅　

真 But with homework counting for **no more than** 10% of their grades, students can easily skip half their homework and see very little difference on their report cards. 但是，一旦家庭作业只占成绩不到 10% 的比例，学生就很容易忽略掉一半的作业，而在成绩单上也看不出多少差别。　　[2012 年英语（二）阅读]

financial assistance　财政资助

真 Even demographics are working against the middle class family, as the odds of having a weak elderly parent—and all the attendant need for physical and **financial assistance**—have jumped eightfold in just one generation. 甚至连人口统计数据也对中产家庭不利，因为家庭中出现一个年老衰弱的父亲或母亲——以及随之而来的体力和经济上的援助需求——的几率在一代人的时间内增加了八倍。

[2007 年英语（一）阅读]

as well　也，又

真 That said, there is a way in which grade forgiveness satisfies colleges' own needs **as well**. 也就是说，"成绩宽恕"在某种程度上也满足了大学自身的需求。　[2019 年英语（一）阅读]

拓 as much 也 ‖ as such 同样地；也

store away　贮存，储存；储备；收起来

真 My mind seems to be able to cope and the information is **stored away** neatly. 我的大脑似乎有能力处理这些信息，并将其有序地存储于大脑中。　[2013 年英语（二）翻译]

拓 put sth. away 贮存某事物，把某事物收起来

in common　共同，共有，共用

真 find the things which you and that person have **in common** 找到你和那个人的共同之处

[2018 年英语（二）阅读]

academic community　学术界；学术团体

真 The solution is to change the mindset of the **academic community**, and what it considers to be its main goal. 解决办法是改变学术界的心态，以及它认为的主要目标。

[2013 年英语（一）阅读]

learn about　了解；得知；学习

真 allow archaeologists to **learn about** what lies beneath the ground without digging 使考古学家不用挖掘就可以了解地下的情况　[2014 年英语（一）阅读]

integrate with　与……结合；与……合并

真 The idea is to force social scientists to **integrate** their work **with** other categories, including health and demographic change; food security; marine research and the bio-economy; clean, efficient energy; and inclusive, innovative and secure societies. 这一想法将迫使社会科学家将他们的工作同其他领域的工作相结合，包括健康和人口变化，食品安全，海洋研究，生物经济，清洁、高效的能源，以及包容、创新、安全的社会。 [2013 年英语（一）阅读]

conflict with　　与……矛盾，与……冲突

真 The White House argued that Arizona's laws **conflicted with** its enforcement priorities, even if state laws complied with federal statutes to the letter. 白宫认为，即使亚利桑那州的法律与联邦法规严格相符，该州的法律也与联邦的执法优先权冲突。 [2013 年英语（一）阅读]

take to　　开始做，逐渐习惯于做；喜欢，亲近

真 Ericsson and his colleagues have thus **taken to** studying expert performers in a wide range of pursuits, including soccer. 埃里克松和他的同事们因此开始研究许多领域（包括足球领域）中的精英。 [2007 年英语（一）阅读]

as well as　　以及；既……又，除……之外（还）

真 It is hard to get right, and requires a remarkable degree of vision, **as well as** cooperation between city authorities, the private sector, community groups and cultural organisations. 这很难做好，它需要远见卓识，以及城市当局、私营部门、社区团体和文化组织之间的合作。 [2020 年英语（一）阅读]

at hand　　可能很快发生的，即将到来；在手边，在附近

真 But that doesn't mean crucial ethical issues involving AI aren't **at hand**. 但这并不意味着涉及人工智能的重要伦理问题不会很快发生。 [2019 年英语（一）阅读]

press for　　迫切要求；催促；敦促

真 Instead of a plan of action, they continue to **press for** more research—a classic case of "paralysis by analysis." 他们没有出台行动计划，只是继续迫切要求进行更多的研究，这是"分析导致行为麻痹"的一个典型案例。 [2005 年英语（一）阅读]

bear/keep in mind　　记住，记在心里

真 "Whether you're a politician or a parent, it might be helpful to **keep in mind** that trying to maintain eye contact may backfire if you're trying to convince someone who has a different set of beliefs than you," said Minson. 明森说："无论你是政客还是家长，如果你试图说服与你有不同信仰的人，保持眼神交流可能会适得其反。记住这一点可能会有所帮助。" [2020 年英语（一）阅读]

真正的交流不在于你说了什么，而在于对方听了什么。 **197**

no matter how (what, when, who)　无论怎样（什么、何时、何人）

真 Mental health allows us to view others with sympathy if they are having troubles, with kindness if they are in pain, and with unconditional love **no matter who** they are. 心理健康可以让我们在别人陷入麻烦之时，同情他人；在别人痛苦之时，友善待人；无论是谁，都能给予其无条件的关爱。

[2016 年英语（一）阅读]

be made of　由……所组成；由……造成

真 But under anti-bribery laws, proof must **be made of** concrete benefits, such as approval of a contract or regulation. 但是依照反贿赂法，只有获得实际的好处才能算作证据，诸如签署一份合同或批准一项法规。

[2017 年英语（一）阅读]

multiply by　乘以；乘上

真 Scoring is now based on a statistical population distribution among age peers, rather than simply dividing the mental age by the chronological age and **multiplying by** 100. 现在，计分是基于同龄人之间的统计人口分布，而不是简单地将心理年龄除以时间年龄再乘以 100。

[2007 年英语（一）阅读]

neither...nor　既不……也不……

真 We **neither** understand **nor** respect each other, and we have no basis for compromise or cooperation. 我们既不理解也不尊重彼此，没有妥协或者合作的基础。

[2019 年英语（一）阅读]

break down　分解；拆分；失败；出故障

真 **break down** problems into bite-sized chunks 将问题分解为小的模块　[2016 年英语（二）阅读]

in pursuit of　寻求，追求

例 They were encouraged to sort out priorities, to cut expenses, and then to seek passive income **in pursuit of** financial independence. 他们被鼓励列出优先顺序、裁减支出以及寻求工作以外的收入以追求经济独立。

build up　逐步建立；增加，增进；增强；发展；形成

例 **build up** a culture of cooperation 建立起合作的文化氛围

gain/make profit　获利；盈利

真 The report, by John Houghton of Victoria University in Australia and Graham Vickery of the OECD, makes heavy reading for publishers who have, so far, **made** handsome **profits**. 澳大利亚维多利亚大学的约翰·霍顿和经合组织的格雷厄姆·维克里共同撰写的这份报告使至今一向获利丰厚的出版商们如芒在背。

[2008 年英语（一）阅读]

owe...to　把……归功于；把……归因于

例 He is so humble that he **owes** his success more **to** luck than to ability. 他如此谦逊，以至于将自己的成功更多地归结为运气，而不是能力。

decline in　在……方面下降

词 decline [dɪ'klaɪn] *n./v.* 下降；变少 *v.* 拒绝；谢绝

真 The sharp hit to growth predicted around the world and in the UK could lead to a **decline in** the everyday services we depend on for our well-being and for growth. 全世界和英国经济增长预期将会遭遇重挫，这会使我们提升幸福感和推动发展所依赖的日常服务逐渐式微。

[2017 年英语（一）阅读]

as if/though　好像，仿佛

真 treat robots **as if** they are fellow beings 把机器人当成好像是同类一样

[2020 年英语（二）阅读]

all over　遍及，到处

真 recruit players from **all over** the world 从世界各地招募球员　[2018 年英语（一）阅读]

拓 in all places 到处

take...as　认为；把……当作

真 First, consumers may **take** CSR spending **as** a "signal" that a company's products are of high quality. 首先，消费者可能将 CSR 支出视为公司产品具有高品质的一个"信号"。

[2016 年英语（一）阅读]

out of the way　把……移开；袖手旁观

真 Parents, he says, can get a lot out of using their devices to speak to a friend or get some work **out of the way**. 他说，通过使用数码设备和朋友聊天或者完成一些工作，父母可以获益良多。

[2017 年英语（二）阅读]

拓 pull out 脱离；退出

act on 按照……行事；对……起作用

真 "The basic compact underlying representative government", wrote Chief Justice John Roberts for the court, "assumes that public officials will hear from their constituents and **act on** their concerns". "代议制政府默认的基本契约，"法庭的首席法官约翰·罗伯兹写道，"是假定公务人员将会听从其选民的要求，并为他们办事。"
[2017 年英语（一）阅读]

拓 in accordance with 按照，遵照

stay out of 置身于……之外

真 That the antismoking lobby was out to destroy our way of life and the government should **stay out of** the way? 还记得怀疑者们坚持认为反对吸烟的游说者们是为了毁掉我们的生活方式，而政府对于吸烟这件事应该置身事外吗？
[2005 年英语（一）阅读]

拓 keep out of 远离

work through 完成，解决

真 All of us **work through** problems in ways of which we're unaware, she says. 她说，我们都是通过一些自己意识不到的方法来解决问题的。
[2009 年英语（一）阅读]

soak up 吸收，摄取

真 Even as we humans count on forests to **soak up** a good share of the carbon dioxide we produce, we are threatening their ability to do so. 即使我们人类要指望森林来吸收我们产生的很大一部分二氧化碳，我们也确实在威胁着森林的这项能力。 [2019 年英语（二）阅读]

charge sb. with 以……指控某人；赋予某人（某种职责）

真 I have excluded him because, while his accomplishments may contribute to the solution of moral problems, he has not been **charged with** the task of approaching any but the factual aspects of those problems. 我之所以将他排除在外，是因为尽管他的成就可能会有助于解决道德问题，但他承担的任务只不过是探究这些问题的事实层面而已。 [2016 年英语（一）阅读]

拓 accuse sb. of sth. 以某事指控某人 ‖ entrust sb. with sth. 托付给某人某事

beef up 改善；加强；改进；提高

真 Yet as distrust has risen toward all media, people may be starting to **beef up** their media literacy skills. 然而，随着人们对各类媒体的信任逐渐缺失，人们开始提升自己的媒体素养。

[2018 年英语（一）阅读]

拓 polish up 改善，提高

access to　　　　通往……的道路；有权使用

真 But it did so while holding its nose at the ethics of his conduct, which included accepting gifts such as a Rolex watch and a Ferrari automobile from a company seeking **access to** government. 尽管这家公司对他的道德准则嗤之以鼻，因为他接受一家公司的劳力士手表和法拉利汽车，但这家公司也试图以此打通政府关系。　　　　[2017 年英语（一）阅读]

neglect of　　　　对……的忽视

真 This seems a justification for **neglect of** those in need, and a rationalization of exploitation, of the superiority of those at the top and the inferiority of those at the bottom. 这似乎是对有需要的人的忽视，对剥削的合理化，对上层人士优越和底层人士卑劣的合理化解释。

[2011 年英语（一）阅读]

拓 give a cold shoulder 冷漠对待；使受到冷遇

out of date　　　　过期；过时

真 This top-down conception of the fashion business couldn't be more **out of date** or at odds with the feverish world described in *Overdressed*, Elizabeth Cline's three-year indictment of "fast fashion." 这种自上而下的时尚行业理念已经完全过时了，与伊丽莎白·克莱因在其《过度着装》一书中所描述的疯狂世界大相径庭，这本书是她耗时三年完成的对"快时尚"的指控。　　　　[2013 年英语（一）阅读]

拓 behind the times （思想、方法等）落伍，过时，陈旧

a handful of　　　　少数；少量；一小部分

真 Quite a lot, according to **a handful of** scientists quoted in the News Feature. 据新闻专栏所采访的一些科学家所说，有很多。　　　　[2014 年英语（一）阅读]

be married to sb.　　　与某人结婚

真 By the third generation, one third of Hispanic women are married to non-Hispanics, and 41 percent of Asian-American women **are married to** non-Asians. 到了第三代，三分之一的西班牙裔女性嫁给了非西班牙裔人，41% 的亚裔女性嫁给了非亚裔人。[2006 年英语（一）阅读]

拓 make a match of it 结婚

at all costs　不惜任何代价，无论如何

真 Privacy protection must be secured **at all costs**. 必须不惜一切代价保护隐私。

[2018 年英语（一）阅读]

拓 at all accounts 无论如何

know of/about　听说，知道，了解

真 One of the astonishing revelations was how little Rebekah Brooks **knew of** what went on in her newsroom, how little she thought to ask and the fact that she never inquired how the stories arrived. 有一个令人吃惊的真相：丽贝卡·布鲁克斯竟然对发生在她的编辑部的事情知之甚少，她几乎不想加以过问，实际上她也从不询问这些新闻报道的来源。

[2005 年英语（一）阅读]

拓 hear of 听说；据说

the more...the more　越……越……

真 In fact, **the more** new things we try—**the more** we step outside our comfort zone—the more inherently creative we become, both in the workplace and in our personal lives. 事实上，我们尝试的新事物越多——离自己的舒适区越远——就会在职场及个人生活中都拥有更强的内在创造力。

[2009 年英语（一）阅读]

拓 the less...the less 越少……越少…… ‖ more and more 越来越……

for the sake of　为了……；看在……的份上

真 It is only in recent years that we hear the more honest argument that predators are members of the community, and that no special interest has the right to exterminate them **for the sake of** a benefit, real or fancied, to itself. 直到最近几年，我们才听到比较坦诚的论点，那就是肉食动物也是这个生态群落的成员，没有任何特殊利益群体有权为了自身利益——无论是真实的，还是假想的——去消灭它们。

[2010 年英语（一）翻译]

拓 for sb./sth.'s sake 为了某人／某事物（起见）

subscribe to　预订；订阅

词 subscribe [səbˈskraɪb] v. 预订；订阅；申购

真 Copyright rested with the journal publisher, and researchers seeking knowledge of the results would have to **subscribe to** the journal. 论文版权归期刊出版商所有，其他想了解实验结果的研究者要订阅期刊才能阅读该论文。

[2008 年英语（一）阅读]

拓 subscribe for 认购；预订

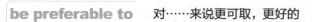

be preferable to　　对……来说更可取，更好的　　○○○

词 preferable ['prefrəbl] *a.* 更可取的；更合意的

真 In the world of capuchins, grapes are luxury goods (and much **preferable to** cucumbers). 在僧帽猴的世界中，葡萄是奢侈品（要比黄瓜更受青睐）。 　　[2005 年英语（一）阅读]

a matter of　　一个关于……的问题 / 事情　　○○○

真 We have no land ethic yet, but we have at least drawn nearer the point of admitting that birds should continue as **a matter of** intrinsic right, regardless of the presence or absence of economic advantage to us. 尽管我们还未形成土地伦理观，但是我们至少更接近问题的要点，即承认鸟类应该继续存在，这是生物物种权利的问题，不管它们对我们是否具有经济价值。 　　[2010 年英语（一）翻译]

ever since　　从那时起，自那时以来　　

真 Now the nation's top patent court appears completely ready to scale back on business-method patents, which have been controversial **ever since** they were first authorized 10 years ago. 现在美国的最高专利法院似乎已经做好了减少商业方法专利数量的充分准备，而这类专利从十年前首次获得批准以来就备受争议。 　　[2010 年英语（一）阅读]

拓 since then 从那时起 ‖ from now on 从现在开始

be conscious of　　意识到……，注意到……，知道　　

词 conscious ['kɒnʃəs] *a.* 意识到的；故意的；神志清醒的

真 This forces users to **be more conscious of** their role in passing along information. 这要求用户更加留意自己在信息传递中所扮演的角色。 　　[2018 年英语（一）阅读]

拓 realize ['riːəlaɪz] *v.* 认识到；了解；实现

have little/no use for　　很少 / 没有用处　　

真 Journalistic tastes had changed long before his death, and postmodern readers **have little use for** the richly upholstered Vicwardian prose in which he specialized. 早在他去世之前，新闻业的品位就已经发生了变化，后现代的读者们几乎不再需要他所擅长的辞藻华丽的维多利亚 - 爱德华风格的散文。 　　[2010 年英语（一）阅读]

transform...into　　把……转变成　　

词 transform [træns'fɔːm] *n.* 改变；使变形；转化

真 But it takes collective scrutiny and acceptance to **transform** a discovery claim **into** a mature discovery. 但是将科学发现的声明转变为成熟的科学发现，则要经过集体的检验并被人们所接受。

[2012 年英语（一）阅读]

拓 turn into 变成；进入

give birth to   生育

真 Adeline Alvarez married at 18 and **gave birth to** a son, but was determined to finish college. 阿德琳·阿尔瓦雷斯 18 岁结婚并生有一子，但她却决心要完成大学学业。

[2008 年英语（一）阅读]

拓 in labor 临产；分娩

easy game   容易捕获的猎物；容易受骗的人

真 The large, slow-growing animals were **easy game**, and were quickly hunted to extinction. 大型的、生长缓慢的动物很容易成为猎物，很快就被猎杀灭绝了。   [2006 年英语（一）阅读]

put down to   归因于

真 The former has been **put down to** social effects, such as a strong tradition of valuing education. 前者一直被归因于社会效应，例如重视教育的深厚传统。

[2008 年英语（一）完形填空]

拓 put down 写下；放下；镇压

come to light   显露出来，被众人得知

真 Thousands of Aztec artifacts **came to light** during the digging of the Mexico City subway in the 1970s. 20 世纪 70 年代挖掘墨西哥城的地铁时，成千上万件阿兹特克人的手工制品才得以面世。

[2014 年英语（一）阅读]

civil servant   公务员

真 If the trade unionist Jimmy Hoffa were alive today, he would probably represent **civil servants**. 如果工会主义者吉米·霍法今天还活着的话，他很可能会代表公务员了。

[2012 年英语（一）阅读]

at stake   有风险；在胜败关头；成败难料

真 And more is **at stake** here than individual objects. 除了单个的物品，还有更多的东西岌岌可危。

[2022 年英语（一）阅读]

be concerned about　关注，关心；对……有兴趣

真 Surveys show that younger generations **are** more **concerned about** climate change. 诸多调查显示，年轻一代更关心气候变化。 [2022 年英语（二）阅读]

deal with　处理；克服；讨论；打交道

真 learn to **deal with** disappointment 学会应对失望 [2022 年英语（二）翻译]

eliminate...from　从……删除、消除、清除

真 It's past time for transparency with these institutions, and it's past time to **eliminate** zoos **from** our culture. 这些机构的公开透明已经是过去的事了，把动物园从我们的文化中剔除也已成为往事。 [2022 年英语（一）阅读]

spare no effort to　不遗余力，全力以赴

真 Zoos, which **spare no effort to** take care of animals, should not be subjected to unfair criticism. 不遗余力地照顾动物的动物园不应该受到不公正的批评。 [2022 年英语（一）阅读]

拓 try one's best to 竭尽全力

be bound up with　与……密切相关

真 His status in Lord Wellington's headquarters and the recognition given to him for his work **were bound up with** the class politics of the Army at the time. 他在威灵顿勋爵总部的地位以及他因工作而得到的认可与当时军队的阶层政治密切相关。 [2022 年英语（一）翻译]

拓 be connected with 与……相关

fit for/to　适合，适于

真 The survey conducted by Harris Poll indicates that over half of the retirees are physically **fit for** work. 哈里斯民意测验所做的调查表明，超过一半的退休人员身体健康，适合工作。

[2022 年英语（二）阅读]

take root　生根，扎根；建立，确立

真 The idea that plants have some degree of consciousness first **took root** in the early 2000s. 植物有一定程度的意识，这一观点是在 21 世纪初首次确立的。 [2022 年英语（一）完形填空]

cut down (on)　减少……的数额或数量；少用或少买（某物）

真 You might have to **cut down on** the amount of exercise or sport you do. 你可能不得不减少你所做的锻炼或运动的量。 [2022 年英语（二）完形填空]

lock away	将……妥善锁起

真 Museums **locked** some of them **away** in the dark. 博物馆把其中一些锁在了暗处。

[2022 年英语（一）阅读]

single (sb./sth.) out	选出，挑出

真 Indeed, in "An International Perspective on New Zealand's Productivity Paradox" (2014), the Productivity Commission **singled out** the low quality of managerial capabilities as a cause of the country's poor productivity growth record. 事实上，在《关于新西兰生产率悖论的国际视角》（2014 年）中，生产力委员会将管理能力低下选作该国生产率增长记录不佳的一个原因。

[2022 年英语（一）阅读]

allow for	在计算、估计、考虑时包括

真 No matter how you "enhance" enclosures, they do not **allow for** freedom, a natural diet or adequate exercise. 无论你如何"改善"围栏，它们都不会将自由、自然的饮食或充分的锻炼考虑进去。

[2022 年英语（一）阅读]

in one's own right	凭借自身的权利、资格、力量等

真 His story of self-improvement and hard work would make a fascinating biography **in its own right**, but represents something more than that. 他自我提升和努力工作的故事本身就可以成为一部引人入胜的传记，但它所代表的意义远不止于此。

[2022 年英语（一）翻译]

本单元资源

in response to 　　作为对……的回答或反应

真 **In response to** another petition last year about banning fake lawns, which gathered 30,000 signatures, the government responded that it has "no plans to ban the use of artificial grass". 去年，另一份关于禁止使用人造草坪的请愿书收集了 3 万个签名，对此政府回应说，政府"并未打算禁止使用人造草坪"。　　　　　[2023 年英语（二）阅读]

拓 react to 对……作出反应 ‖ respond to 回应；应对

make a profit 　　盈利，赚钱

真 Here's a common scenario that any number of entrepreneurs face today: you're the CEO of a small business, and though you're **making a** nice **profit**, you need to find a way to take it to the next level. 现在许多企业家都面临着这样一个常见的情况：你是一家小企业的首席执行官，虽然你当下利润可观，但你需要想办法让它更上一层台阶。　　[2023 年英语（二）完形填空]

拓 any number of 许多 ‖ make money 赚钱

steer clear of 　　避开，绕开

真 And for authors who wish to **steer clear of** citation cartel activities: when an editor, a reviewer, or a support service asks you to add inappropriate references, do not oblige and do report the request to the journal. 对于那些希望避开引用卡特尔活动的作者来说：当编辑、审稿人或支持服务要求你添加不适当的参考文献时，不要勉强，而务必要向期刊报告这一要求。　　　　　[2023 年英语（一）阅读]

be subject to 　　可能受……影响的；易遭受……的

真 It **is subject to** family influence. 它受到家庭的影响。　　[2023 年英语（二）阅读]

拓 be subjected to 受到，经受

in the quest for 　　追求；探索，设法找到

真 **In the quest for** the perfect lawn, homeowners across the country are taking a shortcut—and it is the environment that is paying the price. 为了追求完美的草坪，全国的房主都在走捷径，而付出代价的是环境。　　　　　[2023 年英语（二）阅读]

put out 　　发布；出版；扑灭；生产；把……外包

真 AI can also be used to identify the lifestyle choices of customers regarding their hobbies, favourite celebrities, and fashions to provide unique content in marketing messages **put out** through social media. 人工智能还可以用来识别客户的生活方式选择，包括他们的爱好、最喜欢的名人和时尚，从而在社交媒体上发布的营销信息中提供特定的内容。

[2023 年英语 (一) 翻译]

| rent out | 租出 | |

真 I think individuals being able to **rent out** their second home is a good thing. 我认为个人能够出租他们的第二套房子是一件好事。

[2023 年英语 (一) 阅读]

| go ahead | 进行；前进 | |

真 Any plans submitted before that date are considered to be under the previous rules, and can **go ahead** as long as work starts before 15 June next year. 在这一日期之前提交的任何计划都被认为符合之前的规定，只要工程在明年 6 月 15 日前开始，就可以进行。 [2023 年英语 (二) 阅读]

| drive up | 抬高；迫使……上升 | |

真 The moves are the most significant change to building regulations in years, and industry experts say they will inevitably lead to higher prices at a time when a shortage of materials and high labour costs are already **driving up** bills. 这些举措是多年来对建筑法规所作的最重大调整，行业专家表示，在材料短缺和劳动力成本高已经推高成本的情况下，它们将不可避免地导致价格上涨。

[2023 年英语 (二) 阅读]

| interfere with | 干扰，干涉；妨碍 | |

真 There is no experimental evidence showing that it **interferes with** our ability to focus, for instance, wrote psychologists Christopher Chabris and Daniel J. Simons. 例如，没有实验证据表明它 (互联网) 会干扰我们的注意力，心理学家克里斯托弗·沙布里斯和丹尼尔·J. 西蒙斯写道。

[2023 年英语 (二) 阅读]

| cut through | 快速处理；抄近路穿过；开辟 (出路或通道) | |

真 A Twitter account, which claims to "**cut through** the greenwash" of artificial grass, already has more than 20,000 followers. 一个推特账号声称要对人造草的"漂绿快刀斩乱麻"，这个帐号已经有 2 万多名粉丝。

[2023 年英语 (二) 阅读]

注 greenwash 是由"绿色"（green，象征环保）和"漂白"（whitewash）合成的一个新词。用来说明一家公司、政府或是组织以某些行为或行动宣示自身对环境保护的付出但实际上却是反其道而行。这实质上是一种虚假的环保宣传。

be made up of   由……所组成

真 A growth team **is made up of** members from different departments within your company, and it harnesses the power of collaboration to focus exclusively on finding ways to grow. 增长团队由来自公司不同部门的成员组成，它利用协作的力量专注于寻找增长的方法。

[2023 年英语（二）完形填空]

act as   担当

真 These journals can **act as** milk cows where every single article in an issue may cite a specific paper or a series of papers. 这些期刊就像奶牛一样，每一期的每一篇文章都可能引用一篇特定的论文或一系列论文。

[2023 年英语（一）阅读]

serve to   用来；有助于

真 However, the use of artificial grass must comply with the legal and policy safeguards in place to protect biodiversity and ensure sustainable drainage, while measures such as the strengthened biodiversity duty should **serve to** encourage public authorities to consider sustainable alternatives. 然而，人造草的使用必须遵守现有的法律和政策保障措施，以保护生物多样性和确保可持续排水，而加强生物多样性责任等措施应有助于鼓励公共当局考虑可持续的替代方案。

[2023 年英语（二）阅读]

bring...to life   使更生动；使更有趣

真 The parks also help keep America's past alive, working with thousands of local jurisdictions around the country to protect historical sites and to **bring** the stories of these places **to life**. 这些公园还有助于保持美国历史的活力，与全美数千个地方司法机构合作，保护历史遗迹，让这些地方的故事变得生动起来。

[2023 年英语（二）阅读]

on a regular basis   定期地；经常地

真 According to Paragraph 5, most respondents in the survey would go to the national parks **on a regular basis**. 根据第 5 段可知，调查中的大多数受访者会定期去国家公园。

[2023 年英语（二）阅读]

at...cost   以……的成本或代价

真 The function of the "milk cow" journals is to help scholars publish articles **at low cost**. "奶牛"期刊的作用是帮助学者以低成本发表文章。

[2023 年英语（一）阅读]

on top of	另外；熟练掌握；在……之上；紧接着	

真 **On top of** this, they produce value from their extensive educational programs, their positive impact on the climate through carbon sequestration, their contribution to our cultural and artistic life, and of course through tourism. 除此之外，他们还通过众多的教育项目创造价值，通过碳封存对气候产生积极影响，对我们的文化和艺术生活做出贡献，当然还有通过旅游业（创造价值）。

[2023 年英语（二）阅读]

hit home	使深刻认识到（事物的不愉快或困难）；击中要害	

真 "The visualization, particularly those photographs, really **hit home** that this is something that has to be protected," says Alicia Murphy, Yellowstone's park historian. 黄石公园历史学家艾丽西亚·墨菲说："可视化，尤其是那些照片，真的让人深刻认识到，这是必须保护的东西。"

[2023 年英语（一）阅读]

拓 hit the mark 击中要害；击中目标

hand in hand	密切关联；手拉手	

真 A new study published in the journal *Child Development*, by Eveline Crone of the University of Leiden and colleagues, suggests that the positive and negative sides of teenagers go **hand in hand**. 莱顿大学的伊芙琳·克罗恩及其同事发表在《儿童发展》杂志上的一项新研究表明，青少年的积极一面和消极一面是密切相关的。

[2023 年英语（二）阅读]

close in on	（尤指为了进攻）逼近，靠近	

例 The lions tend to **close in on** their prey. 狮子试图逼近它们的猎物。

go in for	爱好（某活动）	

例 I didn't **go in for** poetry seriously, but now I'm beginning to take an interest in it. 我以前不太喜欢诗歌，但现在我开始对它感兴趣了。

do one's utmost to	尽最大努力	

真 We are not boycotting PRH titles but we are **doing our utmost to** ensure that availability for customers remains good despite the lower overall levels of stock. 我们并没有抵制企鹅兰登

书屋，而在尽最大努力确保在企鹅兰登书屋出版的书整体库存较少的情况下，仍能充分满足顾客所需。 [2023 年英语（一）阅读]

拓 do/try one's best to 竭尽全力

on the back burner　搁置一旁

真 While attractive new ideas can be distracting, the team leader must recognize when these ideas don't serve the current goal and need to be put **on the back burner**. 虽然有吸引力的新想法可能会让人分心，但团队领导者必须意识到，当这些想法与当前目标无关时，就需要把它们搁置一旁。 [2023 年英语（二）完形填空]

impact on　对……有影响，有作用

真 Some believe that AI is negatively **impacting on** the marketer's role by reducing creativity and removing jobs, but they are aware that it is a way of reducing costs and creating new information. 一些人认为，人工智能削弱了创造力并减少了工作机会，从而对营销人员的角色产生了负面影响，但他们意识到这是一种降低成本和创造新信息的方式。 [2023 年英语（一）翻译]

stock up on　存储；置办

真 Indeed, it was frequently the first stop for merchants looking to sell their wares and **stock up on** supplies for their own journeys. 事实上，这里经常是商人们期待能出售商品和为自己的旅行储备物资的第一站。 [2023 年英语（一）完形填空]

in comparison　相比之下

例 The amount of carbon dioxide released by human activities such as burning coal and oil is small **in comparison**. 相比之下，燃烧煤炭和石油等人类活动所释放的二氧化碳量很小。

in favor　得到……的支持；得宠

真 The bill proved largely popular and sailed through Congress with large majorities **in favor**. 事实证明，该法案大受欢迎，并以绝大多数人的支持顺利通过了国会。 [2023 年英语（一）阅读]

拓 out of favor 失去……的支持；失宠

make a change　做出改变

真 Horn said similar registration requirements could benefit struggling cities and towns, but "if we want to **make a change** in the housing market, the main one is we have to build a lot

more." 霍恩说，类似的登记要求可能会使陷入困境的城镇受益，但"如果我们想改变住房市场，最主要的是我们必须建造更多的房子"。 [2023 年英语（一）阅读]

拓 make a difference 产生影响；有关系

on course 可能会做成某事；在正确的航线上

真 It needs someone who can unite the interdisciplinary team and keep them **on course** for improvement. 它需要一个能够团结跨部门团队并使其保持改进的人。

[2023 年英语（二）完形填空]

unaware of 不知道；没有意识到

真 Most customers were simply **unaware of** the premium version and what it offered. 大多数客户根本不知道有高级版本以及它具有什么功能。 [2023 年英语（二）完形填空]

under...control 受到……的控制

真 Its home prices are **under** strict **control**. 它（新英格兰地区）的房价受到严格控制。

[2023 年英语（一）阅读]

in short term 短期内

真 "A lot of workers are servicing the tourist industry, and the tourism industry is serviced by those people coming **in short term**," Castle said, "and so it's a cyclical effect." "很多人都在为旅游业服务，而旅游业是由那些短期来的人提供服务的，"卡塞尔说，"所以这是一种周期性效应。" [2023 年英语（一）阅读]

拓 in long term 长期内

an average of 平均

真 The industry also claims that people who lay fake grass spend **an average of** £500 on trees or shrubs for their garden, which provides habitat for insects. 该行业还称，种植假草的人平均花费 500 英镑在花园的树木或灌木上，这些树木或灌木为昆虫提供了栖息地。

[2023 年英语（二）阅读]

increase by 增加了

真 Meanwhile, the number of annual visitors has **increased by** more than 50% since 1980, and now stands at 330 million visitors per year. 与此同时，自 1980 年以来，每年的游客数量增长了 50% 以上，现在每年达到 3.3 亿人次。 [2023 年英语（二）阅读]

range from...to... 从……到……；（在一定幅度内）变化 ○○○

真 Despite these challenges, Jackson captured dozens of striking photos, **ranging from** majestic images like his now-famous snapshot of Old Faithful, **to** casual portraits of expedition members at the camp. 尽管面临这些挑战，杰克逊还是拍下了数十张令人震撼的照片，从他现在著名的"老忠实者"快照，到探险队成员在营地的随意肖像照，不一而足。

[2023 年英语（一）阅读]

(be) associated with 与……有关；和……联系在一起 ○○○

真 "There may be costs **associated with** our increased reliance on the Internet, but I'd have to imagine that overall the benefits are going to outweigh those costs," observes psychology professor Benjamin Storm. 心理学教授本杰明·斯道姆说："我们对互联网的依赖程度越来越高，这可能会需要付出一些代价，但我不得不想象，总的来说，好处将超过这些代价。"

[2023 年英语（二）阅读]

take care of 照顾；处理；负责 ○○○

真 In adolescence, helpless and dependent children who have relied on grown-ups for just about everything become independent people who can **take care of** themselves and help each other. 在青春期，无助和依赖成年人的孩子成为独立的人，他们可以照顾自己，互相帮助。

[2023 年英语（二）阅读]

in order for 为了 ○○○

真 But **in order for** your growth team to succeed, it needs to have a strong leader. 但是为了让你的增长团队成功，它需要一个强大的领导者。

[2023 年英语（二）完形填空]

lead the way 引领，带路，示范 ○○○

真 The national parks are valuable in that they **lead the way** in tourism. 国家公园的价值在于它们引领着旅游业的发展。

[2023 年英语（二）阅读]

in ruins 毁坏；严重受损；破败不堪 ○○○

真 It is believed that around 12,000 to 15,000 caravanserais were built along the Silk Road, although only about 3,000 are known to remain today, many of which are **in ruins**. 据信，丝绸之路沿线建造了大约 1.2 万至 1.5 万间商队客栈，但目前已知仅存约 3000 间，其中许多已成为废墟。

[2023 年英语（一）完形填空]

| **in crisis** | 处于危机之中 |

真 But the government is right about one thing: U.S. national parks are **in crisis**. 但是（美国）政府说的有一件事是对的：美国的国家公园正处于危机之中。 [2023 年英语（二）阅读]

| **in debt** | 负债；欠情 |

例 He was a compulsive gambler and often heavily **in debt**. 他嗜赌成性，经常负债累累。

| **remove...from** | 把……从……移开，拿开；去掉；从……开除 |

真 The trade magazine *The Bookseller* reported that Waterstones branch managers were being told to **remove** PRH books **from** prominent areas such as tables, display spaces and windows, and were "quietly retiring them to their relevant sections". 行业杂志《书商》报道称，水石书店的分店经理被告知，要把企鹅兰登书屋的书从桌子、展示区和橱窗等显眼区域移走，并"悄悄地把它们撤回相关区域"。 [2023 年英语（一）阅读]

| **stay out late** | 在外面待到很晚 |

真 The participants filled out questionnaires about how often they did things that were altruistic and positive like sacrificing their own interests to help a friend, or rebellious and negative, like getting drunk or **staying out late**. 参与者填写了一份问卷，内容是关于他们做利他和积极的事情的频率，比如牺牲自己的利益来帮助朋友，或者是叛逆和消极的事情，比如喝醉或在外面待到很晚。 [2023 年英语（二）阅读]

| **integrate into** | 使融入；结合在一起 |

真 Another issue is that, while climate change is well **integrated into** some subjects and at some ages—such as earth and space sciences in high schools—it is not as well represented in curricula for younger children and in subjects that are more widely taught, such as biology and chemistry. 另一个问题是，尽管气候变化在某些学科和某些年龄段被很好地融入了——比如高中的地球和空间科学——但在儿童课程和更广泛教授的学科（如生物和化学）中却没有得到很好的体现。 [2023 年英语（一）阅读]

拓 be part of 成为……的一部分

| **trust...to** | 相信（某人会做某事） |

真 The main disadvantage of using AI to respond to customers is that there are concerns about **trusting** personal interactions **to** machines, which could lead not only to the subsequent loss of interpersonal connections, but also to a decrease in marketing personnel. 使用人工智能来回应客户的主要缺点是，人们担心将个人互动托付给机器，这不仅可能导致人际关系随后丧失，还可能导致营销人员减少。 [2023 年英语（一）翻译]

拓 trust...with 托付

buy up	全部（或尽量）买下某物；收购	

真 Now, with record-high home prices and historically low inventory, there's an increased urgency in such regulation, particularly among those who worry that developers will come in and **buy up** swaths of housing to flip for a fortune on the short-term rental market. 如今，在房价创历史新高、库存处于历史低位的情况下，出台此类管控措施的紧迫性变强，这种紧迫感在那些担心开发商会进入市场，买下大片房屋，以求在短租房市场上大赚一笔的人当中尤甚。 [2023 年英语（一）阅读]

拓 flip for 对……感到兴奋不已

go up	上升；上涨；（建筑物）被建造；着火；（喊声）响起	

真 Its rental vacancy rate is **going up** slowly. 它（新英格兰地区）的出租空置率正在缓慢上升。 [2023 年英语（一）阅读]

scale up	增大，扩大（规模或数量）	

真 "As the marketplace adapts to the new requirements, and the technologies that support them, the **scaling up** of these technologies will eventually bring costs down, but in the short term, we will all have to pay the price of the necessary transition," he says. 他说："随着市场适应新的要求以及支持这些要求的技术，这些技术的扩大最终将降低成本，但在短期内，我们都必须为必要的过渡付出代价。" [2023 年英语（二）阅读]

拓 scale down 减少（数量）；缩小（规模或范围）

bring (...) down	（使）降低；把……拿下来；使垮台，推翻	

例 They plan to **bring down** prices on all their products. 他们计划降低所有产品的价格。

result from	起因于；由……造成	

真 It **results from** the wish to cooperate. 它（亲社会行为）产生于合作的愿望。 [2023 年英语（二）阅读]

far behind	与……相差很远	

真 The birth of predatory journals wasn't **far behind**. 掠夺性期刊的诞生也不远了。

[2023 年英语（一）阅读]

plug a/the gap of...	填补……缺口	

真 It's easy to dismiss as absurd the federal government's ideas for **plugging the** chronic funding **gap of** our national parks. 联邦政府填补国家公园长期资金缺口的想法很容易被认为是荒谬的。

[2023 年英语（二）阅读]

stop...from doing sth.	防止……做某事	

真 the necessity to **stop** developers **from** evading taxes 制止开发商逃税的必要性

[2023 年英语（一）阅读]

拓 keep...from... 阻止，抑制；隐瞒

line up	排队；将……排成队；安排（比赛等）；组织准备（人员）	

真 Can anyone really think it's a good idea to allow Amazon deliveries to your tent in Yosemite or food trucks to **line up** under the redwood trees at Sequoia National Park? 有人真的认为，让亚马逊送货到你在约塞米蒂国家公园的帐篷里，或者让快餐车在美洲杉国家公园的红杉树下排队是好主意吗？

[2023 年英语（二）阅读]

attempt to	试图，尝试，企图	

真 Communities throughout New England have been **attempting to** regulate short-term rentals since sites like Airbnb took off in the 2010s. 自 2010 年代 Airbnb 等网站兴起以来，新英格兰地区的社区一直在试图规范短租。

[2023 年英语（一）阅读]

注 **take off** 突然开始流行，突然成功

so that	以便	

真 For this reason, caravanserais were strategically placed **so that** they could be reached in a day's travel time. 出于这个原因，商队客栈都是精心选址而建的，以便商队在一天的旅程内就可以到达。

[2023 年英语（一）完形填空]

as a result	结果，因此	

真 **As a result**, these structures became important centres for cultural exchange and interaction, with travellers sharing their cultures, ideas and beliefs, as well as taking knowledge with them, greatly influencing the development of several civilisations. 结果，这些客栈成为文化交流和互动的重要中心，旅行者分享他们的文化、思想和信仰，并带走知识，极大地影响了几个文明的发展。

[2023 年英语（一）完形填空]

拓 consequently ['kɒnsɪkwəntli] *adv.* 因此 ‖ accordingly [əˈkɔːdɪŋli] *adv.* 因此 ‖ as a consequence 因此，结果

come down　　　下降；流传下来；倒塌；落魄，失势

真 John Kelly, a construction lawyer at Freeths law firm, believes prices will eventually **come down**. Freeths 律师事务所的建筑律师约翰·凯利认为，房价最终会降下来。

[2023 年英语（二）阅读]

come from　　　来自，出自；出生于

真 After all, many of the most interesting books in recent years have **come from** small publishers. 毕竟，近年来许多最有趣的书都出自小型出版商之手。　　[2023 年英语（一）阅读]

a large number of　　　大量的；很多

真 Red flags include **a large number of** citations to an article within the first year. 危险信号包括一篇文章在第一年内被大量引用。　　[2023 年英语（一）阅读]

拓 a small number of 少量的 ‖ a good deal of 大量的

play a (...) role in　　　在……中起（……）作用；在……中扮演（……）角色

例 **play a key role in** the fight to protect the area 在保护该地区的斗争中发挥关键作用

[2023 年英语（一）阅读]

serve as　　　作为，用作

真 Caravanserais **served as** an informal meeting point for the various people who travelled the Silk Road. 商队客栈是沿着丝绸之路而行的各色人的非正式交汇点。

[2023 年英语（一）完形填空]

add to　　　增加；加入，加到

真 **add to** the cost of housebuilding 增加房屋建设成本

step up　　　增加

例 Such debates reflect fierce discussions across the US, as researchers, policymakers, teachers and students **step up** demands for a greater focus on teaching about the facts of climate change in schools. 这样的辩论反映了美国各地的激烈讨论，研究人员、政策制定者、教师和学生都提出了更多要求，要更加重视在学校对气候变化事实进行教学。[2023 年英语（一）阅读]

拓 step forward 前进 ‖ step down 辞职

adhere to   坚持；粘附；拥护，追随

真 Windows and doors will have to **adhere to** higher standards, while there are new limits on the amount of glazing you can have to reduce unwanted heat from the sun. 门窗将必须遵守更高的标准，而同时，对于你可以使用的玻璃数量也有新的限制，以减少来自太阳的多余热量。   [2023 年英语（二）阅读]

注 glazing /'gleɪzɪŋ/ *n.* 玻璃制品

at length   详细地；最后，终于

真 While veterans of previous expeditions had written **at length** about stunning sights, these vivid photographs were another thing entirely. 虽然以前的资深探险家们已经详细地描述了绝美的景象，但这些生动的照片完全是另一回事。   [2023 年英语（一）阅读]

thanks to   由于；幸亏

真 An average extension will probably see around £3,000 additional cost **thanks to** the new regs. 由于这些新规定，一次普通扩建的费用可能会多 3000 英镑左右。 [2023 年英语（二）阅读]

拓 because of 由于；因为

注 reg 是 regulation 的缩写。

hand over   交出；移交

真 Campgrounds are a tiny portion of the overall infrastructure backlog, and businesses in the parks **hand over**, on average, only about 5% of their revenues to the National Park Service. 露营地只占所有待修缮的基础设施的一小部分，而园区里这些做生意的平均只把自己约 5% 的收入上交国家公园管理局。   [2023 年英语（二）阅读]

拓 deliver up 交出，放弃

come to life   表现生动；苏醒；振作起来

真 Poems really **come to life** when they are recited. 诗歌被朗诵出来时才真正变得生动。   [2023 年英语（二）翻译]

head for　　前往；出发；驶向

真 If you're **heading for** your nearest branch of Waterstones, the biggest book retailer in the UK, in search of the Duchess of Sussex's new children's book *The Berch*, you might have to be prepared to hunt around a bit; the same may be true of *The President's Daughter*, the new thriller by Bill Clinton and James Patterson. 如果你要去离你最近的英国最大的图书零售商水石书店的分店寻找苏塞克斯公爵夫人的新童书《海滩》，你可能得准备好四处寻找；找比尔·克林顿和詹姆斯·帕特森的新惊险小说《总统的女儿》可能也是如此。

[2023 年英语（一）阅读]

拓 depart for 去往，动身去…… ‖ start off 出发；离开；起跑

be sensitive to　　对……敏感

真 The non-intrusive delivery of the marketing messages in a way that **is sensitive to** the needs of the target customer is one of the critical challenges to the digital marketer. 以一种对目标客户需求敏感的方式非侵入式地传递营销信息是数字营销人员面临的关键挑战之一。

[2023 年英语（一）翻译]

come into effect　　开始生效，开始实施

真 The rules, which **came into effect** on Wednesday in England, are part of government plans to reduce the UK's carbon emissions to net zero by 2050. 这些规定于周三在英格兰生效，是（英国）政府到 2050 年将英国碳排放降到零的诸多计划之一。　　[2023 年英语（二）阅读]

拓 bring/put sth. into effect 使生效；实行；实施 ‖ take effect 开始实施；开始起作用

be starved of　　缺乏；急需；非常需要

真 If customers are not willing to share data, AI will **be starved of** essential information and will not be able to function effectively or employ machine learning to improve its marketing content and communication. 如果客户不愿意分享数据，人工智能将缺乏必要的信息，无法有效地发挥作用，也无法利用机器学习来改善其营销内容和传播。[2023 年英语（一）翻译]

拓 be badly in need of / be in urgent need of 急需

on a shoestring　　以极少的钱

真 The parks do all this **on a shoestring**. 这些公园用极少的钱在做所有这些事情。

[2023 年英语（二）阅读]

hesitate to	犹豫，不愿意	

真 Waterstones staff **hesitate to** promote big-name authors' books. 水石书店的员工不愿推广知名作家的书。

[2023 年英语（一）阅读]

拓 be reluctant/unwilling to 不愿意

fall off	减少；降低；脱落	

真 Sales of books by mid-list PRH writers **fall off** considerably. 企鹅兰登书屋排名居中的那些作家的图书销量大幅下降。

[2023 年英语（一）阅读]

DAY 17

本单元资源

(be) akin to   与……相似，类似

真 The residents help to look after the children, an arrangement **akin to** alloparenting. 居民们帮忙照看孩子们，这种安排类似于异亲养育。 [2024 年英语（一）阅读]

拓 (be) similar to 类似于

---

on sale   出售，上市；减价出售

真 The size or regularity of markets can vary from season to season, depending on the area's agricultural calendar, and you're likely to find different produce **on sale** at different times of the year. 农贸市集的规模和举办频率可能因季节而异，这取决于该地区的农事日历，你可能会在一年中的不同时间发现不同的农产品在出售。 [2024 年英语（二）翻译]

拓 for sale 待售；供出售

---

work on   努力改善（或完成）；努力说服；研究

真 Then he tried searching for his name to see if a piece he had **worked on** had been published. 然后他试着搜索自己的名字，看看他之前完成的一幅画是否已经发布了。 [2024 年英语（一）阅读]

拓 work at 致力于；努力做

---

be bursting with   爆满；充满

真 With the smell of coffee and fresh bread floating in the air, stalls **bursting with** colourful vegetables and tempting cheeses, and the buzz of friendly chats, farmers' markets are a feast for the senses. 空气中弥漫着咖啡和新出炉面包的香味，摊位上摆满了五颜六色的蔬菜和诱人的奶酪，还有友好交谈的嘈杂声，农贸市集就是一场感官盛宴。 [2024 年英语（二）翻译]

拓 be very full of 爆满；充满

---

burn down   烧毁；（火势）减弱

真 As Roma Agrawal explains in her new delightful book *Nuts and Bolts*, early 17th-century Virginians would sometimes **burn down** their homes if they were planning to relocate. 正如罗玛·阿格拉瓦尔在她颇受欢迎的新书《螺母与螺栓》中所解释的那样，17 世纪早期的弗吉尼亚人如果打算搬迁，有时会烧毁自己的房屋。 [2024 年英语（一）阅读]

---

yield to   屈服；让步；让出（位置等）；给（车辆）让路

例 They chose to fight to the end and would not **yield to** the enemy. 他们选择战斗到底，不向敌人屈服。

---

turn over
翻身；翻转；交，移交；仔细考虑

真 One of the biggest challenges in keeping unsafe aging drivers off the road is convincing them that it's time to **turn over** the keys. 让有安全隐患的老年司机远离道路的最大挑战之一是说服他们是时候交出车钥匙了。 [2024 年英语（二）阅读]

拓 hand in 提交，呈交，上交（尤指书面材料或失物）

call on/upon
请求；号召，呼吁；访问，拜访

真 And so we would **call on** state lawmakers from Richmond to Albany to consider reviewing their own wetlands protections and see for themselves the enormous stakes involved. 因此，我们呼吁从里士满到奥尔巴尼的州立法者考虑一下重新审视他们自己的湿地保护措施，并亲眼看看其中涉及的巨大风险。 [2024 年英语（一）阅读]

in the short term
在短期内，从短期来看

真 As to the prospects for federal legislation, commentators suggest that comprehensive federal privacy legislation seems unlikely **in the short term**. 至于联邦立法的前景，评论人士认为，在短期内，全面的联邦隐私立法似乎不太可能。 [2024 年英语（二）阅读]

拓 in the short run 在短期内，从短期来看

start out as
起初是

真 They **started out as** a novelty feature, but as their use has grown, their benefits have extended within our technologically advanced world. 它们（自动门）起初是一种新奇的设施，但随着使用的增加，其好处在我们这个科技发达的世界里得到了扩展。

[2024 年英语（一）完形填空]

拓 start out by doing sth. 以做某事开始

shore up
加强；改善，提高；支撑

真 States have begun implementing their own solutions to **shore up** protections for consumer-generated health data. 各州已开始实施自己的解决方案，以加强对消费者产生的健康数据的保护。 [2024 年英语（二）阅读]

wipe off
擦干净；消除，除掉；抹去

例 He **wiped off** the words from the blackboard before I could copy them down. 我还没来得及抄下来，他就把黑板上的那些字词给擦掉了。

pull out of　撤离；退出；驶离车站；脱离

真 Nearly 2,000 years ago, as the Romans began to **pull out of** Scotland, they left behind a curious treasure: 10 tons of nails, nearly a million of the things. 大约两千年前，罗马人开始撤离苏格兰，他们留下了一件奇怪的宝藏：十吨钉子，将近 100 万颗。[2024 年英语（一）阅读]

a litany of　冗长的；一连串的

真 High school students eager to stand out in the college application process often participate in **a litany of** extracurricular activities hoping to bolster their chances of admission to a selective undergraduate institution. 渴望在大学申请过程中脱颖而出的高中生通常会参加一连串的课外活动，以期增加他们被筛选严格的本科院校录取的几率。[2024 年英语（二）阅读]

拓 a series of 一系列 ‖ a range of 一系列；一批

be integral to　是……所必需的，不可或缺的

真 Technological innovation **is integral to** economic success. 技术创新对于经济成功来说是不可或缺的。[2024 年英语（一）阅读]

拓 be an integral/essential part of 是……不可或缺的一部分

on one's own　独自；单独；独立地

真 Spending too much time **on your own**, not seeing others, can make you feel lonely and disconnected. 花太多时间独处，不与他人相见，会让你感到孤独和疏离。

[2024 年英语（二）完形填空]

拓 by oneself 独自；单独

bring up　抚养；养育；提出（讨论等）；呕吐

真 Parenting tips obtained from hunter-gatherers in Africa may be the key to **bringing up** more contented children, researchers have suggested. 研究人员表示，从非洲狩猎采集者那里获得的育儿技巧可能是培养出更满足的孩子的关键。[2024 年英语（一）阅读]

拓 bring sb. up against sth. （使）某人直面某事物

put forward　提出（计划、建议等）

真 Write him an email to **put forward** your plan, and ask for his opinion. 给他写一封电子邮件，提出你的计划，并征求他的意见。[2024 年英语（二）写作]

拓 come up with 提出；想出

incorporate...into/in/within 将……包括在内；包含；吸收；使并入

真 Dr Annie Swanepoel, a child psychiatrist, believes that there are ways to **incorporate** them **into** western life. 儿童精神病学家安妮·斯瓦内普尔博士认为，有一些方法可以将它们融入西方生活。 [2024 年英语（一）阅读]

go by （时间）流逝；过去

例 As time **went by** we saw less and less of each other. 随着时间的推移，我们见彼此的次数越来越少。

break with 彻底改变；打破（常规等）；结束与……的关系

真 In a paper published in the *Journal of Child Psychology and Psychiatry*, researchers said that the western nuclear family was a recent invention which **broke with** evolutionary history. 在《儿童心理学和精神病学杂志》上发表的一篇论文中，研究人员说，西方的核心家庭是最近才出现的，它彻底改变了进化史。 [2024 年英语（一）阅读]

type in 键入，输入

真 For example, **type in** "Wizard with sword and a glowing orb of magic fire fights a fierce dragon Greg Rutkowski," and the system will produce something that looks not a million miles away from works in Rutkowski's style. 例如，输入"拿着剑和发光的魔法火球的巫师与恶龙搏斗，格雷格·鲁特科夫斯基风格"，系统就会生成一些看起来与鲁特科夫斯基风格的作品相差不远的东西。 [2024 年英语（一）阅读]

be flooded with 充满；充斥着

真 "It's been just a month. What about in a year? I probably won't be able to find my work out there because the Internet will **be flooded with** AI art," Rutkowski said. "这才过了一个月。那一年后呢？我可能无法在那里找到我的作品，因为互联网将充斥着人工智能艺术。"鲁特科夫斯基说。 [2024 年英语（一）阅读]

拓 **a flood of** 一大批；大量的 ‖ **flood into** 涌入

on the ground 当场；在现场；在地面上；实际

真 While the UK government has stated its ambition for more tree planting, there has been little action **on the ground**. 虽然英国政府信誓旦旦地表示要种植更多的树木，但实际行动却少之又少。 [2024 年英语（二）阅读]

figure out　　找出；想出；弄懂；弄清楚，弄明白　○○○

真 "There is a coalition growing within artist industries to **figure out** how to tackle or mitigate this," says Ortiz. 奥尔蒂斯说："艺术家行业内部正在形成一个联盟，以寻找解决或减少这种情况的方法。"　　　　　　　　　　　　　　　　　　[2024 年英语（一）阅读]

拓 work out 找到（解决办法等）；进展顺利；有满意的结果；锻炼；计算

specialize in　　专门研究（或从事）；专攻　○○○

真 He **specializes in** classical painting digitalization. 他专攻古典主义绘画的数字化。
　　　　　　　　　　　　　　　　　　　　　　　　　　　　　[2024 年英语（一）阅读]

break in　　强行进入；破门而入；训练；**(on)** 打断；搅扰　○○○

例 She longed to **break in on** their conversation but didn't want to appear rude. 她很想打断他们的谈话，但又不愿意显得鲁莽。

conceive of　　想出（主意、计划等）；想象；构想；设想　○○○

真 A more immediate response is to broaden our digital imaginations to **conceive of** AI technologies that don't simply replace jobs but expand opportunities in the sectors that different parts of the country care most about, like health care, education, and manufacturing. 一个更直接的回应是拓宽我们的数字想象力来设想人工智能技术，这些技术并不只是会取代工作，也会在不同地区最关心的领域（如医疗、教育和制造业）扩展机会。
　　　　　　　　　　　　　　　　　　　　　　　　　　　　　[2024 年英语（二）阅读]

make use of　　使用；利用　○○○

真 The problem with open-source AI art generators is that they **make** unauthorized **use of** online images. 开源 AI 绘图生成器的问题在于，它们会在未经授权的情况下使用网上的图像。
　　　　　　　　　　　　　　　　　　　　　　　　　　　　　[2024 年英语（一）阅读]

拓 take advantage of 利用

meet up (with)　　（按照安排）见面，会面　○○○

真 There are groups aimed at new parents, at those who want to try a new sport for the first time, or networking events for those in the same profession to **meet up** and share ideas. 有针对新手父母的团体，有针对那些第一次想尝试新运动的人的团体，也有供同一行业的人士见面并交流分享的社交活动。
　　　　　　　　　　　　　　　　　　　　　　　　　　　　[2024 年英语（二）完形填空]

| **lie in** | 存在；在于 | |

真 The miracle of the Chesapeake Bay **lies** not **in** its depths, but in the complexity of its natural construction, the interaction of fresh and saline waters, and the mix of land and water. 切萨皮克湾的神奇之处不在于它的深度，而在于它复杂的自然构造，淡水和盐水的相互作用，以及陆地和水的交杂混合。

[2024 年英语（一）阅读]

| **benefit from** | 得益于；得利于 | |

真 Shoppers also **benefit from** seeing exactly where—and to who—their money is going. 购买者也从中受益，他们能清楚地看到自己的钱都花在了什么地方，付给了谁。

[2024 年英语（二）翻译]

拓 profit from 从……获利

| **stand up for** | 支持；维护；捍卫；为……辩护 | |

真 It is too easy, and misleading, to see such court rulings as merely **standing up for** the rights of land owners when the consequences can be so dire for their neighbors. 把这样的法院裁决仅仅看作是捍卫土地所有者的权利，这太容易了，也很容易误导人，因为其后果可能对他们的邻居来说是如此可怕。

[2024 年英语（一）阅读]

| **fill out** | 填写（表格等） | |

真 Sue Rexford, the director of college guidance at the Charles E. Smith Jewish Day School, says it is not necessary for a student **filling out** the Common Application to list 10 activities in the application. 查尔斯·E. 史密斯犹太走读学校的大学指导主任苏·雷克斯福德说，学生在填写通用申请表时，没有必要列出 10 项活动。

[2024 年英语（二）阅读]

拓 fill in 填写（表格等）；填满；消磨，打发（时间）

| **not least** | 特别，尤其 | |

真 One possibility was that they merely used their eyes and tried out the plants they found, but that would probably result in a lot of wasted time and energy, **not least** because their eyesight is actually not very good. 一种可能性是，它们（大象）仅仅利用自己的视觉并只尝试它们发现的植物，但这可能会浪费大量的时间和精力，尤其是因为它们的视力实际上不是很好。

[2024 年英语（一）翻译]

拓 not in the least 一点也不；丝毫不

| **hold on** | 握住；坚持不懈；稍等片刻 | ◯◯◯ |

例 They managed to **hold on** until help arrived. 他们成功坚持到了救援到来。

| **make sense** | 有意义；言之有理；明智；合情理 | ◯◯◯ |

真 It would be absurd to try to track the changing price of sports cars since 1695, but to ask the same question of nails **makes** perfect **sense**. 试图追踪自 1695 年以来跑车价格的变化是荒谬的，但针对钉子提出同样的问题是完全有道理的。 [2024 年英语 (一) 阅读]

拓 make sense of 理解 ‖ talk sense 说得有理

| **keep one's promise** | 遵守诺言 | ◯◯◯ |

真 While the FTC is doing what it can to ensure apps are **keeping their promises** to consumers around the handling of their sensitive health information, the rate at which these health apps are hitting the market demonstrates just how immense of a challenge this is. 虽然美国联邦贸易委员会正在尽其所能确保应用程序在处理敏感健康信息方面信守对消费者的承诺，但这些健康应用程序进入市场的速度表明，这是一项多么巨大的挑战。[2024 年英语 (二) 阅读]

| **attach importance to** | 重视；认为……有重要性 | ◯◯◯ |

真 The author holds that the state lawmakers should **attach** due **importance to** wetlands protections. 作者认为，州立法者应给予湿地保护应有的重视。 [2024 年英语 (一) 阅读]

拓 attach... to... 把……附在……上 ‖ attach to (使) 与……有关联

| **(be) exposed to** | 面临；遭受；接触；体验 | ◯◯◯ |

真 For decades we have not taken responsibility for investing in our domestic wood supply, leaving us **exposed to** fluctuating prices and fighting for future supplies of wood as global demand rises and our own supplies fall. 几十年来，我们没有承担起投资国内木材供应的责任，这使我们在全球需求上升而我们自己的供应下降时，面临价格波动，并且还得去争夺未来的木材供应。 [2024 年英语 (二) 阅读]

拓 be faced with 面临

| **on display** | 展览，公开展出 | ◯◯◯ |

真 The monetary value of the objects **on display** is a distant second place in importance. 展品的货币价值在重要性上远远排在第二位。 [2024 年英语 (一) 阅读]

拓 on show 在展出

DAY 17

call for　　　需要；（公开）要求；（去）接

真 The forestry and wood trade body has **called for** urgent action to reduce the country's reliance on timber imports and provide a stable supply of wood for future generations. 林业和木材贸易机构业已呼吁采取紧急行动，减少本国对木材进口的依赖，并为子孙后代提供稳定的木材供应。

[2024 年英语（二）阅读]

拓 call forth 引起；使产生

by all means　　　无论如何；一定；当然可以

真 Ancient art that is displayed in foreign countries **by all means** should be returned to the original country. 在国外展出的古代艺术品，无论如何都应归还给原属国。

[2024 年英语（一）阅读]

拓 by means of 借助……手段；依靠……方法

at first　　　首先；最初；起初；在开始阶段

例 There are ways to regain a social life, but it can feel overwhelming **at first**. 有很多方法可以让你恢复社交生活，但一开始的时候你可能会感到不知所措。

campaign for　　　开展活动以支持或实现……；竞选

真 According to Ortiz, AI companies are advised to **campaign for** new policies or regulation. 在奥尔蒂斯看来，人工智能公司被建议去争取推动出台新的政策或法规。

[2024 年英语（一）阅读]

head off　　　出发，离开；阻止，阻拦；使改变方向

真 When finding their way to waterholes, they **headed off** in exactly the right direction, on one occasion from a distance of roughly thirty miles. 在寻找水坑时，它们（大象）能朝着完全正确的方向前进，有一次还是从距离大约 30 英里的地方出发。　　[2024 年英语（一）翻译]

have one's hands full　　　忙得不可开交；应接不暇

真 Primary care providers **have their hands full** and may not be able to follow through with patients who have trouble driving because they can't turn their heads or remember where they are going—or have gotten shorter and haven't changed their seat settings sufficiently to reach car pedals easily. 初级保健医生忙得不可开交，可能无法跟进那些有驾驶障碍的患者，这

些患者的头部无法转动，或记不住自己要去哪里，或者身材变矮了，但没有把座位相应调整好，以至于无法轻松够到汽车踏板。 [2024 年英语（二）阅读]

(be) entitled to　　有权利、资格做某事

真 Why **are** people who live within a day's drive of London **entitled to** go and see the Elgin Marbles whenever they want, but the people of Athens aren't? 为什么住在距伦敦一天车程内的人有权随时去看埃尔金大理石雕，而雅典人却不行？ [2024 年英语（一）阅读]

put...into practice　　实施，把……付诸实践

真 According to Confor, the UK government's fresh incentives will be too costly to **put into practice**. 根据森林工业联合会所言，英国政府的新激励措施实施起来成本太高。

[2024 年英语（二）阅读]

拓 act out 付诸行动

preclude...from doing sth.　　阻止……做某事

真 What intrinsic factors make the West a suitable home for these artifacts but **preclude** them **from being** preserved and displayed by their countries of origin? 是什么固有的因素使西方成为适合这些文物的家园，而让它们无法在原属国得到保存和展示呢？

[2024 年英语（一）阅读]

拓 prevent...from doing sth. 阻止……做某事

mark out　　画出界限；画出边界；用线画出范围

真 Make sure you **mark out** some time in your diary when you're unavailable for socialising and use this time to relax, rest and recover. 确保在你的记事本上标出一些你不能参加社交活动的时间，利用这段时间来放松、休息和恢复。 [2024 年英语（二）完形填空]

in place　　在正确位置；在工作；准备就绪

真 Without additional protections **in place**, companies may share (and potentially monetize) personal health information in a way consumers may not have authorized or anticipated. 如果没有额外的保护措施就位，这些公司可能会以消费者可能并未授权或预料到的方式共享（并可能变现）其个人健康信息。 [2024 年英语（二）阅读]

拓 in place of 代替；顶替

take the place of 取代；代替；替换

真 Reproductions, even if perfectly made, cannot **take the place of** the authentic objects. 复制品，即使制作得再完美，也不能取代真品。 [2024 年英语（一）阅读]

拓 take sb.'s/sth.'s place 代替；替换 ‖ take place 发生

hold back 拦阻；阻挡

真 Not only will this foster political and social unrest, but it could, as Coyle suggests, **hold back** the sorts of AI technologies needed for regional economies to grow. 这不仅会引发政治和社会动荡，而且正如科伊尔所言，还可能阻碍地区经济增长所需的各种人工智能技术。

[2024 年英语（二）阅读]

refuse to do sth. 拒绝做某事

真 Concern over security is no excuse for **refusing to** return artifacts to their countries of origin. 对安全的担忧不能成为拒绝将文物归还原属国的借口。 [2024 年英语（一）阅读]

拓 turn down 拒绝；把……调低；关小

point at 指，指向；瞄准

例 We set up signs **pointing at** the house so no one would get lost on their way to the party. 我们设置了指向房子的标志，这样就不会有人在去聚会的路上迷路了。

拓 point towards 指，指向 ‖ point out 指出 ‖ point to 指向；提出，指出（重要的事或理由）；暗示；预示

out of sight 在看不见的地方；在视野之外

真 They sometimes travel more than sixty miles to find food or water, and are very good at working out where other elephants are—even when they are **out of sight**. 它们（大象）有时会长途跋涉 60 多英里去寻找食物或水，并且非常善于找出其他大象在哪里——即使那些大象不在它们的视线范围之内。 [2024 年英语（一）翻译]

拓 in sight 可以看见；在视野内

contribute to 为……做出贡献；是……的原因之一；有助于

真 While productive tree planting can deliver real financial benefits to rural economies and **contribute to** the UK's net-zero strategy, the focus of government support continues to be on food production and the rewilding and planting of native woodland solely for biodiversity.

虽然商业林种植可以为农村经济带来实实在在的经济效益，并为英国的净零战略做出贡献，但政府支持的重点仍然是粮食生产及仅出于生物多样性目的的原生林地的再野化和种植。

[2024 年英语（二）阅读]

add up　　把……加起来；合乎情理；有道理

例 The solution—set priorities, **add up** the cost of each item, then consider what else we could buy with the same money. 解决方案——设置优先级，将每件物品所花的钱加起来，然后想一想，用同样这些钱我们可以买些什么其他东西。

拓 add up to 总共是；总计为

play a part　　参与；发挥一部分作用；装模作样

真 Although the cues used by African elephants for long-distance navigation are not yet understood, smell may well **play a part**. 尽管我们尚不清楚非洲象用哪些信号来进行长途导航，但气味很可能起了一部分作用。

[2024 年英语（一）翻译]

work from home　　在家办公

真 This might be especially true if, for example, you are **working from home** and you are missing out on the usual social conversations that happen in an office. 例如，当你在家办公，错过了平日在办公室里总是进行的社交对话时，可能尤为如此。　[2024 年英语（二）完形填空]

what is more　　更重要的是

真 **What is more**, they almost always seem to choose the nearest waterhole. 更重要的是，它们（大象）似乎总是选择距离最近的水坑。

[2024 年英语（一）翻译]

in accordance with　　与……一致；按照……的规定或要求

真 "There could be liability and penalties if a physician does not act **in accordance with** state laws on reporting and confidentiality," she counseled. "如果医生不按照州里有关报告和保密的法律行事，则可能需要担责和面临处罚。"她建议道。

[2024 年英语（二）阅读]

on loan　　通过租借方式；借出的

真 Having said that, I do feel that whatever artifacts find their way to public museums should, in fact, be sanctioned as having been obtained **on loan**, legally purchased, or obtained by treaty. 话虽如此，我确实认为，任何进入公共博物馆的文物，实际上都应该被限定为是通过租借、合法购买或签署协议获得的。

[2024 年英语（一）阅读]

DAY 17

in conclusion 总之；综上所述

例 **In conclusion**, walking is a cheap, safe, enjoyable, and readily available form of exercise. 综上所述，散步是一种廉价、安全、有趣而又随时可以开展的运动形式。

拓 to sum up 总而言之，概括来说

other than 除了……之外；不同；不同于；不

真 By contrast, in hunter-gatherer societies adults **other than** the parents can provide almost half of a child's care. 相比之下，在狩猎采集社会中，父母以外的成年人可以承担起近半数照顾孩子的工作。

[2024 年英语（一）阅读]

meet with 遭遇；受到某种对待；经历；与……会面；满足

真 The American Medical Association's advice has **met with** different responses. 美国医学协会的建议得到了不同的回应。

[2024 年英语（二）阅读]

in many cases 在许多情况下

真 **In many cases** the experts have a hard time agreeing on what is the real object and what is a forgery. 在许多情况下，专家很难就哪个是真品，哪个是赝品达成一致意见。

[2024 年英语（一）阅读]

拓 in any case 无论如何；不管怎样 ‖ in that case 既然那样 ‖ in case of 如果，假使

have a(n) (...) influence on/upon 对……产生（……的）影响

真 High school students who have **had a** strong positive **influence on** their community through an extracurricular activity may impress a college and win a scholarship, says Erica Gwyn, a former math and science magnet program assistant at a public high school who is now executive director of the Kaleidoscope Careers Academy in Atlanta, a nonprofit organization. 埃里卡·格温说，通过课外活动对社区产生强烈积极影响的高中生可能会给大学留下深刻印象，并且可能获得奖学金。埃里卡·格温曾在一所公立高中担任数学和科学磁石计划的助教，现在是亚特兰大一家非营利组织"万花筒"职业学院的执行董事。

[2024 年英语（二）阅读]

miss out 不包括……在内；遗漏；(on) 错失获利（或取乐）的机会

例 Of course I'm coming—I don't want to **miss out on** all the fun! 我当然要来——我可不想错过所有这些乐趣！

be obsessed by 对……着迷，痴迷于

真 I make no apology for **being obsessed by** a particular feature of everyday objects: their price. 我痴迷于日常用品的一个特点：价格。对此我并不感到抱歉。 [2024 年英语（一）阅读]

take a shortcut 抄近路，走捷径

真 The researchers are convinced that the elephants always know precisely where they are in relation to all the resources they need, and can therefore **take shortcuts**, as well as following familiar routes. 研究人员确信，大象总是准确地知道它们相对于其所需要的所有资源的位置，因此可以沿着熟悉的路线走，也可以走捷径。 [2024 年英语（一）翻译]

DAY
17

谢谢你坚持到了这里，

　　逐梦虽难，还请坚持~

PART 02
加分词组

PART
02

give off　　放出，释放

例 **give off** a strong scent 释放一种强烈的气味

bear out　　证实，支持

例 The facts do not **bear out** your assertion that Standard Chartered Bank outperforms Citigroup. 事实并没有证实你的断言，即渣打银行比花旗银行的表现更好。

on the net　　在网上

例 He was much impressed by a saying **on the net** that cities are just like the engine of the society which advances economic growth. 他在网上看到一句话，对其印象非常深刻，它是这么说的："城市就像是一个社会的引擎，促进经济的发展。"

dispose of　　清除，销毁；解决，处理；击败

词 dispose [dɪˈspəʊz] v. 安排；布置

例 It took him 30 minutes to **dispose of** his opponent. 他用了 30 分钟击败对手。

multitude of　　众多，许多

例 The beautiful scenery attracts **multitudes of** tourists. 这片美丽的风景吸引了众多游客。

pave the way for　　为……铺平道路；为……做准备

例 This breakthrough in the negotiation will **pave the way for** the economic recovery. 磋商中的这项突破将为经济复苏铺平道路。

take...to heart　　把……放在心上；关注；牢记

例 That's a lesson that American policy makers will **take to heart**. 美国政策制定者将牢记这个教训。

stock up　　大量储备，备货

例 The authorities have urged people to **stock up** on fuel because of the coming of snowstorm. 由于暴风雪的到来，当局已敦促人们大量储备燃料。

| stick at | 坚持，持之以恒 | ○○○ |

例 If you want to play the guitar well, you've got to **stick at** it. 如果你想练好吉他，你就必须持之以恒。

| at will | 任意，随意 | ○○○ |

例 In ancient times women couldn't travel around **at will**. 古时候，女人不能够随意出行。

| at all events | 无论如何 | ○○○ |

例 **At all events**, the strategy has changed and I have done my best. 无论如何，策略已经发生了改变，而我已经尽力而为了。

| not so much...as | 与其（说）……不如（说） | ○○○ |

例 The Roman poet philosopher Juvenal said men need **not so much** be informed **as** reminded. 古罗马诗人哲学家朱文纳尔说过，人们更需要被记住，而不是被通知。

| wear out | 耗尽；使筋疲力尽；磨损 | ○○○ |

例 The long journey had really **worn** him **out**. 漫长的旅途真让他筋疲力尽了。

拓 give out 筋疲力尽

| come around/round | 来访；如期而至；苏醒 | ○○○ |

例 When he **came around**, he found that he was lying in the bed of a hospital. 当他苏醒过来时，他发现自己正躺在一家医院的病床上。

| at sb.'s disposal | 任某人处理；由某人自行支配 | ○○○ |

例 Tom will have a car **at his disposal** for a whole month. 汤姆将有一辆汽车供他使用一个月。

| on the occasion of | 值此之际 | ○○○ |

例 The book was given to me as a present **on the occasion of** my college graduation ten years ago. 十年前在大学毕业之际，我收到了这本书作为毕业礼物。

| be ready for | 预备好，使准备好 | ○○○ |

例 If you **are ready for** more responsibility, tell your boss you are ready. 如果你已经准备好承担更多的责任，就告诉你的老板你准备好了。

拓 be ready to do sth. 准备好做某事；决心或愿意做某事

as a matter of fact　实际上，事实上

例 **As a matter of fact**, there were 78 million baby boomers born between 1946 and 1964 in the US. 事实上，1946 年到 1964 年美国婴儿潮期间出生的人数有 7800 万。

at the latest　最迟，最晚

例 This new cross-sea bridge will be opened to traffic in July **at the latest**. 这座新建的跨海大桥最晚七月通车。

拓 at the earliest 最早

start out　出发；着手开始做

例 Where you **start out** in your career often has a big impact on where you end up. 你的第一份职业往往对你最终所从事的职业有深远的影响。

life sentence　无期徒刑

例 He was arrested and is currently serving a **life sentence** for the murder of four people. 他因谋杀四人而被逮捕，目前正在服无期徒刑。

in a form　以一种形式

例 The atoms are linked up **in a form**, which comes into being molecules. 原子以某种形式组合起来，形成了分子。

on short notice　在很短的时间内（突如其来，没有充分的准备时间）

例 Lily came around **on short notice** this morning, but I was out for jogging then. 莉莉今天早晨临时来访，但那时候我出去慢跑了。

better off　更好的；生活较优裕的，经济状况好的

例 Even when you win (the fights), you end up no **better off**. 即使你在争执中获胜了，你的状况也不会变得更好。

fight off　击退；抵抗，摆脱

例 The woman **fought off** an armed robber. 那位女性击退了一个持枪抢劫者。

burst upon/on	突然来到；突然明白

例 The rock music dramatically **burst upon** the world stage in the mid-1950s. 20 世纪 50 年代，摇滚乐突然戏剧性地出现在了世界舞台。

stop by	顺便访问；停在……附近

例 Today I will **stop by** the hospital and say thanks to the doctor and nurse who took care of me when I was ill. 今天我要顺便去趟医院，然后向我生病期间照顾我的医生和护士道谢。

no wonder	难怪

例 **No wonder** he didn't pass the final exam; he hadn't reviewed his lessons. 难怪他没有通过期末考试，他都没有复习功课。

splash out	随意花钱，大肆挥霍

例 It's not a good idea to **splash out** on a credit card when the economy is declining. 经济衰退时期使用信用卡大肆消费不是一个明智的举动。

tidy away	把（某物）收拾好

例 When the children have a lot of toys everywhere, parents can call their children to **tidy away** the toys. 当孩子把一大堆玩具扔得满地都是的时候，家长可以让孩子把玩具收拾好。

for (the) purpose of	为了……目的

例 He says Mike created the ID the other day **for the purpose of** sharing information with Facebook users around the world. 他说，迈克前几天创建这个账号是为了与世界各地的脸书用户分享信息。

拓 with the view of 为了做……；为了……目的

wash out	洗掉；冲洗干净；精疲力竭；淘汰

例 When it's above the horizon, the moon can **wash out** all but the most intense of displays with its light. 若是月亮尚在地平线上，它的光亮会冲淡一切，这样就只能看到月光了。

night and day	日以继夜地

例 What's more, he gave the strictest orders that a guard should walk round the castle **night and day**. 另外，他还下了最严格的命令：城堡里的守卫要日夜巡逻。

get going　开始动身，开始做事　○○○

例 How often have you finally steeled yourself to start some difficult project, only to be interrupted the minute you **get going**? 你经常终于下决心开始做某个困难的项目，但是才刚开始就被打断了吗？

in comparison with　与……比较，同……比较起来　○○○

例 **In comparison with** Bill, Mike is more sensitive about his face. 和比尔相比，迈克更注重个人的脸面。

in competition with　与……竞争　○○○

例 In France, by contrast, there are over 50 certification bodies, all **in competition with** one another. 相比之下，法国有 50 多家认证机构，竞争激烈。

sit in on　列席；旁听　○○○

例 In 2006, he perplexed German diplomats by presenting the chancellor with a small dog as a gift and made a habit of having his black Labrador, Koni, **sit in on** their meetings. 2006 年，他送给该国总理一只小狗作为礼物，并经常让他的黑色拉布拉多犬考尼参与他们的会谈，这让德国外交官们感到困惑。

slip up　疏忽；跌倒；遭到不幸　○○○

例 A new study suggests that people considered saints in some aspects of their lives can **slip up** in other arenas, as a way of maintaining a sort of moral balance. 一份新的研究表明，有时人们认为圣人也会在某些方面犯错误，以此来保持一种道义上的平衡。

拓 be forgetful of 疏忽 ‖ make a mistake 出差错，犯错误

hold up　经受得住检验；举起；耽搁；抢劫　◇○

例 It's unclear if the argument **holds up**, but it's stimulating. 目前还不清楚这个论点是否站得住脚，但它很有启发性。

take shape　形成；成形；体现；具体化　○○○

例 Puris says his firm should turn a profit next year as more projects **take shape**. 普里斯说，随着更多项目的成形，他的公司明年应该会盈利。

拓 shape into 形成

at a loss 困惑，不知所措

例 The attacks have been so ferocious that experts have been left **at a loss** to explain the "unprecedented" behaviour. 袭击行为变得如此凶残，专家都不知该如何解释这种"前所未有"的行为。

think out 解决；仔细考虑；发现

例 I was young and ill-educated and I had to **think out** my problems in the utter silence. 我涉世不深，受不良教育毒害，还不得不在一片缄默之中尝试理清我的问题。

拓 work out 解决；算出；实现；制定出；消耗完；弄懂；锻炼

think through 充分考虑；全盘考虑；想透

例 One strategy is to **think through** what changes would make it easier for you to bring lunch from home. 一种对策就是仔细想想能否做些改变，使得从家带午饭变得更便捷。

拓 think out 认真考虑；仔细盘算 ‖ think over （尤指在做决定前）仔细考虑，慎重思考 ‖ think up 想出；发明

turn a deaf ear (to) 充耳不闻；不加理睬；不愿听

例 The officials in particular are given information about the effects of smoking but **turn a deaf ear to** it as they receive cigarettes as gifts. 我们为这些官员特别提供了有关吸烟的有害影响的信息，但他们对此充耳不闻，因为他们收受香烟礼物。

拓 shut/close your ear to （对……）充耳不闻，置之不理

warm to 开始喜欢；同情；爱好

例 The speaker was now **warming to** her theme. 演讲者就她的主题越讲越起劲。

on the hour 准点地；在整点时刻

例 The trains would run **on the hour** but not as many as would run on a normal weekday. 火车将会准点出发，但车次不像正常工作日那么多。

throw away 扔掉，丢弃

例 Worries about food safety prompt many people to **throw away** perfectly good food. 对于食品安全的担忧促使很多人扔掉了一些非常好的食物。

拓 cast off 摆脱；抛弃

roll in　蜂拥而来；到达

例 Information is beginning to **roll in** and we'll be sharing it when it is verified. 信息开始不断涌入，等证实这些信息后，我们就会和大家共享。

拓 flood in 涌入，大量地涌到 ‖ flow in 流入

win out/through　（克服困难）终获成功

例 Nothing's impossible and it all depends on man; you would **win through** if you persist. 一切皆有可能，都取决于人；只要努力坚持，你会赢得胜利的。

be/seem irrelevant to　不切题；与……不相干

例 We say—all of it must **be irrelevant to** us. When in fact there is a lot that is relevant. 我们认为，所有的这些都得和我们无关，而实际上很多是与我们有关的。

differ in　在（某方面）不同

例 They **differ in** size but not in kind. 它们只是大小不同而实质一样。

in cash　用现金

例 You'd better pay **in cash**. 你最好付现金。

to begin/start with　第一，首先

例 **To begin with**, we should doubt if his proposal is going to work. 首先，我们应该怀疑他的提议能否行得通。

拓 in the first place 首先

put to use　使用，利用

例 But if we can learn some general principle that someone else might **put to use**, that is fantastic. 但是，如果我们能够了解一些其他人可能使用的原理，这会很有趣。

拓 utilize ['juːtəlaɪz] v. 使用；利用 ‖ put...to good use 从……中获益 ‖ in use 被使用；在使用中

beyond one's ability　超出某人的能力

例 The exercise was **beyond the abilities** of some of the class. 这个练习超出了班上一些学生的能力。

in the heart of
在……的中心；处于……的核心

例 The peace with Egypt and Jordan has long served as an anchor of stability and peace **in the heart of** the Middle East. 就像一只稳定与和平的锚，与埃及和约旦的和平共处已经长久地在中东的核心地区发挥了作用。

cast aside
踢开；扔掉；抛弃

例 We must **cast aside** outdated policies and thinking. 我们必须摒弃过时的政策和思维。
拓 discard [dɪ'skɑːd] v. 丢弃；抛弃

take against
反对，不赞成；不喜欢

例 It is not a boring story, but my children have **taken against** it. 这个故事并不无聊，可我的孩子们不喜欢它。

show off
炫耀，卖弄

例 The mechanic was **showing off** his skills. 修理师正在炫耀他的技能。

bet on
下赌注于……；敢说，八成

例 She **bet** 1000 dollars **on** the final score of the game. 她下 1000 美金赌比赛最后的分数。

in broad daylight
在大白天；公开地

例 A man was robbed in the street **in broad daylight**. 光天化日之下，一个男子在大街上遭到了抢劫。

work off
（通过消耗体力）宣泄感情；工作以偿还债务

例 They **worked off** their anger by running. 他们通过跑步来消气。

keep a hold on
紧握；掌握

例 They tend to **keep a** tighter **hold on** their purse and consider eating at home a realistic alternative. 他们更倾向于紧紧抓住自己的钱包，认为在家吃饭是一个现实的选择。

wall in
（用墙或障碍）围住，封闭

例 The man is **walled in** by a mountain of papers. 男子被堆成山的文件包围了。
拓 besiege [bɪ'siːdʒ] v. 围困，围住

| sleep off | 用睡眠来消除 | |

例 She has been up all night. Let's leave her to **sleep it off**. 她昨晚熬了一宿，让她睡吧，一觉醒来就没事了。

| stick out for | 坚持要求；坚持索取 | |

例 The workers **stick out for** a higher pay rise. 工人们坚决要求更大幅度地提高工资。

拓 insist on/upon 坚决要求；执意继续做某事

| would sooner | 宁可；宁愿 | |

例 I **would sooner** give up playing football than miss my evening class. 我宁可不踢球，也不愿错过晚上的课。

拓 would rather 宁愿

| in high spirit | 情绪高涨的，喜气洋洋的，兴高采烈的 | |

例 We are **in high spirit** now. 我们现在情绪高涨。

| come and go | 时来时去；时有时无；时隐时现 | |

例 Opportunities **come and go**; it is up to you, the individual, to make the best decision for yourself. 机会来了又走，一切都取决于你，你自己来为自己做出最好的决定。

| on condition (that) | 在……条件下；倘若 | |

例 He agreed to speak **on condition** he not be further identified for fear he could get into trouble. 他同意在不进一步透漏身份的条件下接受访问，以防引来麻烦。

拓 provided [prə'vaɪdɪd] *pron.* 假如；倘若

| last but not least | 最后但同样重要的 | |

例 **Last but not least**, we'll discuss how to carry out the contract smoothly. 最后但同样重要的是，我们将讨论如何顺利执行合同。

| come to nothing | 毫无结果；完全失败 | |

例 All the efforts will **come to nothing** if the new approach isn't economically viable and environmentally beneficial. 如果新的方法在经济层面不可行或不利于环境，所有的努力都将功亏一篑。

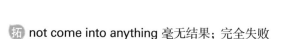

拓 not come into anything 毫无结果；完全失败

file for 申请；提出……申请

例 Michael's company continued to slide and now may have to **file for** bankruptcy. 迈克尔的公司业绩继续下滑，现在可能不得不申请破产。

be skilled at 善于；在……方面熟练的

例 Psychologists **are skilled at** inventing unusual tests of human thought and behavior. 心理学家善于发明一些不寻常的方法来测试人类的思想和行为。

拓 be good at 善于，擅长做…… ‖ be adept in 善于，擅长

fight back 反击；抵抗

例 The scientists **fight back**, but they always have to make some concessions. 科学家们进行抗争，但他们总是要做出一些让步。

have difficulty (in) 在……方面有困难

例 Students for whom English is not the mother tongue may **have difficulty in** getting ideas across, so that numerous revisions are required. 对于那些母语不是英语的学生来说，读英文原著也许会有困难，所以很多修订版就非常有必要。

hold one's own 坚持住；坚守住；支撑住

例 It's miserable if one cannot **hold his own** direction of life. 把握不住自己的人生方向是一种悲哀。

drop to 下降到，跌到

例 Indeed, studies show that after 24 hours without sleep, a person's performance can **drop to** the level of someone who is legally drunk. 确实，研究显示，在 24 小时不睡觉之后，一个人的行为水平能够下降到某些人法定醉酒状态的程度。

talk sb. out of 说服某人不做（某事）；说服某人放弃

例 Don't try to **talk people out of** how they feel at first. 不要试图说服他人放弃他们的第一感受。

拓 persuade sb. not to do sth. /persuade sb. out of doing sth. 说服某人不做某事

| push up | 向上推；抬高；俯卧撑；推起 | ○○○ |

例 Keeping your back straight, **push up** with your arms until your arms are extended. 保持背部挺直，向上推你的手臂直到手臂伸直。

| grow out of | 产生于；因长大而穿不上；因长大而不再做 | ○○○ |

例 Our worries always **grow out of** our fears. 忧虑总是伴着我们的恐惧而生。

| inject into | 把……注入；添加 | ○○○ |

例 To avoid dangerous climate change we will have to limit the total amount of carbon we **inject into** the atmosphere. 为了避免气候发生危险的变化，我们必须限制排放的温室气体总量。

| distinguish between...and... | 区别……和…… | ○○○ |

例 It takes several years of practice to **distinguish between** Sturm wine **and** vinegar. 要将斯蒂尔姆酒和醋区别开来需要多年实践经验。

拓 to make a distinction 区别

| come into use | 投入使用；开始使用 | ○○○ |

例 The system has **come into use** and gotten satisfying effect. 该系统已投入使用，并取得了令人满意的效果。

拓 go out of use 停止使用

| buy out | 买下……的全部产权；出钱使……放弃地位 | ○○○ |

例 The remnant of the car industry is trying to **buy out** its workers. 汽车行业残留下来的公司也正试图买断工人。

| equip with | 装备，配备；备有……，以……装备 | ○○○ |

例 In modern companies, employees have to **equip with** the knowledge structure and ability. 在现代公司，员工必须具备专业的知识结构和能力。

| keep one's word | 遵守诺言，守信 | ○○○ |

例 Tom always **keeps his word**, so if he promises to help you move, then he'll be here. 汤姆总是信守诺言，所以如果他答应帮你搬家，他就会来的。

拓 eat one's word 收回前言；承认自己说错了话

dry out 戒酒；变干

例 I approved the doctor's order to keep him in the room till he was **dried out**. 我同意了医生的命令，把他关在房间里，直到他戒酒为止。

拓 give up drinking 戒酒 ‖ give up alcohol 戒酒

have a good time 玩得高兴

例 Women consider that the point of all getting together is to **have a good time** and develop relationships—not just to sit there like couch potatoes staring at the screen. 女性认为大家聚在一起的目的是玩得开心，发展良好的关系，而不是像个电视迷一样坐在那里盯着屏幕。

拓 have fun with 玩得开心

at intervals 不时，时时；每隔……时间 / 距离

词 interval ['ɪntəvl] *n.* 间隔时间；停顿

例 He said the enemy troops continued firing **at intervals**. 他说敌军继续间断地射击。

time out 暂停，时间到；超时

例 With 21 seconds to go before halftime, Brown wanted to call a **time out**. 距中场休息还有 21 秒时，布朗想叫一次暂停。

拓 time's up 时间到

in the long run 最终，从长远来看

例 It's not cheap to build all of the pipes and pumps for a district cooling system, but it saves money **in the long run**. 一个区域冷却系统的所有管道和泵站建造起来并不便宜，但从长远来看，这可以节约资金。

touch down 着陆，降落

例 The flight **touched down** on time. 航班准时到达了。

avail oneself of 利用

例 Employees should **avail themselves of** the opportunity to buy cheap shares in the company. 雇员应该把握机会购买公司的廉价股份。

not...at all   一点也不

例 Children were **not** colour-coded **at all** until the early 20th century: in the era before domestic washing machines all babies wore white as a practical matter, since the only way of getting clothes clean was to boil them. 20 世纪初期之前，孩子们的衣服是没有对应色码的：在家用洗衣机问世之前的年代，婴儿都穿实用的白色，因为洗净衣服的唯一方法是煮沸。

warm up   做准备活动，热身；使变热；兴奋起来，激动

例 It's important to **warm up** properly before running. 跑步前适当热身很重要。

think up   想出（主意或计划）

例 He **thought up** a plan to get rich quickly. 他想到了一个快速致富的计划。

tear...away   逼（某人）离开；迫使（某人）停止

例 I'll bring John to the party, if I can **tear** him **away** from the TV. 如果我能把约翰从电视机前拉走，我就带他去参加聚会。

play off against   使对抗

例 So, if the provinces want to run the health-care show, they should prove they can run it, starting with an interprovincial health list that would end duplication, save administrative costs, prevent one province from being **played off against** another, and bargain for better drug prices. 所以，如果各省想要掌管医疗保健业务，它们应该证明自己的能力。首先它们需要一个跨省的医疗清单，以此来避免重复，节约管理成本，防止省与省之间发生冲突，并且通过谈判获得更优惠的药品价格。

see to   负责，照料

例 Would you **see to** changing the sheets on the beds upstairs? 你能负责替换楼上的床单吗？

in the interest of   为了……的利益

例 Finding a new model to support journalism is **in the interest of** society as a whole. 寻求一种新的模式来支持新闻业，总的来说是为了社会的利益。

本单元资源

talk sb. into doing sth. 说服某人做某事 ○○○

例 The person might try to **talk** you **into** staying but be firm—respect yourself and your time and the changes you're trying to make. 那个人可能会试图说服你留下。但你要坚定你的信念——尊重自己和自己的时间以及你想要做出的改变。

拓 persuade sb. into doing sth./persuade sb. to do sth. 说服某人做某事

at (the) worst 在最坏的情况下；在最糟的情况下；最糟糕；坏到极点 ○○○

例 He will be expelled from school, **at worst**. 最坏的情况是，他会被学校开除。

pass on 继续下去；传递下去 ◇

例 If you want to **pass on** values to your team, start by defining what those values mean to you. 如果你想在你的团队传递价值观，那就从定义那些价值观对你来说意味着什么开始吧。

拓 hand on 传递下去

top up 充值；装满 ○○○

例 My mobile phone is out of credit, I have to **top up** it. 我手机没钱了，得去给手机充值。

you bet 当然；的确；你说的没错 ○○○

例 **You bet**. You should try it yourself. 当然。你应该亲自体验一下。

tear at 用力撕；撕扯；强拉 ○○○

例 The child tried to **tear at** the box, but he failed to tear it. 那个孩子试图撕开箱子，但是撕不开。

behind someone's back 背着某人；在经历，经受；某人背后 ○○○

例 I don't want to talk **behind someone's back**, but have you noticed the scar on his face? 我不想在背后议论别人，可是你注意到他脸上的疤了吗？

close up 靠近；关闭；愈合 ○○○

例 I think it was Charlie Chaplin who said that **close up**, human life is tragic, but from a distance, it's funny. 我想应该是查理·卓别林说的这句话吧：人生近看是悲剧，远看是喜剧。

take off	脱下；起飞；离开

例 **take off** your shoes 脱下你的鞋子

enter on/upon	开始；正式开始；着手做

例 The President has just **entered upon** another term of office. 该总统刚刚开始另一任期。

on line	网上；上线中；联机；压线球

例 Sometimes you can find kids' programming **on line**, which might have narration of stories or simpler dialogue that is easier for you to follow. 有时候你可以在网上找到儿童节目，其中或许会有讲故事或更简单的对话，对你来说更容易跟上。

walk out	走出；退席；罢工；把（某人）领出

例 It's amazing what can happen when you **walk out** of the room. 当你走出房门，你会惊异于那些可能会发生的事情。

shut up	关闭，打烊；住口；监禁

例 Due to the new policy, a handful of smaller agents were forced to **shut up** shop around him. 由于新出台的政策，他附近的一些更小的房地产中介公司被迫关闭。

on purpose	故意；有意；成心地

例 Likewise, starting your morning **on purpose** 30 minutes early will likely inject at least 30 additional productive minutes into your day. 同样，每天早晨早起 30 分钟相当于给你每天的生活额外增加了至少 30 分钟的高效时间。

拓 deliberately [dɪˈlɪbərətli] *ad.* 故意地；刻意地

equate with	把……等同；使相等；同等相待

例 As the thinking goes, symmetrical faces are then deemed beautiful; beauty is linked to confidence; and it's a combination of looks and confidence that we often **equate with** smarts. 按照这一思路，匀称的脸被认为是漂亮；美貌与自信有关；我们常常把美貌与自信的结合等同于聪明。

be worthwhile to	做……是值得的

例 It will even **be worthwhile to** rest and gain strength during this period. 在这段时间，应该及时休息和获取力量。

keep up with
跟上；不落后；赶上

例 We planned to work together, but he is too prolific and I cannot **keep up with** him. 我们曾计划一起工作，但是他太高产了，我没法赶上他。

拓 keep pace with 并驾齐驱，保持同步 ‖ catch up with 赶上，追上

tangle with
与……争论或打架

例 You shouldn't **tangle with** him because he's stronger. 你不应与他打架，因为他比你强壮。

be relevant to
与……有关

例 List only experience that would **be relevant to** the job you're seeking. 只把和求职有关的经历列举出来即可。

under...circumstances
在……情况下

例 Recent opinion polls show that 60 percent favour a lifting house price **under** certain **circumstances**. 最近的民意调查显示，60% 的人赞同特定情况下的抬高房价。

stand up to
经受住；抵抗；勇敢地面对

例 The carpet is designed to **stand up to** a lot of wear and tear. 这种地毯设计得十分耐用。

close by
在附近，在近旁

例 When the chimps slept **close by**, I stayed up in the mountains near them. 当大猩猩在附近睡觉的时候，我就待在它们附近的山上。

cast about/around for sth.
匆忙寻找或考虑某事物

例 As ministers **cast around for** new sources of growth to make up for crisis-hit financial services, science and technology suggest themselves. 在部长们到处寻找新的经济来源以弥补经济危机给金融服务行业带来的损失时，高科技行业出现了。

back up
支持；往后退

例 I **back up** his no-smoking rule. 我支持他的禁烟规定。

so long
再见

例 **So long**, have a good weekend. 再见，周末愉快！

take/have a hand in
插手，参与

例 Joe insists on **having a hand in** the company, even though he has no real authority at this point. 乔坚持要插手公司的事情，尽管他现在没有实权。

count...in 把……计算在内

例 If you're all going to the party, then you can **count** me **in**. 要是你们全都去参加聚会，就可以把我也算上。

拓 factor in 把……计算在内；将……纳入

take a chance 冒险一试，尝试一下

例 If you find yourself avoiding new chances and disregarding problems, it's time for you to **take a chance**. 如果你发现自己正在回避新的机遇，或逃避面对问题，这时你就该冒险一试了。

拓 chance one's arm 碰碰运气，冒险试一试

turn down （把音量）调小，调低；拒绝

例 **turn down** the volume 把音量调低

拓 excuse oneself from 婉言拒绝

talk back 顶嘴，反驳

例 Many people don't believe that money answers all things, but only he knows how to **talk back**. 很多人都不认为金钱是万能的，但是只有他知道该怎么反驳。

take note (of) 注意到；记笔记

例 Blair wrote in his journal, "It means that we need to **take note** that something abnormal is happening. " 布莱尔在他的日志里写道，"这意味着我们需要注意到一些异常的事正在发生。"

拓 make notes 记笔记

take one's time 慢慢来，从容地

例 **take your time** to carefully reflect on your thoughts 花时间仔细回想你的想法

拓 take it/things easy 放轻松，慢慢来

turn in 归还，交还

例 We left shortly after, and went to the office to **turn in** our keys. 我们很快就离开了，到办公室去归还了钥匙。

拓 give back 归还，送回

for short　　缩写；简言之　　〇〇〇

例 Artificial Intelligence (or AI, **for short**) is the name given to any attempt to have computers gain attributes of the human mind. 人工智能（缩写为 AI）这个名称来源于一些想让计算机拥有某些人类智能属性的尝试。

拓 in a nutshell 简单地说

to perfection　　尽善尽美；恰到好处　　〇〇〇

例 The experienced car racer can always time his start **to perfection**. 那位经验丰富的车手总是能够完美地掌握出发时间。

拓 to the queen's taste 尽善尽美地

upward of　　超过；多于　　〇〇〇

例 The space station costs **upward of** $200 billion, yet some critics call it a "station to nowhere." 该空间站的成本超过 2000 亿美元，然而一些批评人士将它称之为一座"不存在的空间站"。

拓 in excess of 超过，比……多

retreat from　　退出，放弃；逃避　　〇〇〇

例 Governments will become far more involved in some areas of the economy, such as macroeconomic management and financial regulation. But they will **retreat from** others, such as education and medical treatment. 政府会积极参与某些经济领域，比如宏观经济管理和金融监管，但会从教育和医疗等其他领域中退出。

be disappointed at　　对……感到失望　　〇〇〇

例 I suspect many people will **be disappointed at** how keenly he talked down the importance of electoral reform in some interview. 我猜想很多人会对他在一些采访中极力贬低选举改革的重要性感到很失望。

convenient to do　　方便做某事；便于做某事　　〇〇〇

例 It is **convenient to use** dry yeast because its handling is simple and its preservation easy. 使用干酵母比较方便，因为它便于操作，也容易保藏。

if anything　　如果有什么区别的话；如果有……的话　　〇〇〇

例 **If anything**, he worked even more enthusiastically than usual, because on Sundays he could catch the people who were usually out during the workdays. 如果硬说有什么区别的话，就是他比平常更富有激情地工作，因为在星期天他可以找到那些工作日不在的人。

on the move | 移动中；在活动中，在进行中

例 It's much easier than ever to get things done **on the move** without lugging a laptop around. 现在，脱离笔记本电脑的移动办公比以往容易多了。

tear down | 拆除；弄倒

例 The government will order BYD to **tear down** whatever they have built on the land. 政府将命令比亚迪拆除他们在这片土地上建的所有东西。

stand down | 退职；退出（比赛或竞选）；离开证人席

例 The embarrassing scandals and the popularity of the republican left in the recent Euro-elections have forced him to eat his words and **stand down**. 令人尴尬的丑闻和近期欧盟选举中共和党左翼大受欢迎的事实迫使他自食其言，退出王位。

拓 resign from office 辞职

be ignorant of | 无视；不知道，不了解

例 Some experimental measurement comes along that seems to **be ignorant of** the established order and breaks the rules. 有些实验结果似乎带着对已有规则的一种无视，并且似乎要颠覆这些规则。

拓 be insensible of 不知道；对……没有感觉

count as | 视为，当作，看成

例 If you consider yourself a fan of CSR, ask yourself this question: Would such a company **count as** a socially responsible company? 如果你认为你是企业社会责任的爱好者，那么问问你自己这个问题：这样的公司算不算一家有社会责任感的公司？

on the point of | 正要……的时候；在……之际

例 When ambulance staff arrived they saw the woman was **on the point of** giving birth and rushed her to a nearby building where she had her baby. 当医护人员赶到时，他们发现这个女人快要分娩了，就赶紧把她送到附近的大楼里，在那里她顺利生下了孩子。

拓 at the time of 在……的时候

reckon...as/for/to be　把……看作，认为……是

例 We should not **reckon** examination **as** the only means of stimulating pupils to pursue knowledge. 我们不能把考试看作激励学生学习知识的唯一手段。

拓 regard...as 把……看作，认为……是 ‖ look upon...as 把……看作

come/go into effect　开始生效，实施

例 The agreement **went into effect** in 2012. 该协议于 2012 年生效。

拓 go into force 生效，实施

in the matter of　就……而论，在……方面

例 There is no hierarchy to happiness, except **in the matter of** feeling. 幸福是没有等级的，它只关乎感觉。

拓 with regard to 关于，就……而论 ‖ in the case of 至于，就……来说

think better of　重新考虑（后决定不做）；改变主意

例 What a foolish idea! I hope you will **think better of** it. 多么愚蠢的想法！我希望你重新考虑一下。

拓 on second thoughts 经重新考虑

do/try one's best　尽最大努力

例 **try your best** to comfort him 尽你最大努力地安慰他

拓 try one's utmost 竭尽全力

use up　耗尽，用光

例 CD drives can **use up** the laptop's battery very quickly. CD 光驱能迅速地耗尽笔记本的电池。

拓 run out of 用尽，用完

think highly/poorly of　对……评价很高 / 很糟

例 Those talented people who **think highly of** themselves create many career obstacles for themselves due to pride. 那些天才自视甚高，由于自负，他们给自己制造了许多职场上的障碍。

now and then　时而，偶尔，有时

例 It gets boring doing the same things over and over, so it's fun to try something new **now and**

then. 经常重复做同一件事，时间久了就会感到厌倦，所以偶尔尝试一些新鲜事物也是一种乐趣。

拓 once in a while 有时，偶尔

come by　偶然获得；得到（通常靠努力）；短暂拜访，顺道拜访

例 Anyone who has been on a lengthy job hunt can tell you that discouragement is easy to **come by**. 每个有过长时间求职经历的人都会告诉你，你会很容易出现沮丧的情绪。

拓 drop in on 顺路拜访，非正式访问

in words　口头上，用语言

例 Watch for things the professor emphasizes, even if just **in words**. 注意教授强调的内容，哪怕只是口头上的。

拓 by word of mouth 口头地

abound in/with sth.　有大量的；富于

例 They live in a region that **abounds with** rain and snow. 他们住在一个雨雪丰沛的地区。

stand off　避开；疏远，远离

例 He tried to **stand off** his creditors. 他试图避开债主。

拓 keep off 避开，不接近

be content with　满足于，对……感到满意

例 Try to free yourself from the culture of excess and learn to **be content with** fewer possessions and greater simplicity. 尽力把自己从无节制的文化中解放出来吧，学会满足于更少的物质财富，享受更加简朴的生活。

拓 be satisfied with 对……感到满意

vote sb. in　选出某人任某职

例 His father was just **voted in** as the president. 他的父亲刚被投票选为主席。

tune in (to sth.)　调整频率（至），收听

例 British viewers will be able to **tune in to** the show from 3 am on Monday morning. 英国的乐迷们可以从周一凌晨3点开始收听本次演出。

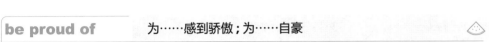

| **be proud of** | 为……感到骄傲；为……自豪 | |

例 We should **be proud of** our Nobel Prize winners. 我们应该为我们的诺贝尔奖获得者感到自豪。

拓 take pride in 为……感到骄傲；为……自豪

| **argue for** | 赞成；支持；论证 | |

例 Indeed, when their regulations fail, they often use the fact to **argue for** more power and more regulation. 的确，当他们的监管失败时，他们为了得到更大的权利和更多的监管而用事实去做争辩。

拓 argue against 反对；据理反对；争辩；反驳

| **speculate about/on** | 推断，推测 | |

例 Speculative questions means that the reader has to **speculate about** things which are unknowable, because they are outside the text. 推测类问题是指读者必须推测未知之事，因为它们在文本之外。

| **take back** | 收回；使回忆起；带回 | |

例 **Take back** control and anything is possible. 夺回控制权，任何事情都是可能的。

| **spread out** | 张开；伸开；传播；铺开 | |

例 Dark clouds began to **spread out** across the sky. 乌云开始在天空中散开。

| **a train of** | 一连串的；一系列；连续的 | |

例 **A train of** nice recollections runs across my mind when speaking about my college years. 一说起大学时代，我的脑中就闪过一段缤纷的回忆。

| **die out** | 消失，灭绝 | |

例 They are actually a sign that a thunderstorm is **dying out** and the bad weather has passed. 它们实际上是雷暴逐渐消失，恶劣天气已经过去的迹象。

| **what is worse** | 更糟糕的是 | |

例 He was unemployed, and **what is worse**, his father suddenly passed away. 他失业了，更糟的是，他的父亲突然去世了。

turn into
变成；进入；变为

例 At last, I **turn into** a spot and start following the crowd heading toward the elevator. 最后，我进到一个地方，开始跟着人群朝电梯走去。

sit by
袖手旁观；坐视不管

例 He issued a statement saying: "We can **sit by** and watch competitors steal our patented inventions, or we can do something about it." 他发表了一份声明，说道："在竞争对手窃取我们的专利发明时，我们可以选择袖手旁观，也可以选择出手做点什么。"

keep/be abreast of
跟上某事物的发展，了解最新情况

例 For example, if you're a heavy investor, it might be important for you to **keep abreast of** what's going on in the stock market on a day-to-day basis. 举个例子，如果你热爱炒股，你也许想知道股市的每日行情。

fall victim to
成为……的受害者；成为……的牺牲品

例 We all **fall victim to** at least a few lies during the course of our lifetime. 在我们的一生中，至少会有一些谎言给我们带来伤害。

let off
放（炮、烟火），放出；开（枪）；宽恕，从宽处理；免除

例 They **let off** fireworks to celebrate the New Year. 他们放烟花以庆祝新年。

in the way
造成不便或阻碍

例 Why let pride be **in the way** of love, unless your ego is your one True Love? 为什么让骄傲成为爱情的绊脚石呢？除非你觉得你的自尊就是你的真爱！

up to the minute
最新的；直到现在的；最新式的

例 It gives you a great way to find out the **up to the minute** news on the market as well as most company stocks. 它给了你非常好的方法来找到最新的股市和大部分公司的股票信息。

拓 up to date 最新的，最近的

throw up
放弃；辞去；匆匆建造；呕吐；扬起（灰尘）

例 She has just **thrown up** a very promising career. 她刚刚放弃了一个很有前途的职业。

circulate to
传递

例 Please **circulate to** those who may be interested. 请传递给有兴趣的人。

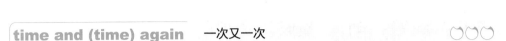

time and (time) again　一次又一次　○○○

例 **Time and time again**, research shows, and people confirm, that there is a pattern to who and how we love. 研究一次又一次地告诉我们，人们坚信，我们寻找爱人和经营爱情有特定的模式。

throw out　否决；扔出去；不受理　○○○

例 They decided to **throw out** the idea because it would have been too expensive. 他们决定放弃这个主意，因为它代价高昂。

be central to　对……来说是重要的　○○○

例 Community involvement **is central to** our plan. 社区的参与对我们的计划很重要。

prepare against　为应付……做准备　○○○

例 We must mobilize the masses to **prepare against** all possible eventualities. 我们要发动群众作好准备，以应付各种可能发生的情况。

bring into　把……拿入，带入；使开始生效；使清楚地被人理解（或知道）　○○○

例 **Bringing** a merger **into** play might be the best option to save the company. 进行合并可能是挽救公司的最佳选择。

speak out/up　大声地说；公开（或坦诚地）表达情感（或意见）　○○○

例 The administration will be forthright in **speaking out** against human rights abuses. 政府将直言不讳地反对侵犯人权行为。

on the spot　当场，立刻；在现场　○○○

例 My boss grilled me about the mix-up in the report, making me explain the whole thing right there **on the spot**. 老板盘问我报告中的错误，让我当场给出解释。

on leave　休假；在休假中　○○○

例 I've been **on leave** for the past few weeks as my illness has gotten worse. 由于我的病情加重，过去几周我一直在休假。

拓 on holiday 在休假

| with a view to | 以……为目的 | ◯◯◯ |

例 They offered her a training course **with a view to** moving her to upper management. 他们为她提供了培训课程，想把她调到高级管理层。

| sweep into | 把……扫进……；涌入；（彻底、果断、突然地）到达或进入 | ◯◯◯ |

例 We need to **sweep** all these crumbs **into** the trash before we can set the table for dinner. 我们需要将所有这些碎屑扫进垃圾桶，然后才能摆好桌子吃饭。

| knock down | 撞倒；拆卸 | ◯◯◯ |

例 I accidentally **knocked down** an old lady on the street today—I felt so bad! 今天我在街上不小心撞倒了一位老妇人，我难受极了！

| put through | 完成；接通；使穿过；使从事，使经受 | ◯◯◯ |

例 The assignment must be **put through** before Friday. 作业必须在周五之前完成。

| pick out | 挑选出 | |

例 **pick out** a red skirt 挑出红色的裙子

| for life | 终生，一生 | ◯◯ |

例 He is sentenced **for life** after all the charges against him has been proven true. 鉴于对他的所有指控都证明属实，他被判了无期徒刑。

拓 throughout one's life 终生

| pass away | 去世，逝世 | ◯◯◯ |

例 This chart shows the percentage of people, across different Asian countries, who are willing to donate their organs after they **pass away**. 这张图表展示了几个亚洲国家的居民愿意在去世之后捐献器官的百分比。

| keep (...) secret | 保守秘密 | ◯◯◯ |

例 He revealed some personal details never heard before in this interview, along with a little tidbit that he was supposed to **keep secret**. 他在这次采访中透露了一些前所未闻的个人轶事，还爆出了一条他本该缄口的小秘密。

拓 button up one's lip 保守秘密

PART 02

to the limit of   达到……的极限 ○○○

例 Orders were placed **to the limit of** our ship-building resources. 这些订单达到了我们造舰能力的极限。

on the decline   在下降，在衰退中；在走下坡路 ○○○

例 Global demand for solar technology is rising, yet the American producers' share of the U. S. and foreign markets is **on the decline**. 全球对太阳能技术的需求是增长的，然而美国本土制造商在美国和国外市场中的份额却在下降。

be distracted by   被……分心，被……搞得心烦意乱 ○○○

例 We **are distracted by** all the things we have to do—not just the stuff we're actually doing, but even the stuff we're not doing. 我们要为所有那些不得不做的事情分心——不仅是我们实际在做的事，还有我们没有在做的事情。

draw up   写出；草拟；画出；停住 ○○○

例 In order to screen callers, I **drew up** one-page form for each caller. 为了筛选电话面试者，我为每个面试者草拟了一份表格。

拓 sketch out 草拟

commit suicide   自杀 ○○○

例 The danger about **committing suicide** in depression patients is very outstanding. 抑郁症患者自杀的风险极高。

once (and) for all   一劳永逸；限此一次 ○○○

例 She asked me to stop, **once (and) for all**, telephoning her late at night. 她让我永远不要再在深夜给她打电话。

swear to   向……发誓 ○○○

例 **Swear to** me that while you still love me you will not divorce. 向我发誓：只要你还爱我，你就不会离婚。

for fun   为了快乐，为了好玩；开玩笑地 ○○○

例 We all want to know that what do we do **for fun**. 我们都想知道如何做才能得到快乐。

| wait on | 焦急地等待（某事发生） | |

例 I know he might turn me down, but I'm going to have to **wait on** his answer. 我知道他可能会拒绝我，但我还是想再等一等他的答案。

| step by step | 逐步地 | |

例 My father told me to set goals **step by step** and then follow them one by one. 我的父亲告诉我要一步步地设定目标，并且逐个地实现它们。

拓 stage by stage 逐步地

| by rights | 按理说；正当地 | |

例 **By rights**, the old-fashioned space probes should no longer be of interest to anyone. 按理说，过时的航天探测器应该已不再能引起人们的兴趣。

| without fail | 务必；必定，无疑 | |

例 Every Sunday, **without fail**, he arrives by bus at 7 a. m. , an hour before the bookstore opens. 每个周日，毫无例外地，他会在上午 7 点钟——书店营业前的一个小时，坐公交车到达那里。

DAY 20

本单元资源

| **grip on** | 控制 | ○○○ |

例 In order to hold on to power, he has kept a tight **grip on** the majority of the company's shares. 为了保住权力，他一直牢牢地控制着公司大部分的股份。

| **be opposed to** | 反对……；与……相对 | ○○○ |

例 Some people **are opposed to** death penalty. 一些人反对死刑。

拓 against/object to 反对

| **on occasion** | 有时，偶尔 | ○○○ |

例 That machine went out of order **on occasion**. 那台机器有时发生故障。

拓 from time to time 有时，偶尔

| **tide over** | 使度过（难关等），克服 | ○○○ |

例 The country may use its foreign exchange reserves to **tide over** the crisis. 该国可以用其外汇储备来度过此次危机。

拓 live through 度过；经受过

| **sleep through** | 酣睡一整夜 | ○○○ |

例 Dave was finally able to **sleep through** the night at home. 戴维终于能够在家酣睡一整夜。

| **acquaint with** | 使熟悉，使认识，使了解 | ○○○ |

例 You should **acquaint** yourself **with** all the content of the application. 你应该熟悉这个应用的所有内容。

| **take exception to** | 反对，抗议 | ○○○ |

例 I **take exception to** some recent comments of Mr. Healy which are totally wrong. 我对希利先生最近的一些言论表示反对，它们完全是错误的。

拓 no exception 无一例外

| **for certain** | 肯定地；确凿地 | ○○○ |

例 The only thing he knew **for certain** was that something was about to happen. 他唯一能够肯定的就是将会有事要发生。

step aside 让开；回避 ◠◠◠

例 Please **step aside** and allow the children into the museum. 麻烦让开一下，让孩子们进入博物馆。

space out 使间隔开；（因服食毒品等）变得昏昏沉沉 ◠◠◠

例 So if you really want to study more efficiently, **space out** shorter, hour-long study sessions. 如果你真想要提高学习效率，那就把目标拆分成几个更短期的内容，以小时为单位来分阶段学习。

in use 在使用中 ◠◠◠

例 The old bridge is still **in use** today. 这座古桥至今仍在使用。

in abundance 大量的，丰富的 ◠◠◠

例 That country has something no other Arab countries has **in abundance**: water, oil and an educated population. 那个国家有着其他阿拉伯国家所不具备的大量的水、石油和受过教育的民众。

hardly...when/before 刚一……就…… ◠◠◠

例 **Hardly when** I got home, it started to rain. 我刚到家，天就开始下雨了。

拓 no sooner...than 一……就……，刚刚……就……

be in debt 欠债，负债 ◠◠◠

例 I will never spend beyond my checkbooks and I think it is wrong to **be in debt**. 我永远都不会超额消费，并且我认为负债是不正确的。

give credit for 认可；赞扬 ◠◠◠

例 Don't be upset. We should **give** ourselves **credit for** our strengths. 别沮丧，我们应该认可自己的优势。

拓 give credit to 归功于；赞许

turn a blind eye to 对……视而不见 ◠◠◠

例 How can you **turn a blind eye to** such practices yet purport to be concerned with animal welfare? 既然你声称深切关心动物福利，又怎么能对这种做法视而不见呢？

| rest with | 在于；取决于 | ◯◯◯ |

例 Part of the blame does **rest with** changes in Medicare and Medicaid payment policies. 部分指责确实归咎于医疗保险和医疗补助的付费政策。

| watch over | 照管；守护；看守，监视；负责 | ◯◯◯ |

例 I have to **watch over** my friend's child tomorrow afternoon. 明天下午我不得不帮我朋友照看一下孩子。

拓 keep an eye on 照看；留意；密切关注

| on no account | 绝对不能；决不 | ◯◯◯ |

例 The parents warned their children **on no account** to open the door for anyone during their absence. 这对父母警告他们的孩子，在他们不在的时候，绝对不能给任何人开门。

拓 in no way/in no case/in no circumstances 决不；绝对不能

| think over | 仔细考虑 | ◇ |

例 You should **think over** the matter before you take action. 你需要在采取行动之前再仔细考虑一下这件事。

| fill with | 装满，充满 | ◇ |

例 Her eyes **filled with** tears when her favorite toy was crushed into pieces . 当她心爱的玩具被摔个粉碎的时候，她的眼中噙满了泪水。

| out of doors | 露天，在户外 | ◯◯◯ |

例 When the evening chores were done, she did not want to be with the rest of them, and went **out of doors** wandering along she knew not whither. 做完了傍晚的家务后，她不想和其他人待在一起，于是就来到户外，在连她自己都叫不上名来的地方游荡着。

| call off | 取消 | ◯◯◯ |

例 The outdoor football match was **called off** because of the bad weather. 由于天气恶劣，室外足球赛被取消了。

| tear away from | 舍不得离开 | ◯◯◯ |

例 She could hardly **tear** herself **away from** the fascinating story. 她几乎不能将自己从这个引人入胜的故事中抽离出来。

DAY 20

run wild　　失控；变得荒芜

例 I'm looking forward to returning to Pandora, a world where our imaginations can **run wild**. 我希望回到潘多拉星球，在那儿我们的想象力可以自由地驰骋。

cut in　　插嘴，打断

例 She was always **cutting in** on others' conversations. 她总喜欢打断别人的谈话。

拓 strike in 插嘴 ‖ break in 打断；闯入；使逐渐习惯

(not) for anything　　无论如何（用于否定句中）

例 I wouldn't change my life **for anything**. 我无论如何都不会改变自己的生活。

拓 for the world （否定句内）无论如何；（肯定句内）每一方面都……

stick together　　（粘）在一起；团结一致；互相支持

例 The two substances **stick together**, crystallize and exit the body long before there's a chance to form kidney stones. 这两种物质粘在一起，会在有机会形成肾结石之前结晶并排出体外。

talk sense　　说话有道理

例 **Talk sense** and behave yourself. You are not a kid any more. 说话讲道理，行为举止规矩些。你已经不是小孩了。

拓 see sense 变得明智起来；开始明白事理

drag sb. /sth. down　　使某人 / 某事物垮掉；使某人 / 某事物感到厌烦

例 If she fails, she will **drag** us all **down** with her. 要是她失败了，我们大家都会被连累。

拓 drag sb. in/into sth. 把毫不相干的人插入谈论；毫无必要地扯到某人

operate on　　给……做手术；对……起作用

例 The doctors **operated on** the patient but failed to save his life. 医生给这位病人做了手术，但是没能挽救他的生命。

lead into　　导致；引起

例 It is easy to mistranslate words and it will slow down your progress eventually, or even worse might **lead into** embarrassing situations. 误翻很容易，而且这样会最终放缓你的进程，或者更糟糕的是会导致尴尬的情况发生。

hear from 从……那里听到；接到……的信或电话

例 I **hear from** many writers that Prague is the place to live in, or at least to visit for a while. 我从多名作家那里听说，布拉格是值得居住或至少游玩一阵子的地方。

on the table 公开地；在桌面上

例 In today's meeting there were several new proposals **on the table**. 今天的会议上公开了几项新建议。

fix up 为……做好安排；商妥；修理；解决；改进

例 I know you are all filled up this week, let's **fix up** about the next time we meet. 我知道你这个星期全部排满了，咱们来安排一下下次见面的时间吧。

拓 arrange for 安排；为……做准备

keep a close watch on 密切注意，关注

例 We had to **keep a close watch on** the gas tank because there were no gas stations anywhere except at the village. 我们必须时刻留神油表，因为在村子以外是没有加油站的。

拓 pay close heed to 密切注意

cheer sb. on/cheer on sb. 鼓励某人，为某人打气

例 A big crowd had gathered around the tower to see the race and **cheer on** the runners. 一大群观众早已聚在高塔附近准备看比赛，并为跑步的人加油。

on hand 在手边；临近

例 There are fundamental tools and capabilities that we should all have **on hand**. 有一些基本的工具和功能是我们手边全都应该具备的。

拓 within reach 伸手可及的，在附近

vote against 投票反对

例 People called on their representatives to **vote against** the new tax policy. 人们请求他们的代表投票反对新出的税收政策。

拓 ballot against 投票反对

scale down 缩小（规模或范围）；减少（数量）

例 Decisions were made to **scale down** the celebration after a number of sponsors were forced to cut back on financial support. 在一群赞助商被迫削减财政支持后，（众人）决定缩减庆祝

活动的规模。

拓 scale sth. back/scale back sth. 减少（数量）；缩小（规模或范围）

give place to　　让位于，被……所代替

例 These days a laptop can **give place to** various smart phone applications coming from various genres. 目前，笔记本电脑越发地让位于各种类型的智能手机应用程序。

拓 be replaced by 被……替代 ‖ make room for 让地方给……

submit to　　提交；向……提出；服从，屈服

词 submit [səb'mɪt] v. 服从，顺从；提交；主张

例 He refused to **submit to** this unjust verdict. 他拒不服从这不公正的判决。

拓 bring up 提出；养育

sort of　　有几分地；到某种程度；稍稍

例 My boss was fired, but I **sort of** liked his way of management. 我的老板被解雇了，但某种程度上我挺喜欢他的管理方式。

拓 kind of 有点；有几分

辨 **sort of** 指"有几分；稍稍；到某种程度"，多用于动词之前，相当于 "rather, kind of"。如：She sort of pretends that she doesn't really care. 她有点装作不在乎。

a sort of 指"一种"，相当于 "a kind of"。如：The team gave mice a drug that targets a sort of endurance gene. 研究小组喂给老鼠能作用于一种耐力基因的药。

take/get/have a nap　　打盹，小睡片刻

例 **Taking a nap** after a heavy study session would allow your brain some time to rest. 在刻苦学习一段时间后打个盹，可以给大脑一些时间休息。

拓 nod off 打盹 ‖ take a rest 休息

drive sb. to do sth.　　驱使、促使某人做某事；强迫某人做某事

例 The urge to survive **drove them to keep** swimming. 求生的欲望驱使他们继续游泳。

拓 compel sb. to do sth. 强迫某人做某事

talk nonsense　　胡说八道，胡言乱语

词 nonsense ['nɒnsns] n. 胡说；废话

例 Our valuable time will not be wasted if we don't let others **talk nonsense** to us. 只要我们不

听信别人胡说八道，宝贵的时间就不会浪费。

bid up 哄抬（价钱），竞相出高价

词 bid [bɪd] *v.* 出价

例 If they **bid up** the price higher than the market can bear, oil stockpiles will increase, which in turn will put downward pressure on prices. 如果他们抬高的价格超过市场的承受能力，石油储备量就会增加，反过来价格的下行压力也会增加。

拓 raise price 抬价

on order 已订购；在途；已经订购的

例 I have mostly learned what I know from your articles about genetic engineering, but I also have a book **on order**. 虽然我已经从你关于基因工程的文章中学到了很多，但我还是订购了一本书。

拓 place/make an order 预定；订购

go over 检查，审查；复习，重温

例 **go over** some of these concepts mentioned above 重温一下上面提到的概念

拓 brush up on sth. 复习，重温 ‖ review [rɪˈvjuː] *v.* 复习（功课）；复查

go into action 开始行动；投入战斗

例 The adrenal glands release adrenaline and other stress hormones which prime certain organs to **go into action**. 肾上腺释放肾上腺素和其他压力荷尔蒙，这些都能够激发某些器官，让它们行动起来。

拓 fall upon 开始行动；进攻

be/become absorbed in 专心于，全神贯注于

例 Again, George **became absorbed in** the unfolding of the book. 乔治又一次沉浸在这本书的故事情节中。

die down 减弱；逐渐平息

例 We're hoping that the storm can **die down** before we go out surfing. 我们希望暴风雨在我们出去冲浪之前平息。

拓 fade away 逐渐消失；褪色

DAY 20

complain of 抱怨；诉苦；抗议

例 Some people who go on low carbohydrate diets **complain of** low energy and quit, not because such diets couldn't work, but because they consume insufficient calories. 有些采用低碳水化合物饮食的人会抱怨体能不足并放弃，不能说这样的饮食方法没有用，而是因为他们消耗的卡路里不足。

拓 complain about 抱怨

as often as not 往往；时常

例 The questions sometimes get me thinking about a problem in a different way, and I'll learn something new **as often as not**. 这些问题有时能让我换个角度思考，我也往往会因此学到一些新的东西。

拓 more often than not 通常；多半

to sb.'s credit 某人值得赞扬；在某人名下；归功于某人

词 credit ['kredɪt] *n.* 信用，信誉；贷款 *v.* 相信；归功于……

例 **To his credit**, John Mack was one of the first Wall Street CEOs to say publicly that his industry needed stricter regulation. 值得称赞的是，约翰·麦克是华尔街最早公开表示自己所在行业需要更严格监管的首席执行官之一。

拓 give credit to sb. 归功于某人

be in sympathy with 赞同，支持，和……一致

词 sympathy ['sɪmpəθi] *n.* 同情；慰问；赞同

例 I'm sure he will **be in sympathy with** your proposal. 我肯定他会赞成你的提议。

拓 go along with 赞同；陪同前往

tire out 使……十分疲劳；筋疲力尽

例 The bursts of speed needed to catch their prey **tire** cheetahs **out**—meaning they need to rest after a kill. 猎豹在追杀猎物时的冲刺速度已经透支了体力，这意味着它们在捕杀结束后需要养精蓄锐。

check up on 检查，核对，校对

例 Tiny biology-based computers could **check up on** the health of individual cells, and then treat those cells based on what they find. 微型生物计算机可以检查单个细胞的健康情况，还可以根据所发现情况对这些细胞进行治疗。

take down　记下，写下；拿下，取下；拆卸　

例 In order to host a dinner party for the entire family, she **took down** a bunch of recipes, planned the dishes and made a shopping list. 为了给全家人办个晚宴，她记下了一大堆食谱，计划了要做的菜肴，并且列了购物清单。

拓 note down 写下；记录

touch off　触发；引发；爆炸　

例 The expert claimed that simply getting electric cars to market will **touch off** a cycle of new research, investment and product improvement. 专家宣称仅仅将电动车推向市场，就会引发一系列的新研究、投资和产品改良。

拓 trigger ['trɪgə(r)] v. 触发，引起 n. 扳机；起因

on the air　在广播，广播中　

例 Women also call to request songs, but prefer not to be named **on the air**. 女士们也会打进电话来点歌，但她们不会在广播中留下名字。

辨 **on the air** 指 "在广播中，播出"。如：These three reporters are on the air frequently. 这三位记者经常在节目中播音。
in the air 指 "在空中；悬而未决；在流传中"，如：Snowflakes were swirling in the air. 雪花在空中飞舞。

act for　代理；代表；代办　

例 These organizations **act for** groups of rights holders such as songwriters or authors and collect money from businesses that use copyrighted work. 这些组织是词曲家或作家等版权人的代理，并从使用这些版权产品的商务活动中收取费用。

拓 represent [ˌreprɪ'zent] v. 代表；表现

reply to　回答，回复　

例 We will **reply to** your e-mail address with further information. 我们会把更详细的信息回复到您的电子邮件地址。

to date　至今；到目前为止　

例 The new proposal is simply a new opinion of a new group based on a limited assessment of the research **to date**. 这项新提议只是一个新的工作小组对到目前为止已经做过的研究进行有限评估而做出的新结论罢了。

拓 up to now 至今；到目前为止 ‖ as yet 到目前为止；至今仍……

keep down	压制，镇压；使处于低水平

例 My mom put a pack of ice on my forehead to **keep down** the fever. 妈妈把冰袋放在我的额头上，让我退烧。

拓 suppress [sə'pres] *v.* 抑制；镇压

accede to	加入；同意

例 The EU expressed support to this country's efforts to **accede to** the *Government Procurement Agreement*. 欧盟表示支持这个国家为加入世界贸易组织《政府采购协定》而做出的努力。

assault on	对……的袭击；猛然袭击

词 assault [ə'sɔːlt] *v./n.* 攻击；袭击

例 He was charged for **assaulting on** a police officer. 他因攻击警察而被起诉。

拓 attack on 攻击；对……进攻

turn round	转身；转向；改变意见

例 There was a sign that the cumulative impact of the new policy may eventually **turn round** the recession. 有一迹象显示新政策的累积效应可能最终会扭转经济的衰退。

draw into	使卷入；吸收；吸取

例 The speed increases of these new processors prompt users to update their smartphone and **draw** them **into** the tablet market. 新的处理器在速度上的提高会吸引用户更新智能手机，并把他们吸引到平板设备市场。

check in	登记，入住；报到

例 Since we were early to **check in**, the hotel allowed us to leave our luggage with the receptionist. 由于我们办理入住时间比较早，酒店允许我们把行李先寄存在前台。

be alien to	与……相异；违反……

例 These images **are alien to** the prophetic mode of the Old Testament prophets. 这些图像与旧约先知的预言模式不符。

to one's knowledge	据某人所知

例 **To my knowledge**, this is the only album written to accompany a work of written prose. 据我所知，这是随同散文作品而写的唯一的专辑。

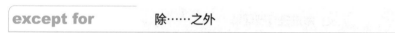

except for　除……之外　○○○

例 Our shortcomings and encountered problems are the same **except for** the fields and their appearances. 除了领域和表现方式不同之外，我们的缺点和遇到的问题都是一样的。

be keen on　爱好，喜欢，热衷　◇

例 In addition to the goals and projects which we love, most of us have a few commitments which we **are** not so **keen on**. 除了我们热爱的目标和项目，大多数人都有一些我们不太热衷的承诺。

call up　打电话；召集，动员；使想起　◇○

例 The manager will **call up** and discuss the terms of employment with me. 那名经理会打电话跟我谈论雇佣条件。

try on　试穿；试验　◇

例 **try on** her new running shoes 试穿她那双新买的跑步鞋

turn back　回头；往回走；翻回；挡住（某人）；折转（某物）　○○○

例 It was never too late for him to **turn back**. 对他来说，现在回头为时不晚。

coincide with　符合；与……相一致　○○○

例 Russian concessions so far have been halfhearted and Russian policies do not **coincide with** those of America. 俄罗斯的让步不是真心实意的，而且俄罗斯的政策与美国的政策是不相吻合的。

compatible with　与……兼容，与……不矛盾，与……一致；和……能和睦相处的　○○○

例 Although we have lots of smartphone apps to choose today, they're all different and not **compatible with** other smartphone operating systems. 尽管我们今天有很多智能手机应用可供选择，但它们不相同，并且与其他智能手机操作系统不兼容。

at fault　出毛病；感到困惑　○○○

例 I'm sorry. My memory was **at fault**. 对不起，我记错了。

to all appearances　显然地；就外表来看　○○○

例 Testers have become the bottleneck and, **to all appearances**, they should be responsible for any further delay. 测试人员成了瓶颈，显然，他们应该对任何进一步的延迟负责。

| sink in | 沉没；渗进去；被理解 | ◯◯◯ |

例 If we stop moving forward, we will **sink in** the water, like sharks. 如果我们停止前进，我们就会像鲨鱼一样沉入水中。

拓 submerge in 沉没

| add up to | 合计，总计 | ◯◯◯ |

例 If household and corporate debt together **add up to** as much as 200% of GDP, they will jeopardize the broader economy. 如果家庭债务和公司债务加起来达到 GDP 的 200%，那么它们将危害整个国家的经济。

| build on/upon | 以……为基础；依赖，依靠……；建立于 | ◯◯◯ |

例 In this way, you start with a single customer and **build on** that profile. 利用这种方式，你从一个消费者出发，并以他的概况为基础进行划分。

| step down | 辞职；走下；逐步减低 | ◯◯◯ |

例 The Prime Minister has said he will **step down** as soon as the country is on the recovery track. 首相表示，一旦该国步入复苏轨道，他将辞职下台。

拓 leave office 辞职，下台，离任

| stir up | 激起；煽动；搅拌；唤起 | ◯◯◯ |

例 We should be careful in case of **stirring up** narrow-minded, extreme nationalism. 我们应该谨慎，以免激起狭隘的、极端的民族主义情绪。

| talk down to | 轻视地（对人）说话；用高人一等的口气说话 | ◯◯◯ |

例 You'd better not **talk down to** coworkers, including subordinates. 你最好不要用居高临下的口吻和同事说话，包括下属。

| be jealous of | 嫉妒；妒忌 | ◯◯◯ |

例 People usually don't admit they **are jealous of** their friends. 人们通常不会承认嫉妒自己的朋友。

拓 be envious of 羡慕；嫉妒

| at leisure | 空闲；从容地 | ◯◯◯ |

例 I filter all of these emails into a "Review Optional" folder, intending to browse them **at**

leisure. 我把这些邮件全都过滤到一个名为"随意查看"的文件夹，打算空闲的时候再打开查看。

extend to
延伸至；扩至；适用范围扩及；给予

例 Now it seems that their boycotts will **extend to** all levels of government, and all parts of the country. 现在看来他们的抵制将会延伸到各级政府，以及该国的所有地区。

run out (of)
用光，耗尽；到期，期满

例 He argued in an annual report that the labor surplus would not **run out** for another decade. 他在年度报告中辩称，剩余劳动力在未来十年内还不会用完。

in perspective
正确地（看待或判断）

词 perspective [pəˈspektɪv] *n*. 观点，看法；景色；透镜，望远镜

例 If you want to put the problem **in perspective**, you should be a patient listener. 如果你想正确认识这个问题，你需要耐心地倾听别人的话。

incur criticism
招致批评

词 incur [ɪnˈkɜː(r)] *v*. 招致；遭受

例 This study has **incurred criticism** for being too narrowly focused. 这一研究因为关注范围太过狭窄而遭到批评。

in proportion (to)
与……成比例的

例 Her short legs are not **in proportion to** her long body. 她的短腿和身长不成比例。

on the go
忙个不停，四处奔走

例 She has been **on the go** ever since this morning. 她从早上开始就忙个不停。

play with
以……为消遣，玩弄；（不太认真地）考虑；同……一起玩

例 Billy has much money to **play with** in his manhood. 比利成年时有许多钱供他挥霍。

to the contrary
相反地

例 Despite constant assurances **to the contrary**, the country still retains its nuclear program. 尽管这个国家再三保证停止核项目，但事实却恰恰相反。

| at a glance | 看一眼；马上 | ◠◠◠ |

例 One could recognize **at a glance** that she is a kindhearted person. 人们一眼就能看出她是个很有同情心的人。

拓 at first blush 乍一看；一瞥

| nowhere near | 远不及；离……很远 | ◠◠◠ |

例 The concert hall is **nowhere near** full. 音乐大厅里远未满座。

| in and out | 进进出出 | ◠◠◠ |

例 Eve slipped **in and out** of the cinema by the side door. 伊芙从影院的侧门溜进溜出。

| on the alert | 提防；密切注意；随时准备着 | ◠◠◠ |

例 Drivers should be **on the alert** for traffic signals. 驾驶员需要密切注意交通信号。

拓 beware of 谨防

| take heart | 鼓起勇气，振作起来 | ◠◠ |

例 It's great to see that you **take heart** and work harder than before. 看到你振作起来，比以前更加努力工作，真是太好了。

| fix on | 决定；使集中于；确定 | ◠◠◠ |

例 I'm not in the mood to **fix on** anything today. 我今天不在状态，无法做任何决定。

| land in | 使……陷入；在……着陆 | ◠◠◠ |

例 Sally's hot temper has **landed** her **in** trouble before. 莎莉的火爆脾气曾给她带来麻烦。

| step in | 介入；插手干预；短时间的非正式访问 | ◠◠◠ |

例 The team coach **stepped in** to stop the two football players from coming to blows. 球队教练出面制止了那两位球员之间的斗殴。

拓 come between...and... 干预或破坏……与……之间的关系；离间

| run over | 浏览；溢出，超出限度；略述；碾过 | ◠◠◠ |

例 She **ran over** her notes before giving the public speech. 她演讲前把稿子浏览了一遍。

| at the instant of | 在……的时刻 | ◠◠◠ |

例 **At the instant of** the panic attack, the whole city was in sound sleep. 在恐怖袭击发生的时刻，整个城市处于沉睡中。

be indicative of 暗示……；表示…… ○○○

词 indicative [ɪnˈdɪkətɪv] *a.* 象征的；指示的，表示的

例 Fever could **be indicative of** a pathogen infection. 发烧表明可能受到了病原体感染。

make nothing of 不了解；把……看得轻而易举，不认为……困难 ○○○

例 The tourist guide showed me a hand-drawn map but I could **make nothing of** it. 导游给我画了张地图，但我却看不懂。

word for word 逐字地，一字不变地 ○○○

例 She explained the ordinance to us **word for word**. 她逐字逐句地替我们解释这项条例。

explain away 敷衍搪塞；为……辩解，声辩 ○○○

例 I had noticed blood on my friend's clothing but he **explained** it **away**. 我注意到朋友的衣服上有血迹，但是被他搪塞过去了。

trade on/upon （不公正地）利用 ○○○

例 He was a selfish man who **traded on** the achievements of others. 他是个自私自利、不惜利用他人的成就作垫脚石的人。

check out 结账离开；核实，查实；符合要求 ◐○

例 She has gone to the reception desk, presumably to **check out**. 她去前台了，可能是要办理退房手续。

come at 扑向，向……逼近；找到，得到，弄明白 ○○○

例 She maintained that she was protecting herself from Mr. Cox, who **came at** her with a knife. 她坚持说自己是在正当防卫，因为考克斯先生拿着刀向她逼近。

gender inequality 性别不平等 ○○○

词 gender [ˈdʒendə(r)] *n.* 性；性别

例 Paying attention to gender issues not only helps reduce **gender inequality** but promotes social progress. 重视性别问题不仅有助于减少性别不平等，也有利于社会进步。

take a delight in 以……为乐 ○○○

例 He appears to **take a** particular **delight in** singing the song at rallies. 他在集会上唱起这首歌的时候似乎非常开心。

| **be worthy of** | 值得，配得上 | |

例 I did not consider her to **be worthy of** trust. 我认为她不值得信赖。

| **plough through** | 费力地通过……；费劲地阅读，吃力地钻研 | |

词 plough [plaʊ] *v./n.* 用犁耕田；开路；投（资）

例 Mr. Darley watched her **plough through** the brook. 达利先生看着她艰难地蹚过小溪。

| **by reason of** | 由于；因为 | |

例 Their plan failed **by reason of** bad organization. 由于组织不当，他们的计划失败了。

DAY 21

本单元资源

---

in a small way　　小规模地；节俭地　　○○○

例 More non-workers will be encouraged into the labor force if the government takes measures to cut payroll taxes **in a small way**. 如果政府能够小规模地减少所得税，这将刺激更多的就业。

拓 in a big way 大规模地，彻底地

---

piece together　　渐渐弄清（真相）；拼凑　　○○○

例 Thinking calmly for several days, Alice was able to **piece together** what had happened. 冷静思考了几天之后，艾莉丝能够渐渐弄清所发生的事情了。

拓 scratch up 拼凑；凑集

---

triumph over　　击败；得胜；成功　　○○○

例 I believe that love is the greatest thing in the world; that it alone can **triumph over** hate. 我相信，世界上最伟大的事物就是爱，只有爱能够战胜仇恨。

---

step out　　走出去；暂时外出　　○○○

例 Every time you **step out** of your comfort zone, you're going to feel fear. 每当你跨出你的"舒适区"，你就会开始感觉到恐惧。

---

to my mind　　依我的看法，据我看来　　○○○

例 **To my mind**, in order to find happiness, we must look for positive causes that are peaceful and appealing to our mind. 据我看来，为了得到幸福，我们要寻找能为我们的心灵带来平安喜乐的善因。

拓 in my opinion 依我看来，在我看来

---

head into　　走向　　○○

例 Next week we will **head into** Thailand to enjoy our honeymoon. 下周我们将出发去泰国度蜜月。

---

be up in the air　　（问题等）悬而未决；不肯定；异常兴奋，十分激动　　○○○

例 Your marriage may **be up in the air** if your spouse has been going through a change of heart. 若配偶的想法有所改变，你的婚姻生活将会处于一种悬而未决的状态。

拓 be in suspense 悬而未决

| **fall down** | 跌倒；失败；倒塌 | |

例 The only way they'll learn to ride a bicycle is to let them ride on their own and **fall down** a time or two. 唯一能让他们学会骑自行车的方法，是任由他们自己学着骑车，跌倒几次。

拓 fall over 跌倒

| **safe and sound** | 安然无恙 | |

例 What made us surprised is that they survived and escaped from the accident **safe and sound**. 我们感到惊异的是他们竟安然无恙地逃离了车祸。

拓 in a whole skin 安然无恙 ‖ fall/land on one's feet 安然无恙

| **stop short** | 突然停止；中途停下，停止 | |

例 Sometimes, a passerby who crosses the street right in front of cars makes them all **stop short**. 有时，路人横穿马路，出现在汽车前面，使得汽车突然停止。

拓 cease from 停止 ‖ desist from 停止

| **fit into** | （使）适合，适应；符合 | |

例 An ideal life for me is that I can find some friends who **fit into** my life philosophy in some manner. 我的理想生活就是有一些在某种程度上符合我的人生观的朋友。

| **bid for** | 出价；投标；许诺获支持 | |

例 Customers had to **bid for** 50 items, and then one bid was taken and compared with a counterbid generated at random by a computer. 客户必须对 50 个物品进行出价，出的每一次价都会和电脑随机产生的价格进行比较。

拓 bid on 投标；出价 ‖ tender for 投标

| **take...by surprise** | 使吃惊；撞见；奇袭 | |

例 Let's keep this gift under wraps, so we can **take** him **by surprise**. 让我们先将这个礼物保密，这样才能给他惊喜。

拓 take aback 使吃惊；惊吓

| **be typical of** | 有代表性的，典型的，象征性的 | |

例 That is the type of easily getting impulsion that **is** so **typical of** teenagers. 这种容易冲动的情况在青少年中非常典型。

persist in 坚持不懈，执意 ○○○

例 If you **persist in** practicing tone, scales and trouble spots, gradually you'll become an excellent singer. 如果你坚持练习音色、音阶和难点，渐渐地你就会成为一名优秀的歌手。

the moment (that) 一……就…… ○○○

例 I loved you **the moment (that)** I saw you. 我对你是一见钟情。

slip through 溜走；滑过；蒙混过关 ○○○

例 Don't let life **slip through** your fingers by always living in the past. 不要总怀念过去而让生命从你的指尖溜走。

拓 slip away 悄悄溜走

turn away 不准……入内；解雇；走开；转过脸 ○○○

例 Universities are not allowed to **turn away** any student who is disabled or has physical ailments. 大学是不允许拒绝残疾或有身体疾病的学生入学的。

under pressure 面临压力，在压力之下；受到压力 ○○○

例 **Under pressure** from consumers they gradually improved their quality and have won recognition from customers. 在消费者施加的压力下，他们逐渐改善质量并且赢得了消费者的认可。

follow one's example 以……为榜样 ○○○

例 As a public figure, he should always pay attention to his words and deeds, because others may **follow his example**. 作为公众人物，他应该时刻注意自己的言行，因为别人可能会以他为榜样。

at present 目前，现在 ◇

例 There is no evidence of the effectiveness of these interventions **at present**. 目前，没有证据能够表明这些干预措施的有效性。

stumble on/upon/across 偶然发现，偶然遇到 ○○○

例 You can **stumble upon** ideas in books that give you AHA moments, and hence lead to a different experience for your life. 你会在书中偶然发现让你恍然大悟的点子，从而给你的生活带来不一样的体验。

pull through　　渡过难关；恢复健康

例 The authorities' concern is that the banks will have trouble determining who will **pull through**, and this can easily wind up with a lot of dud loans. 当局担心的是，银行将难以确定谁将渡过难关，这很容易导致大量不良贷款。

take on　　承担；从事；穿上；呈现

例 No one knows whether they volunteered or were ordered to **take on** the difficult task. 没有人知道他们是自愿还是奉命承担这项艰巨的任务的。

take a fancy to　　喜欢上

例 I never used to like fruits as a kid, but I've **taken a fancy to** them as I've grown up. 我小时候从来都不喜欢水果，但我长大后就喜欢上了。

at a stretch　　一下子

例 She can only drive two hours **at a stretch**, so you'll have to take over soon. 她一次只能开两个小时，所以你很快就得接手。

tie up　　（船）系泊；捆绑；安排好

例 **tie up** your boat at the dock 把你的船系在码头上

buy off　　买通，贿赂，收买

例 They entered the meeting without tickets because they **bought off** the staff. 他们没有票就进入了会场，因为他们收买了工作人员。

core values　　核心价值观

例 This society needs to review their **core values** and to see just where they are headed. 这个社会需要重新审视其核心价值观，看清楚自己在朝何方前进。

stand in　　暂时代替

例 If you can't attend the party tonight, I'll find someone to **stand in** for you. 如果你今晚无法参加宴会，我将找人代替你去。

find fault with　　找茬，挑剔；抱怨

例 If you always try to **find fault with** others' shortcomings, then it means that you have gained another shortcoming. 如果你总是试图挑剔别人的缺点，那这就意味着你自己因此而多了一个缺点。

make certain　　弄清楚；确保

例 I just want to **make certain** that who allowed you to copy the data without permission. 我只想弄清楚到底是谁允许你擅自复制了数据。

turn up　　出现；到达；调大；发现

例 They didn't expect too many people to **turn up** at the party because it was Wednesday. 他们没指望有太多人来参加聚会，因为那天是星期三。

level off　　变得平稳；保持水平

例 Recently, after the government took some effective measures, prices began to **level off**. 最近，政府采取了一些有效的措施后，物价开始平稳下来。

on the increase　　在增加

例 A recent report shows that juvenile delinquency is **on the increase**. 最近的一份报告显示，青少年犯罪正在呈上升趋势。

on the verge of　　即将……；濒于……

例 The show is **on the verge of** being canceled because of the poor ratings. 由于收视率太低，这档节目即将被取消。

up to date　　最新的；现代的；新式的

例 It's a modern factory and everything was really **up to date**. 这是一个现代化的工厂，一切都是最新式的。

up against　　面临；遭遇

例 Recent studies have shown that farmers will be **up against** environmental limits by 2050, as industry and consumers compete for water. 最近的研究表明，由于工业和消费者争夺水资源，到 2050 年，农民将面临环境的限制。

come/draw to a close　　结束

例 There are no other issues to discuss, and this meeting can **come to a close**. 没有其他问题要讨论了，这次会议可以结束了。

| **bottom line** | 底线；要旨 | |

例 The **bottom line** is that you have to go to this special meeting and no one else can replace you. 归根结底，你必须去参加这次的特别会议，别人替代不了。

| **on that score** | 关于那一点，关于那个问题 | |

例 The accommodation in the school is excellent, so I don't think we need to worry about the children **on that score**. 学校的住宿条件很好，所以我认为我们不必担心孩子们在这方面的问题。

| **size up** | 判断；估计，估量 | |

例 It only took a few seconds for the detective to **size up** the situation at the scene. 侦探只用了几秒钟就对现场的情况作出了判断。

| **to the extent of** | 到……地步，到……程度 | |

例 The food imports could rise, but it will not **to the extent of** shaping the monetary policy. 食品进口可能会增加，但不会达到影响货币政策的程度。

| **clean out** | 把……打扫干净 | |

例 **clean out** the garage 把车库清理干净

| **in brief** | 简单地说，简而言之 | |

例 **In brief**, he has the unique ability to contribute to this position and the long-term development of your company. 简而言之，他有着可以为这个职位以及贵公司长久发展做出贡献所需要的独特能力。

拓 to be brief 简言之

| **year after/by year** | 年复一年；年年，每年 | |

例 **Year after year**, I find myself less and less interested in nightlife and more focused on enjoying the outdoors. 年复一年，我发现自己对夜生活越来越不感兴趣，而是更专注于享受户外生活。

| **in a position** | 能够；在……位置 | |

例 I believe that they are **in a position** to recognize financial opportunities and risks in advance. 我相信他们能够预先认识到财务风险和机会。

give access to　向……开放；接见；准许进入　○○○

例 But if the goal is to truly **give access to** high-quality postsecondary education to most people, well, for that you need to do a lot more. 但是如果目标是真的给大多数人提供高等教育的机会，那么需要你做的事情还有很多。

拓 have a chance/an opportunity to 有……的机会

by common consent　大家都同意；（被）公认　○○○

例 In a nation of stoics, the most patient sufferers—**by common consent**—are those from Tohoku, the poor north-eastern area struck by earthquake and tsunami on March 11th. 在这个主张忍耐的国家，大家公认的最能忍耐的受灾人群来自东北，这个贫困的地区于 3 月 11 日经历了地震和海啸。

拓 universally/generally acknowledged 普遍承认

out of hand　无法控制；马上，立刻　○○○

例 When we can't explain logically why we think something is a bad or even for that matter a good idea, we can tend to either ignore it completely or use faulty logic to dismiss it **out of hand**. 当我们无法逻辑清晰地解释为什么我们认为一些事情是坏事，甚至是个好主意时，我们可以选择完全忽视它，或运用错误的逻辑立刻将其驳回。

throw oneself into　积极从事；投身于　○○○

例 The panacea for a broken heart is a busy mind and a tired body; so **throw yourself into** work even though you don't really feel like working, and focus all your energy into your professional life. 忙碌的头脑和疲倦的身体是医治心碎的灵药，因此请将自己投入到工作中去，即使你并不是那么喜欢工作，也最好集中所有的精力到自己的职业生活上。

拓 devote oneself to 献身于，专心于；致力 ‖ apply oneself to 致力于

tell the white lie　说善意的谎言　○○○

例 Who doesn't **tell the** occasional **white lie**, to avoid social awkwardness or hurting someone's feelings? 为了避免社交时的尴尬或伤害某人的感情，谁没说过暂时的善意的谎言呢？

pour out　倾诉；流出　○○○

例 Of course, you don't **pour out** all of your innermost secrets the first time you meet someone—it has to be a gradual opening up. 当然，你不必在与其他人第一次见面时就倾

诉你内心深处的秘密——这需要一个循序渐进的过程。

拓 pour forth 倾诉；不断流出 ‖ confide sth. to sb. 向某人吐露（隐私、秘密等）

walk away/off　　走开；离去

例 The best kind of friend is the kind whom you can sit on a porch, never say a word, and then **walk away** feeling like it was the best conversation you have ever had. 最好的朋友是，你可以和他坐在门廊上，不说一句话，分别的时候你会觉得这是你们之间有过的最好的对话。

get around/round to　　找时间做……，开始考虑……

例 In the case of bloggers, we invest all of our time into getting attention, but many of us never **get around to** monetizing that attention. 在博客中，我们把自己所有的时间用来吸引流量，但是我们中的很多人从未考虑把这些流量变现。

come into existence　　（事物、局面等）产生；形成；成立；开始存在

例 In this view all technological breakthroughs emerge as novel combinations of existing technological components, which have themselves **come into existence** through the same process. 以这种观点来看，所有的技术突破都是现有技术元素的创新合并而产生的，这些元素也是经历同样的过程产生的。

拓 come into being 产生；开始存在

run for　　竞选

例 Each group selected candidates to **run for** president and vice-president. 每组选出候选人去竞选总统和副总统。

拓 campaign for 为……而斗争

supply with/to　　供给；提供

例 But with sensible policies, nations could set a goal of generating 25 percent of their new energy supply with WWS sources in 10 to 15 years and almost 100 percent of new **supply** in 20 **to** 30 years. 但是有了理性的政策，国家可以设定一个目标：在 10 到 15 年里，它们给 WWS 能源提供 25% 的新能源，在 20 到 30 年里，它们实现 100% 供给。

拓 provide sth. for 为……提供，供应某物

burn up　　烧起来；烧掉；发怒

例 Biting, chewing, swallowing and digesting food takes energy—it's known as the thermic effect of food and it can **burn up** to 30 percent of the calories on your plate. 咬下、咀嚼、吞咽和消化食物都需要能量——这就是我们熟知的热疗效应，它可以燃烧掉你所吃食物的30%的热量。

拓 burn away 烧掉，烧光 ‖ burn off 烧掉；烧除；消耗能量

| turn one's back on | 不理睬；避开；拒绝接受；抛弃，背弃 | ○○○ |

例 He **turned his back on** his friends when he became famous. 他成名以后对自己的朋友连理都不理。

拓 turn a deaf ear to 对……置之不理

| dry up | 干涸，枯竭 | ◇ |

例 It is feared the mine could **dry up** dozens of perennial streams and two rivers that run through the hills, while pollution could damage fruit orchards and plants said to possess medicinal properties. 人们担心采矿会导致流经山脉的数十条存在多年的溪流和两条河流干涸，而且废料会污染果园和据说具有药物特性的植物。

| have connection with | 与……有联系 | ○○○ |

例 Does the central bank's ability to orchestrate inflation **have** any **connection with** the government's involvement in war? 那么，中央银行调节通货膨胀的能力和政府参战之间有联系吗？

拓 be affiliated with 附属于；与……有关系

| rare bird | 稀有的人，不寻常的人；珍品 | ○○○ |

例 She is that **rare bird**, a physicist who works independently of any institution. 她就是那个稀有之人，是一位不依赖于任何机构的独立的物理学家。

| no way | 绝不，一点也不；不可能，没门 | ○○○ |

例 The only problem is that there is **no way** to verify the accuracy of those images, since only the dreamer ever "sees" them. 唯一的问题是没有办法检验这些图像的准确性，因为只有做梦的人"看见"过这些图像。

拓 out of the question 不可能的；不允许的

beat to the punch　先发制人；抢先下手

例 He **beat** me **to the punch** and asked me the very same question first. 他先我一步问了跟我一模一样的问题。

拓 fire the first shot 先发制人；打头炮 ‖ get the drop on sb. 先发制人；胜过某人

arm with　供给……武器；装备；备战

例 **Armed with** knowledge, you'll be a good teacher. 用知识武装自己，你会是一个好老师。

take a loss　承担损失；遭受损失

例 If the central bank were forced to **take a** major **loss** on its Greek bonds, it too would need a capital infusion. 如果中央银行被迫承担希腊国家债券的主要损失，中央银行也同样需要资本注入。

拓 bear the loss of 承担……的损失

on schedule　按时；按照预定时间

例 I was a real workaholic in the past, putting in 60 hour work weeks to make sure I had every minute scheduled, working as fast as I could to get things done on time, **on schedule** and perfectly. 曾经，我是个十足的工作狂，每周工作 60 个小时，以确保每一分钟都充分利用，尽可能快地按时并保质保量地完成工作。

be on the ropes　处于困境，接近失败（或毁灭）

例 The first victim of an ecological crisis could be the Mekong giant catfish, which has **been on the ropes** for years. 这场生态危机的第一个受害者是湄公河鲇鱼，它们已经濒临灭绝很多年了。

trade off　权衡

例 Yes, individuals generally prefer to be happier, but sometimes they are willing to **trade off** happiness for other behavior that gives them greater utility. 确实，人们普遍追求快乐，但有时人们也愿意用快乐换取对他们更有用的行为。

make a sacrifice　作出牺牲

例 Other than 5% of the public who will willingly **make a sacrifice** to buy green vehicles, the other 95% of people will ask, "What am I getting—what's the deal?" 除了 5% 的人愿意作出牺牲去购买节能汽车，其他 95% 的人会问："我能得到什么——有什么用？"

drop off　　　　下降；减少

例 And so as more and more commerce migrates to the Internet, there is a potential **drop off** in tax revenues to these states and localities. 并且随着越来越多的商业转向互联网，那些州和当局都面临税收下降的潜在风险。

stick around　　　　在附近徘徊；逗留

例 But right now, I have no idea what will happen, so I guess you'll just have to **stick around** and find out. 但是现在，我不知道将会发生什么，所以我猜你会在附近徘徊并找出答案。

拓 wander about 徘徊，转来转去

badly off　　　　穷困的，没钱的；境况不佳的

例 This might be true, but it doesn't leave you **badly off** either. 这也许是真的，但是也不会更糟了。

拓 be badly off for sth. 缺乏某物

finish up　　　　完成；结束；用光

例 The project, which started last year, will not **finish up** until 2025. 这个从去年就开始的项目，预计到 2025 年才能完成。

expert in/at　　　　熟于；在……方面是行家

例 He's **expert in** cooking good cheap meals. 他善于烹制好吃又便宜的饭菜。

tie in with　　　　与……一致；配合

例 "The Victorian image of Jesus doesn't **tie in with** the historical evidence," he said. 他说："维多利亚时代的耶稣形象与历史证据不一致。"

cheer up　　　　使高兴；高兴起来；使振奋

例 When your child is sick, you can make him some chicken soup, a cup of hot chocolate, or whatever he needs to **cheer up**. 当你的孩子生病了，你可以为他做些鸡汤，冲一杯热巧克力或者任何能让他高兴起来的东西。

拓 buck up 使振作；打起精神 ‖ delight [dɪ'laɪt] v. 给……乐趣；使愉快

DAY 21

spread over　传遍；遍布，覆盖

例 The spill of pollution **spread over** 170 square miles and posed a serious threat to both sea life and water quality. 污染的蔓延扩散超过了 170 平方英里，对海洋生物和水质造成了严重威胁。

拓 spread across 传遍；席卷

be addicted to　对……上瘾

例 Part of the problem is that many homeless adults **are addicted to** alcohol or drugs. 该问题的部分原因是许多无家可归的成年人对酒精或毒品上瘾。

拓 addiction to 对……成瘾

(be) on edge　紧张不安的；兴奋的

词 edge [edʒ] *n.* 边缘

例 Kate **was on edge** when waiting for her exam results. 在等候考试结果时，凯特坐立不安。

PART 02

290 即使烟花不曾光顾，也有仰望的笑脸。

PART 03
索引

D

Y

图书在版编目(CIP)数据

恋练不忘：考研英语词组识记与应用大全 / 新东方
考试研究中心编著. -- 北京：群言出版社，2024.2
　　ISBN 978-7-5193-0892-6

　　Ⅰ. ①恋… Ⅱ. ①新… Ⅲ. ①英语 – 词汇 – 研究生 –
入学考试 – 自学参考资料 Ⅳ. ①H319.34

中国国家版本馆CIP数据核字(2024)第022449号

责任编辑：侯　莹
封面设计：黄　蕊

出版发行：群言出版社
地　　址：北京市东城区东厂胡同北巷1号（100006）
网　　址：www.qypublish.com（官网书城）
电子信箱：dywh@xdf.cn　qunyancbs@126.com
联系电话：010-62418641　65267783　65263836
法律顾问：北京法政安邦律师事务所
经　　销：全国新华书店

印　　刷：河北泓景印刷有限公司
版　　次：2024年2月第1版
印　　次：2024年2月第1次印刷
开　　本：710mm×1000mm　1/16
印　　张：20.5
字　　数：359千字
书　　号：ISBN 978-7-5193-0892-6
定　　价：58.00元

Kites rise highest against the wind, not with it.

— Winston Churchill